Good Grief

Exploring Feelings, Loss and Death with Under Elevens

A Holistic Approach

2nd edition

Barbara Ward and Associates

Jessica Kingsley Publishers
London and Bristol, Pennsylvania

First published by Barbara Ward in 1987 (ISBN 0-9512-882-2)
First published by Jessica Kingsley Publishers in 1993
Jessica Kingsley Publishers Ltd
116 Pentonville Road
London N1 9JB, England
and
1900 Frost Road, Suite 101
Bristol, PA 19007, U S A

Second edition 1996

Companion Volume:

Good Grief: Exploring Feelings, Loss and Death with Over Elevens and Adults 2nd edition ISBN 1 85302 340 X

Also available

- A one day training course to accompany the pack
- Healing Grief – Book by Barbara Ward

Further details from:

Barbara Ward, 3 Wheelwright Court, Walkhampton, Yelverton, Devon PL20 6LA

Library of Congress Cataloging in Publication Data
Ward, Barbara, 1937-
Good grief 1 : exploring feelings, loss, and death with under 11's
/ Barbara Ward and associates. -- 2nd ed.
p.   cm.
ISBN 1-85302-324-8 (pbk.)
1. Loss (Psychology) in children. 2. Bereavement in children.
3. Grief in children. 4. Children and death. 5. Loss (Psychology)-
-Study and teaching (Elementary) 7. Grief--Study and
teaching (Elementary) 8. Deth--Study and teaching (Elementary)
I. Title.
BF723.L68W37   1995
155.9'37'083--dc20   95-16041
                                                CIP

British Library Cataloguing in Publication Data
Ward, Barbara
Good Grief. - Vol.1: Exploring Feelings,
Loss and Death with Under Elevens. -
2rev.ed
I. Title
155.937

ISBN 1 85302 324 8

Printed and Bound in Great Britain by
Cromwell Press, Melksham, Wiltshire

CONTENTS

Section 1 – Introduction

Section 2 – Activities

Section 3 – Appendices

Dedication

To all those who suffer loss
To educators who use this book
To friends and colleagues for their patience, support and encouragement.
B.W.

Acknowledgements

My thanks go to the wonderful team of contributors for their input, support and encouragement and the people/organisations mentioned in the attributions. This book could not have been written without them.

I wish also to thank the following members of the London Borough of Hillingdon for their expertise and encouragement: Gerry Ackroyd, Senior Educational Psychologist; Trisha Grimshaw, Assistant Borough Librarian; Linda Pennington, Religious Education Support Teacher; Richard Wales, Advisor/Inspector; and Paul Bamber, Health Education Authority Regional Co-ordinator.

Also, Barbara Kahan, Chairwoman of the National Children's Bureau, for writing the Foreword, Laurel Newman for providing the framework for three of the 'Activities', John Balding of the University of Exeter for providing the 'Just a Tick' information.

Last and not least my associates without whom *Good Grief* would not exist: Sally Crosher my personal assistant, for her endless patience and for putting the book on computer, her husband John for his technical advice and Cynthia Hendley for her typing. In conclusion I'd like to thank my publishers Jessica Kingsley for their hard work on this final edition.

Foreword

It is easy to assume that children do not experience the same depths of feeling as adults when faced with grief and loss. Nevertheless, though their ways of expressing themselves and their interpretations of what is happening may be different, the intensity and impact of their experiences should not be underestimated. Although their understanding of cause and effect and sense of time are different from adults', the pain, guilt and anger engendered by loss and grief may be very great.

But the child lives in an adult world in which the expression of feelings – particularly grief – may be discouraged and their only recourse may be to try to contain them within themself. To do so may give rise to behaviour which is poorly regarded by adults and in consequence grief may be compounded by rejection, leaving the child even more alone with his painful feelings.

Good Grief is addressed to parents, carers, teachers; those who spend time living and working with children under twelve years old. It starts from the premise that children need to be able to mourn and to know that other people understand and respect their need to do so. This, the author suggests, not only will enable them to cope with their own grief or sadness, but help them in turn to become compassionate, understanding people.

The pack is rich in teaching material, ranging through many practical situations and also showing imagination and sensibility to feelings and needs of children from the youngest upwards. It draws attention to the many events, experiences and situations which give rise to feelings of loss and grief as well as death itself. Car accidents, with their accompaniment of injury and sometimes death; the experiences of children of multi-racial origins, some of whom may have known intensity of fear, witnessed others die, or suffered, at the least, loss of their familiar culture; the exceptional sensitivity of autistic children who can suffer deeply from a house move or even a change in appearance of familiar surroundings: these are a few of many examples which provoke the student to think more widely and recognise the common elements in otherwise very disparate situations. Children can be very disturbed by the death of a loved pet; they also are exposed to daily violence and death on the national news programmes. All of these are likely to prompt them to want to know what it means, and to want to talk – and teachers and parents often need help in responding. The book can provide help, not just in responding to children whose ability may assist understanding, but also to children of mixed abilities, and those who are less articulate.

Ideally it is suggested that the educators need to have come to terms with loss in their own lives. Those who have very recently experienced a major loss might do better to wait until they themselves have learned to cope. If time and opportunity can be found for a short training preparation, this is likely to be particularly helpful. Parents and teachers cannot avoid being role models and young children are keenly alert to adult attitudes.

Moving into the implementation of the ideas presented the book suggests that schools which give information only are likely to be ineffective. Many practical suggestions are offered, such as involving parents in projects, using visitors to help talk with children and recognising the hundred and one situations which will leave a sense of loss. Divorce, homelessness, unemployment, serious illness, child abuse, still births and miscarriages, the birth of a handicapped child – they all call for understanding. The child needs to know that she, and particularly he, is permitted to cry, to be angry and to know that although they feel guilty they are not responsible for the loss. The time scale for understanding needs expanding. Teachers often underestimate this, but special attention may be needed for long periods. If adults grieve deeply for two years, why assume children 'get over' it much more quickly?

Towards the latter end of the book many creative activities are suggested and described together with some of the equipment of special attention – warmth, night lights, cuddles, special food. There are also warnings against 'killer statements' – 'We don't have time for that now' – 'only babies behave like that'.

Good Grief has been put together with love and deep understanding of children's needs in facing loss and death. It is essentially practical and suggests attitudes and activities well within parents' and teachers' scope. It is a valuable contribution to child care in the broadest sense.

Barbara Kahan
Chairwoman of the National Children's Bureau
Director of Gatsby Project, incorporating the Child Care Open Learning Project

Statistics for Britain

It's the last and greatest taboo of the Western World – our fear of death and dying...we are afraid of death, we deny it, we are even ashamed of it.

'Death is one of the greatest taboos. It doesn't square with our worship of youth' But the truth, after all, is that we are all terminally ill. Once we recognize that, we can enjoy the life we have left.

Elizabeth Kubler Ross, 1982

In Britain there are 3,200,000 widows
                  750,000 widowers
approximately 180,000 children under 16 who have lost a mother or a father through death

1 woman in 7 is a widow
1 man in 8 is a widower
1 woman in 2 over age 65 is a widow
1 man in 6 over age 65 is a widower

Every day approximately 500 wives become widows and 120 husbands become widowers

Of the bereaved children under 16 approximately 120,000 are widows' children and 60,000 are widowers' children.

(1984 OPCS)

DIVORCE

'The divorce rate was 74,000 in 1971 – 146,000 in 1981 and 151,000 in 1987. Official estimates indicate that if divorce rates prevailing in the mid 1980s were to contine, then 37% of marriages are likely to end in divorce.
Death still terminates the majority of marriages.
1 in 5 children will expereince a parental divorce by the age of 16.

Family Change Future Policy
Kathleen Kiernan Malcol Wicks 'Family policy Studies Centre' 1990

In 1994 there were 160,684 under 16s affected by divorce. Four out of ten marriages now end in divorce.

Relate

Organizations

The Compassionate Friends is an international organization of bereaved parents, offering friendship and understanding to other bereaved parents through local regions or national membership.

Cruse is an organization which offers, through local branches or national membership, a service to the bereaved such as counselling, someone to share things with, information on practical matters, and opportunities for contact with others.

The National Children's Bureau is an organization specializing in research into the care and well-being of children in the family, school and society in the areas of health, education, child welfare and the law.

The National Association for the Welfare of Children in Hospital. The main aim of this organization is to raise awareness of the emotional needs of children when in hospital. It provides information and advice on where to find hospitals with, for example, totally free visiting, beds for overnight stay of parents and play-workers who stimulate activities on the wards.

Psychosynthesis and Education Trust. Psychosynthesis is based on a psychology which offers a broad perspective of human life, with special focus on human potential. The Trust trains people in counselling and psychotherapy.

Schools Outreach is a registered charity that facilitates the placement and support of fully-trained, high-callibre gifted persons who will enhance the lives of school children by being based long term in a school and its local community.

How to Use this Book

'If children were allowed to externalize pain, anger and guilt, they would love to go to school.'

Elizabeth Kubler Ross

This book aims to create an atmosphere where everyone feels cared for and where they can share their feelings, both the sorrows and the joys. It aims to help students to

- Create a common core of experiences, upon which they can refer and share.

- Understand that loss and death are a natural part of existence.

- Become aware of the needs of others and themselves at times of loss.

- Be aware, following loss or death, of how we grieve.

- Prevent death becoming the unmentionable.

- Appreciate that cultural groups express feelings differently.

Occasions when Questions May be Asked

- When a child loses someone who is close to them.

- When a friend or a member of staff dies.

- Following media coverage of the death of a famous person.

- Following disasters and serious accidents.

- After personal experience of a fatal accident, serious illness or disaster.

Section 1

Introduction

Why Teach About Loss and Death?

Background to Book

'Pain can be physical, emotional or spiritual – whichever aspect it starts with, it will always spread to the others, so the earlier we start dealing with the pain of loss and death the less likely it is to affect the other aspects.' (Laura Mitchell, International Stress and Tension Control – Annual Conference 1987)

'Because of the changes in lifespan and the fact that many deaths now occur in old age, many people are caught unprepared, not knowing how to behave or the practical procedure to follow. Mourning is treated as if it were a weakness, a self-indulgence, a reprehensible bad habit, instead of a psychological necessity.' (Gorer 1965)

A series of fatal accidents on school trips in recent years have highlighted the need for teachers to prepare pupils to face death and bereavement.

The recognition of the effects on health and changing patterns in bereavement led to Loss and Death Education becoming an important part of the School Curriculum in the 1970s.

When I first introduced these books in 1987, there was no recognized scheme for teaching the subject in Great Britain, despite the fact that Loss and Death was included in the content area of many Personal, Social and Health Education and Religious Education courses. (See Educator's Notes *National Curriculum*.)

Many different types of loss can be the cause of grief and mourning. Death of or separation from a loved one is the most obvious and painful sort of loss.

In our experience in the field of education we have encountered many young people who are unable to learn because of losses not recognized and worked through. This experience showed us that the changes young people experienced had the same potential for loss as death but went largely unnoticed, with no recognition that the grieving process was necessary (see *Understanding Loss*). All these losses require us to give up a familiar state or way of life for a new one. This is the basis of all grief.

Gill Combes, a contributor to this book, discussed various aspects of health with six- and ten-year-olds in several multiracial primary schools in Birmingham. Three strong themes that emerged to do with loss were as follows:

(1) Loss of family to and from Pakistan – most of the children still had family in Pakistan and wanted them to be here; some relations also returned for long visits or permanently and caused a lot of anxiety among the children.

3

(2) Nearly all the groups, when we asked about 'big changes that had happened recently' talked about re-decorating the house, much to our surprise – they found new decorations hard to adjust to and mourned the previous wallpaper/paint!

(3) One of the schools we worked in had had major road works going on nearby, and most of the children commented that they didn't like the changes, roads would be busier and harder to cross.

If we don't mourn losses at the time they happen, major problems, for example, severe depression, can be triggered off when later losses occur. Rutter (1970) found that psychiatric disorders were greatly increased where children had lost a parent by death. Bowlby (1980) in his work on *Loss* proposed that there is a specific connection between prolonged deprivation in the early years and the development of an affectionless psychopathic character extremely difficult to treat and given to persistent delinquent conduct. Toffler in his book *Future Shock* says that many young people are in this state due to the rapid changes that are happening on all levels in modern society. Another reason for approaching the subject through loss is that one in five children will be affected by divorce.

> 'Teacher observation indicated that approximately two thirds of all youngsters showed some notable changes in school, subsequent to parents' separation. While youngsters differed both in the manner and intensity in which their distress was expressed, responses affecting academic achievement were most common. For more than half the students teachers reported a high level of anxiety. Most often this was described to us as new and unaccustomed restlessness. Children who used to sit and do their work now roamed about the room constantly, and in the process began to interrupt classroom activities.'

In addition, the importance of the help schools could give at this time was emphasized as follows:

> 'It was clear that school was useful precisely because it provided structure in a child's life at a time when the major structure of his life, the family, was crumbling. Going to school daily, being required to perform certain tasks in and out of school, having routine social contacts, all these structural… supports potentially assist a child in his adaptation to divorce. It was clear that many children were supported by school in this basic way, regardless of the quality of their academic and social functioning within the classroom.'

It is generally accepted that the ability we have to deal with any crisis depends on our preparation for it. We prepare people for birth and marriage, but when it comes to death we like to feel we are immortal. All the other 'losses' we encounter in life from the moment we leave our mother's womb can be seen as 'little deaths' and how we deal with each will affect how we deal with our own death and that of others close to us. Sudden tragedy, for example, a car accident, may happen at any time in a school or community, with fellow pupils completely unprepared to handle the death of a friend, teacher or loved one.

In some Special Schools this need particularly applies where it is more usual for one of the pupils to die.

Delphine Fredlund, USA, believes that children are interested in death at an early age, but soon learn from adults that 'you don't talk about it'. In a study with parents, she found they felt very inadequate in handling this aspect of their children's development and, although they agreed it was primarily their responsibility, said over and over again 'Churches and schools must help'.

An example of a parent's inadequacy was the eight-year-old child who asked her mother at bedtime 'what happens when you die?' Her mother replied 'I'll bring you some cocoa'.

A pupil of seven years at a school of which I am a governor wrote the following on 'Anger', when taking part in a class activity on 'Feelings'. 'I'm angry they didn't tell me my father was dying. I wasn't able to say goodbye.' (She was five at the time of his death.)

Data collected through the National Survey in Primary Schools using the 'Just a Tick' questionnaires in 1985 suggested marked differences between adults' and children's views on the relevance of the topic 'Death and bereavement' in the primary school programmes.

Within a check list of 43 topics which the various adult groups rated for importance for inclusion in the curriculum in the middle school, the rank order position derived from their responses were as follows:

For	10,208 parents	40th
	639 teachers	41st
	236 health care professionals	41st

For the boys and girls responding to the same check list of 43 topics according to their levels of interest in each topic, the derived rank order positions for 'Death and bereavement' were as follows:

For	1,744 3rd year boys (age 9–10)	11th
	1,831 4th year boys (age 10–11)	16th
	1,628 3rd year girls (age 9–10)	11th
	1,737 4th year girls (age 10–11)	16th

The supporting prompt when the topic was being considered by the pupils was

'25. Death and bereavement
This would be about the feelings people have when someone they love dies, and what can be done to help them.'

In a more recent smaller survey in secondary schools, the adults' response was found to be very similar. But higher responses were found from the boys and girls.

In answer to the question 'Can children really understand death?', Grollman (1977) maintains that a child growing up today is 'all too aware of the reality of death, i.e. a pet is killed, a funeral procession passes by, a grandfather dies, a leader is assassinated. TV nightly bombards us with death in many forms in glorious colour'.

Thanatologists generally agree that death education for children, when developmentally appropriate, helps reduce fears and anxieties about death and dying.

It has been said that those who get the most out of life are those who are at ease with the fact they must die. Preparing for loss and bereavement then is part of the preparation for living.

'Man was made for joy and woe
And when this we rightly know
Thro' the world we safely go'

(*Auguries of Innocence*, William Blake)

The benefits of accepting the words of the poem could perhaps help young people to think of their losses or 'little deaths' as opportunities for new beginnings.

Teachers may believe that children need to be protected from the facts of death: yet an overview of child development suggests that the discovery of loss begins during infancy. Perhaps it is the teachers' *own* fears and attitudes which prevent them from mentioning the subject.

As part of the research phase of the HEA Primary Project an investigation was carried out into children's perceptions of the world of relationships. Children aged between four and eleven were asked to write about the saddest thing they could remember. Then responses revealed that loss of friends, family and pets, for a variety of reasons, including death, was their main source of unhappiness. It was clear that children wanted – and needed – to talk about their feelings and it was interesting to note their increasing ability to understand other people's pain, suffering and sadness (see p.4).

American research and my experience of teaching loss and death showed that the majority of educators felt inadequately prepared to teach the subject and that information and guidance was needed. Hence the reason for producing this book.

If we believe that education is about prevention and developing potential, and not just academic success, we need to help children recognize loss and death as an inevitable part of all existence. They can then use these situations as opportunities for growth – hence the title of this teaching book 'GOOD GRIEF'.

References

Bowlby, J. (1980) *Attachment and Loss, Volume 3: Loss*. London: Hogarth Press.

Fredlund, D.J. (1977) 'Children and death from the school setting viewpoint.' *The Journal of School Health*.

Gorer, G. (1965) *Death, Grief and Mourning in Contemporary Britain*. London: Cresset.

Grollman, D. (1977) 'Explaining death to children.' *The Journal of School Health*.

Children and death for the school setting viewpoint.

'Just a Tick' National Survey in Primary Schools. 1988 HEA Primary Schools Project. Schools Health Education Unit. University of Exeter.

Rutter, M. (1970) *Helping Troubled Children*. Penguin.

Toffler, A. (1971) *Future Shock*. Pan.

4 and 5 year olds

THE SADDEST THING YOU CAN REMEMBER

(S = 28)

Death of grandparent	3·6%
Death or loss of pet	7·2%
Personal/illness	3·6%
My behaviour on others	7·2%
Others behaviour on me	21·4%
Punishment	17·9%
Nil	21·4%
Family death	
Family illness	
Injury/illness of others	
Missing special events or coming to an end	

10 and 11 year olds

THE SADDEST THING YOU CAN REMEMBER

Death of grandparent	30·2%
Death or loss of pet	19·8%
Personal injury/illness	7·3%
My behaviour on others	3·1%
Others behaviour on me	11·5%
Punishment	5·2%
Family death	
Family illness	
Injury/illness of others	
Missing special events or these coming to an end	

Educator's Notes
Introducing the Teaching Programme

Good Grief has been designed to provide a framework for exploring the sensitive issues around Feelings, Loss and Death.

Who is it Suitable For?

This book has been developed for children of different abilities under the age of 12. Because of the basic philosophy and active learning methods, it is suitable to be used in a wide variety of teaching and pastoral situations.

Equal Opportunities – Race, Gender and Special Education Needs

The activities in the book have been designed to incorporate equal opportunities.

The National Curriculum

Various approaches are suggested which may be incorporated into the different subject headings. Examples are given at the start of each topic.

All schools are now required by law to provide a broad and balanced curriculum which promotes the spiritual, moral, cultural, mental and physical development of pupils and prepares them for the opportunities, responsibilities and experiences of adult life (Section 1, Education Reform Act, 1988). Promoting pupils' personal and social development (PSD) means supporting them as they develop from dependent children into independent young people with a wide range of adult roles. At the heart of PSD is the promotion of personal qualities, skills, attitudes and values which enable individuals to think and act for themselves, to manage relationships with others, to understand moral issues and to accept social responsibilities.

The cross-curricular elements described by the National Curriculum make a significant contribution to PSD and the teaching of Loss and Death, as does the guidance laid down in NCC's Curriculum Guidance (3) 'The Whole Curriculum'. In addition, NCC Curriculum (5) 'Health Education', which I was asked to contribute to, has Feelings, Loss and Change and Death included in every key stage. The subject is also included in all key stages of Religious Education. The 1994 NC Guidance allows each school to develop their own PSD and RE Policy and from that to prepare 'Programmes of Study' for practical guidance in the classroom.

Terms — Nursery/School/Parent/Teacher/Educator

Nursery: includes all groups for under fives.

School: includes all learning situations involving children between five and twelve years old.

Parent: includes all carers of children outside the school setting.

Teacher/ Educator: the terms are interchangeable and include any adult involved with children in a learning situation.

Who Should Teach It?

Educators need to have come to terms with losses in their own lives and not to have experienced a major loss recently. They, too, should have a good support network and be used to teaching sensitive areas.

Training

Ideally all educators should have a short training to explore their own experiences of loss, look at the issues raised in this book, and learn appropriate listening skills. Please write to Barbara Ward, author of *Good Grief*, for details of the one day training she has developed to complement the book.

Creating the Climate

'If children were allowed to externalise pain, anger and guilt, they would love to go to school.' (Elizabeth Kübler-Ross)

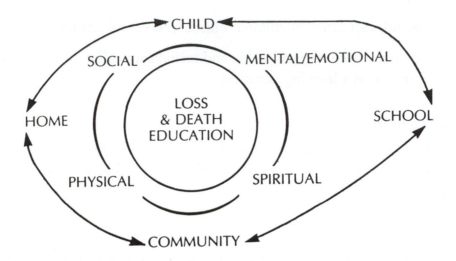

The ethos of the school will be at least as important as any formal context of teaching. A happy, caring institution is obviously the first priority. A major contribution can be made by its physical environment, aesthetic appeal and provision for different cultures, interests and needs.

However, the greatest impact on any young person is their home life. Therefore the most crucial factor will be the quality of relationships both within the school and with the parents and the community at large.

At times of loss and death, the staff need to be alert to the needs of the family and the support that is needed. Opportunities need to be given for children and their families to talk when ready, but staff must also respect their right not to talk if that is their choice.

Once the climate has been created the hidden curriculum groundwork of this subject has been achieved.

Parents

It is essential that parents are aware of and experience the school as a caring institution and one in which they have faith, so they can share any losses or deaths that should affect their children. The formation of a Home/School Association, parent meetings, day-to-day involvement and regular availability of the staff and headteacher assist greatly in making the relationships constructive and valuable. If the school's policy on Loss and Death Education can be developed together with parents, so much the better; at the very least the policy needs to be made explicit to parents and be part of a wider 'The School as a Health Promoting Community Policy'.

Suggested Policy

- When new children start school, ask their parents to inform you of any major losses such as death or divorce. The appropriate teacher(s) then need to tell the children they know about their loss and are available to talk. Tell parents you want to work together. Ask them to keep the school informed of any major changes that could affect their children.

- Include loss and death education in the curriculum, which should include self-esteem, so there is always a point of reference. This should incorporate training for staff and a policy for dealing with individual or group loss or death.

- Make sure all the teaching and non-teaching staff are aware of the loss or bereavement, so that the child is not hurt by some chance remark.

- Explain to the child's class or group what has happened before the child returns to the school. Remind them that tears are OK; that they are a natural and normal response when we are sad. Involve a friend or friends in the class as extra support.

- Talk to the bereaved child/children and family before they return to school so that the families' needs and patterns of grieving and coping can be understood. (Some children prefer not to talk about the loss in school as they want somewhere to escape from the grief at home and want to be treated as normally as possible.) Support is about providing opportunities, but recognizing that not everyone will want to take them up.

- Where appropriate acknowledge the death(s) by having a memorial service.

- Have suitable books available in the class or library for the child to read.

- There may be times when the child, if upset, needs to go somewhere quiet on his or her own or with someone else. For young children and those who have special needs, have a 'cuddle corner' in the classroom. It could have a large soft armchair or bean bags and soft toys and/or blanket or duvet.

- Encourage support systems in the form of small groups in the classroom from an early age. They can meet at the end of each day to share their feelings. This could start by sharing 'something I enjoyed today was…' and go on to 'something that made me sad/angry/frightened was…' In this way children get to realize that everyone has similar feelings and this prevents alienation, one of the main effects of loss. For further ideas see Section 2, 'How Can we Help?'

- Notice any change in behaviour. Quiet children may become noisy or *vice-versa*. Aggression, moodiness, anxiety, lack of concentration and minor illnesses can be quite common in the first few weeks. Depression or suicide attempts are also possible with older children.

- Watch for specific school problems, for example falling behind in school work, cruelty from other children, need for more attention and security. Recent research has shown that children that are bullied have often experienced loss or death.

- Be aware of professional/voluntary agencies in the area which can support you or the parents, or to which the child can be referred, if necessary. They can also help you set up a group for bereaved children, where necessary. (See also Dora Black's book in *Educator's Book List* and the videos in *Additional Resources*).

- Finally, use all examples possible to show that loss and death are a normal and natural part of life. This can include discussing 'soaps' and media happenings.

Governors

The 1986 Education Act encouraged the more positive involvement of governors in their schools, giving them extra representation and responsibilities.

Directors of Education

Directors of Education like to be notified immediately of a death in school so they can write to the family concerned.

Educational Psychologists

The involvement of educational psychologists with bereavement and loss might include:

- Working directly with young people who have experienced loss.

- Advising the educators concerned on a likely response to the loss and the help they can give. This would include emphasizing the importance of the stability and routine of school life at a time of disruption and unhappiness at home.

- Providing more general information to educators or other interested groups – for example, an educational psychologist may lead a staff discussion on the impact of family break-up on young people.

When intensive help is needed for a child or the family, the psychologist might recommend approaching the local Child Guidance Service.

Access to an educational psychologist is usually open – anyone can contact the local School Psychological Service for advice – but teachers would normally do so through their Headteacher.

Educational Welfare Officers (EWOs), School Nurses, Social Workers and Family Counsellors

EWOs and School Nurses can provide valuable links between the school, parents and the community.

Teaching Approaches

'Tell them and they hear
Show them and they see
Do it and they understand.'

How people learn, why people behave as they do, whether and how or even if they want to change, are complex notions. Evidence suggests that a variety of approaches make for the most effective teaching of Personal, Social and Health Education, of which Loss and Death Education are a part.

It is important to utilize the more active teaching methods already in practice with the under twelves. They will form a sound basis for technical and vocational education (TVE) in secondary schools.

The exploration of knowledge and beliefs, the development of self-esteem and group support, are vital components when teaching about feelings, loss and death. The giving of information alone has been shown to be largely ineffective.

The 'Teaching Approach' Needs:

(1) To recognize that there will be children in every group who will have experienced the loss or death of someone close to them, for example parental divorce/separation or death of a grandparent.

(2) To treat bereavement as a natural and normal part of life.

(3) To take cues from the group on the depth they want to go to (bereaved children may want to go further than the other members of the group or *vice-versa*).

(4) To watch for signs of children who may need support; for example, gigglers are often the most scared.

(5) To reassure, where necessary, that tears are natural and normal. Stress that you or other members of the staff are available on a confidential basis for them to talk to at any time should the need arise.

(6) In order to fulfil this, to tell other teaching, and non-teaching, staff that the lessons are taking place, and be given the appropriate reading from section 1.

(7) To create an atmosphere of trust where children feel free to share their feelings. It is often most helpful to sit the children in a circle where everyone can have eye contact; this can be either in pairs, small groups or the whole class.

Grounding the Activities

Children should be encouraged to share and discuss these experiences. It usually helps to 'ground' the experience.

It may be necessary to form smaller groups to give each child the opportunity to share, and it may be easier to start by sharing with just two people rather than a larger group.

It is important that children are not forced to share something if they really do not want to. In this case, where possible, an opportunity needs to be given to share with an adult outside the class. Often children can be surprised to find that others have had similar experiences and/or difficulties. The realization can not only be liberating but also prevents long term feelings of alienation, especially in situations where children have experienced loss of a parent, through separation/divorce or death, or other forms of loss.

Both positive and negative experiences need to be shared, with emphasis placed on the positive alternative. Often other children who have experienced similar situations are best at this.

Integrating the Subject into the Curriculum

The topic can be introduced by:

(1) A planned topic for one year group or the whole school, which could include assemblies involving parents and the community.

(2) A situation arising at home/school or in the community which sparks off discussion in class. This can take place at any time and is not planned. This can often be the most effective way, i.e. starting from children's own experiences.

Both of these ways ensure that children of each age group cover topics most suited to their needs, either initiated by the teacher or children. The aim is for the children and teacher to work together, building on previous experiences, ensuring that the subject is taught in a natural way.

How Can the Subject be Co-Ordinated and Developed Throughout the School?

○ Incorporate the concept of the spiral curriculum and the needs of the children and their families.

○ Incidental work, as well as planned topics, can be recorded as children progress through school. Successive teachers can then build on what has gone before. (See teaching scheme on Life Cycle and Ageing.)

It is interesting, even at this early stage, to see the work that has been done, and which areas to build on.

Visitors to the School

The purpose of having a visitor, rather than a speaker, to a lesson is to place responsibility, both for the visitor and for the questions asked, with the children. A visitor can respond to the needs of a group, whereas a speaker presumes the need(s).

Suggestions for Using a Visitor

- Decide with the children whom to invite, for example a representative from a voluntary organization.

- The children are then asked to write to the suggested name(s) inviting them to come at a special time and place, and to explain what the framework of the session will be. Alternatively the proposed visitor could be telephoned.

Questions/Needs for the Class to Decide

- Who will meet the visitor and where?
- How to greet them.
- Will any refreshments be needed?
- Who will be the time keeper?
- How will the visitor be introduced to the class?
- How will the class introduce itself to the visitor?
- How will the session be ended?
- Who will see the visitor out and thank them?
- Who will write to say thank you to the visitor?

Asking Questions

Depending on the age of the children it is useful first to brainstorm ideas. The class will then need to decide who will ask the first question, who will go next, etc.

Time needs to be given for the visitor to ask questions.

Evaluation

Encourage the children to evaluate the session by asking all or some of the following questions, depending on age and ability:

- What did we learn/find out?
- Were we well organized?
- Was the visit enjoyable?
- Did the visitor seem comfortable?
- Are there any questions still unanswered?
- Was there anything we could change before another visit?

Planning

The first task when planning is to identify objectives. We have included these for the different activities, but we hope educators will develop their own before starting any course.

(1) REMEMBER THE BASICS WHEN PLANNING ANY COURSE

Why – Objectives   When – Date and time

What – Content   Where – Place

How – Method   Who – Teachers and resources

N.B. Be realistic about timing and always have an extra activity ready but be prepared to go at the pace that is right for each group.

(2) ACTIVITIES NEED TO BE FITTED INTO THE CONTEXT OF YOUR OBJECTIVES

They are designed as a means to an end not an end in themselves.

(3) CHOICE OF ACTIVITIES

The best resource in any teaching programme will be the children, educators and the surrounding community. The activities in *Good Grief* have, therefore, been designed to utilize these resources to their best advantage.

The activities in this teaching book are in a logical sequence. You may like to add ideas of your own or use only one or two activities to enhance other activities you have already planned.

Each part is designed to stand on its own after the background reading of Section 1. We realize we have included far more under each heading than anyone could use in the limited time available. We therefore suggest you use the following check list before selecting an activity:

(1) Is it suitable for the age and ability of my class/group or do I need to change it?

(2) Does the activity make sense on its own or do I need an introduction or follow up?

(3) Have I read the background notes and relevant resources and have I checked the background of all the members of the group?

(4) Have I alerted the other members of the staff and given them the appropriate background reading?

(5) Does it fit the time I have available or does it need adapting?

(6) Do I feel comfortable and familiar with the subject or do I need to discuss or practise the activity with a colleague first?

Evaluation

Evaluation is the way we tell whether we have met our objectives, and whether our approach, activities and children's involvement have been effective.

Always debrief at the end of each activity by asking the children to discuss their feelings. This will enable you to assess the effectiveness of the activity both from your own and the children's point of view.

Learning relies on sharing and exploring children's experiences, attitudes, and values.

Evaluation needs to assess the process of these sessions, not just the content, that is: how did the children feel during these activities; what caused their feelings and reactions; what did they think; also what did they learn and how can they apply that learning to their lives.

The following are typical 'processing' questions:

- How did you feel during the activity?

- How are your feelings at this activity?

- What did you think during the activity?

- What are you thinking now?

- Did you change anything you were doing? Give examples.

- Will you change anything you do in the future as a result of the activity? Give examples.

Other Approaches Could Include

(1) ASKING THE CHILDREN:

- What they enjoyed most/least about a lesson.

- How they are feeling, for example, I'm feeling sad/happy/etc. at the moment, is anyone else feeling the same?

(2) HOW ARE WE FEELING NOW:

- Ask the children to draw a circle and divide it into four sections and then write a word or draw something in each section to show how they are feeling.

The checklist below can be used to indicate how well the objectives for each session have been met. There may well be some changes in the children's behaviour during the course of a session, although it is probable that significant changes will take longer. It is important, therefore, to look at the situation again in the weeks and months that follow.

Try to involve the children in monitoring their own progress. By doing this the children will have a deeper insight into their own behaviour, and the teacher can show them that their opinion is valued.

Checklist

Refer to this checklist during the weeks that follow the session. It can be used to monitor changes in the class as a whole, or for individuals. The following questions can be answered with:

(1) 'Occasionally'   – 'OC'

(2) 'Quite often'   – 'QT'

(3) 'Nearly all the time'   – 'NY'

FOR EXAMPLE, 'DO THE CHILDREN':

	OC	QT	NY
• Explain their needs and express their own feelings openly when appropriate?		–	—
• Treat each other with consideration?	–	–	–
• Show an understanding of other people's needs and feelings?	–	–	–
• Help anyone who has special needs or who is disabled, if appropriate?	–	–	–
• Show sensitivity for and acceptance of cultural differences in others?	–	–	–
• Seek ways of helping others where appropriate?	–	–	–

N.B. Add any other statement of your own.

Understanding Loss

'There is no growth without pain and conflict and no loss that cannot lead to gain.'

(Lily Pincus, 1961)

Loss touches all of us throughout life, yet its existence is generally not recognized except in extreme cases such as death and divorce.

Every time people make a change in their life, they take on a new role or let go of an old one, they lose something. The potential for loss is rarely considered part of changing school or teacher. Generally the capacity to adapt is recognized.

The loss event is likely to become and remain a source of stress rather than a potential for growth unless the loss aspect is recognized and acknowledged, and grieving encouraged.

Bereavement can be described as 'the loss of something that is precious'. The word is most often used in the context of a person, but it may include, for example, the loss of an inanimate object or the ending of relationship, or a change in a particular situation.

No child can live very long without encountering loss. By the time a young person is ready to leave school they will have experienced most of the following:

- **Growing up.** This process may also be seen as a loss of accustomed forms of support and attention as well as the gain of autonomy.

- **Going to school**, which means temporary separation from parents as well as the gain of education, playmates etc.

- **Changing** Play Group/Nursery School to Primary School to Secondary/Middle School to College means a periodic loss of familiar surroundings and people as well as gains of new experiences, e.g. teacher, playmates.

In addition there will be other losses, some predictable, some unpredictable, affecting either the child themselves, family or friends. These could include:

- NEW SIBLINGS to adjust to, which can cause a loss of parental attention.

- DEATH OF A SIBLING. This can result in preoccupied parents with resulting feelings of isolation as well as the loss of someone close to you.

- PARENTS CHANGING JOBS which can mean the move to another area and giving up their friends, schools and familiar environment.

- MOTHERS RETURNING TO PAID EMPLOYMENT – sometimes resulting in the loss of someone to greet and listen to them on returning from school.

- BEREAVEMENT as grandparents grow older and die.

- LOSS OF PARENT THROUGH SEPARATION/DIVORCE OR DEATH. In 1994 there were 160,684 under sixteens affected by divorce. Four out of ten marriages now end in divorce. Over a third of marriages are re-marriages (where either or both parents have been divorced before). This can mean adjustment to a new step-parent too.

- FAMILY OR FRIENDS MOVING AWAY or ending or changing relationships. Change of country/culture.

- CHILDREN IN CARE. In 1994 there were 76,000 children in care in Britain, with approximately 38,000 in foster homes. Sonia Jackson of Bristol University outlined the factors contributing to the 'high risk of educational failure'. These included disrupted schooling, low expectations, low self-esteem and lack of continuity – all compounded 'by the low priority given to education by social workers who bear the main responsibility for the welfare and progress of children in care'.

- SPECIAL NEEDS. During the school years about 20 per cent of all children will at some time experience being identified as having special educational needs (DFE 1994). Many difficulties (physical, sensory, emotional, behaviour or learning) are not identified at birth, but come to light during the early years at home or school. These can include minor difficulties such as discovering diabetes, wearing glasses or a hearing aid or more serious physical or learning ones. These difficulties can result in loss of status, self-esteem, friends, participation in activities, achievements, and sometimes loss of family. The degree of loss will depend on the child's perception and the reaction of those around them.

- UNEMPLOYMENT. An increasing number will have experienced their parents' and elder sibling's unemployment and may in fact face unemployment on leaving school. Many 16–18 year olds will find the government training scheme the only opening for them.

- HOMELESSNESS. A growing problem facing young people in Great Britain. Shelter say there are 8500 sleeping rough every night. In the first half of 1994 there were 64,120 households accepted by local authorities as being homeless.

- HOSPITAL STAY. This can mean temporary loss of familiar surroundings.

- CHILD SEXUAL ABUSE. Defined as 'any sexual exploitation between an adult, whether by coercion or consent'. Ten per cent of children are thought to have experienced some form of sexual abuse. This can result in a variety of losses on different levels including loss of innocence and self-esteem.

- SERIOUS ILLNESS. e.g. cancer, heart disease and AIDS. In 1994 in the United Kingdom there were 551 under fourteens in schools who were HIV positive and up to July 1994 there were 175 under fourteens with AIDS, 89 of whom have died. AIDS (Acquired Immune Deficiency Syndrome) is a condition which develops when the body's defences are severely damaged. As a result, people are more likely to get illnesses which the body would normally be able to fight off easily. At the moment there is no cure for AIDS. Some drugs are used to prolong life for people with AIDS. This disease may result in harassment, rejection and isolation as well as death.

- DRUG MISUSE. A world-wide problem which is causing particular concern with/for children and young people. Drug misuse and abuse can occur with legal drugs as well as illegal ones. Legal drugs include alcohol, tobacco, tranquillizers and coffee.

  > Drug abuse can result in loss of that which makes us a person, our personality. With the loss of personality is the restriction on our freedom of choice; our life is restricted, our horizons narrowed. Other losses may include loved ones, career, happiness, health and life itself. In addition giving up drugs may involve loss of a way of life and the contacts that go with it.

Some of the following losses mentioned by Peter Speck in his book *Loss and Grief in Medicine* may mean young people having to deal with the grieving process of family or friends:

(1) A miscarriage or stillbirth can often make a woman feel that she is a failure as a woman.

(2) A couple who cannot conceive may feel a loss of status and purpose.

(3) When a baby is born with a defect the parents may grieve for the normal child they have lost.

(4) The most commonly experienced loss resulting from a hysterectomy is the knowledge that a woman can no longer conceive and bear children and that her reproductive life is over.

(5) If the body image is disrupted by amputation, or other surgery, it can lead to a grief-like reaction which requires a period of mourning before resulting trauma is resolved and a new, acceptable, body image is formed. The acceptance of this by others is important.

(6) The initial reaction to loss of vision may render the person immobile, expressionless and depressed. The person may be preoccupied with the total dependency they feel and the loss of individual freedom.

(7) To be designated 'disabled' can be an important change in status which seems to emphasize the loss of capability and self-esteem for many. The loss of a sense of future and of security can lead to a sense of hopelessness.

(8) 'Redundancy Neurosis' affects mainly young or middle-aged people who cannot find employment. Their feelings of loss of status, self-respect and earning power have lead to depressive illness.

The way young people deal with any of these losses or 'little deaths' will affect the way they deal with the ultimate one of their own death or someone close to them. It is now possible to go for up to 50 years without experiencing the death of anyone near to us, so that when death does touch us closely it is difficult to know how to react or what to do. The intensity of the grief reaction will depend on how they have experienced the other losses, their personal characteristics, their religious and cultural background and the support available.

Divorce and Separation

How the School Can Help

Background Reading

- **Section 1** 'Understanding Loss'
  'Why Teach Loss and Bereavement'
  'Statistics for Britain'

- **Section 2** 'Living with Loss'

- **Section 3** 'Unhappy Ever After'
  'Caught in the Middle'

One in five children experience the loss of a parent through divorce or separation. In many cases the effect on their psychological development may be more traumatic than the death of a parent.

Helpful Hints for Teachers

Parents often discuss their marital breakdown with teachers.

- Be aware of the agencies available in your area, and advise parents to go for help as soon as possible (see 'Useful Addresses' in Section 3).

Helpful Hints for Parents

Professor Caplan, the Scientific Director of the Family Center for the Study of Psychological Stress, makes the following suggestions for parents:

'Parents intending to divorce should discuss the issues with their children before the separation to prepare them for what is about to happen in a manner geared to their ages and developmental levels. With pre-school children this discussion should take place a week or two before the family's break up; with 5–8 year olds the discussion should be a month or two beforehand; older children should be given longer notice.

If possible parents should talk to their children together to show that they agree. They should expect that, after this first discussion, they will need to continue talking about the issues with children as a group or individually depending on the children's reactions and the questions they raise. The initial discussion should cover the following points:

(1) The parents intend to end their marriage, live in separate homes, and no longer be husband and wife, because they have stopped loving each other and cannot live

peacefully with each other; the divorce has not been caused by anything the children have done.

(2) The couple intend to continue as parents of their children, to love them and care for them throughout childhood. They promise this without regard to what may happen in the future, when one or other may remarry and have additional children.

(3) The children will live in the home of one parent and visit the other parent regularly. The parents know that the children need continuing contact with both of them for healthy growth and development, and both want the children to maintain close links with each parent.

(4) The parents realize that the children will probably oppose the divorce because it breaks up their home, but the children cannot alter their decision and should not try to do so. It has been made by the adults because of adult problems.

(5) The parents know that the children may feel angry, upset or insecure. They have taken these reactions into account and are sorry about them. They will help the children master these feelings; most children succeed in this after a few months.

(6) Divorce is common; every second or third marriage ends in this way. Thus the children should not feel different from others; they should not feel ashamed because their parents have divorced. Like other family matters this is private, but the children should feel free to talk about it to their close friends and their teachers. It often helps to share such matters with others who can provide support in times of difficulty. If, for a few weeks, thoughts about family troubles interfere with the children's capacity to concentrate in the classroom or on homework it would be good for their teachers to know what is happening and help the children overcome their temporary difficulties.

(7) The children should stay out of the quarrels between the parents; they should definitely not take sides. Even though the parents have stopped loving each other they continue to love their children and will always do so. They each want the children to love the other parent. They will do their best not to say bad things about each other to the children; if, because of anger they do not always succeed, the children should forgive them.

(8) The parents do not wish the children to carry messages from one to the other, and promise to try not to send messages through the children. They do not wish the children to tell them what the other parent has been doing.

(9) The parents jointly or individually will talk to the children about these matters from time to time before and after the divorce. They know that it will be hard for the children to understand and come to terms with what is happening and that it will take a long time for them to adjust to the division of their family into two separate homes. The children should express their feelings in any way that is comfortable and should feel free to ask questions, which the parents will try to answer.'

Helpful Hints for Children

- ° Provide a caring atmosphere at school to help balance the disruption at home (see 'The School as a Caring Community' in Section 1.)

- ° Involve the Educational Psychologist where appropriate to support the children and teachers.

- ° Read the two articles in Section 3 mentioned above.

How to Help Someone Who is Suffering from Loss

- DO let your genuine concern and caring show.

- DO be available…to listen or to help with whatever else seems needed at the time.

- DO say you are sorry about what happened and about their pain.

- DO allow them to express as much unhappiness as they are feeling at the moment and are willing to share.

- DO encourage them to be patient with themselves, not to expect too much of themselves and not to impose any 'shoulds' on themselves.

- DO allow them to talk about their loss as much and as often as they want to.

- DO talk about the special, endearing qualities of what they've lost.

- DO reassure them that they did everything that they could.

- DON'T let your own sense of helplessness keep you from reaching out.

- DON'T avoid them because you are uncomfortable (being avoided by friends adds pain to an already painful experience).

- DON'T say how you know how they feel. (Unless you've experienced their loss yourself you probably don't know how they feel.)

- DON'T say 'you ought to be feeling better by now' or anything else which implies a judgement about their feelings.

- DON'T tell them what they should feel or do.

- DON'T change the subject when they mention their loss.

- DON'T avoid mentioning their loss out of fear of reminding them of their pain (they haven't forgotten it).

- DON'T try to find something positive (e.g. a moral lesson, closer family ties, etc.) about the loss.

- DON'T point out at least they have their other…

- DON'T say they can always have another…

- DON'T suggest that they should be grateful for their…

- DON'T make any comments which in any way suggest that their loss was their fault (there will be enough feelings of doubt and guilt without any help from their friends).

Tracing Western Attitudes to Death

'Since men cannot cure death, they have made up their minds not to think about it'   *(Camus)*

In pre-Christian times there was little fear of death itself but people would fear the 'spirits' of the dead returning to harm them.

From around the time of the advent of Christianity onwards, a view of the world was formed with the earth at the centre, heaven above and hell below. However, early beliefs of an existence after death were accepted in the simple form that all those attending church would automatically go to heaven and those who did not would become extinct.

Life for nearly everyone at this time was rural-based with the church and manor being the centre of their lives. As local crafts developed with the subsequent trading of goods and the growth of towns, so beliefs started to alter, albeit slowly, in all areas of life.

Death had always taken place at home in the bedchamber with the family present, including the children. This continued into the nineteenth century, but during this time a change came in the way the Day of Judgement was perceived. At first it was thought all would sleep until the final day and, on awakening, be judged; it was seen as a long way off. Then the Day of Judgement was thought to occur at the time of death itself, mainly due to a reinterpretation of the Bible, whereby death came to be seen as 'a symbol of the disastrous alienation between men and God due to sin' (**Ninian Smart**). Hence the element of 'fear' of death was introduced and reproduced in art and literature of that period (13th–14th century). On the whole though, death remained familiar and was an accepted part of everyone's life. This long chain of centuries when death was familiar is called 'Tamed Death' by the historian Philippe Aries.

From the mid-eighteenth century onwards, all this started to change with the emergence of new radical thought whereby individualism replaced collectivism, rationalism, scientific discoveries and industrialization led to eventual mass migration of people to live in towns.

Two aspects of this made a great difference to the attitude towards death. One was the change in religious perceptions. Darwin's theory of evolution brought with it a questioning of all previously-held beliefs and, as this century has progressed, all beliefs have been re-examined and analysed by many in varying ways. Now the central beliefs of the Virgin Birth and the Resurrection are under scrutiny, causing a rift in the institution of the Churches. Initially a 'Second Coming' and the Resurrection was expected within a comparatively few years. Now that 2000 years have almost passed, many are wondering – why so long? They are uncertain, so little is spoken. This ambivalence of thought causes a difficult state of affairs for the dying and the bereaved. There is no set belief and code of behaviour to follow because accompanying this the rites of mourning have been discarded.

The second reason for a change in attitude was the advent of hygiene, hospitals, medical advances and technology. It was not considered hygienic for the dying person to be lying at home surrounded by family and friends. If a person does die at home, then the body is instantly removed. Unless death is caused by an accident, most die in hospital, with the situation being controlled by strangers in an alien atmosphere where we have little control, so apprehension and fear ensue. Sometimes no family member is present at the time of death. The professionals handling the situation are often as unused to the emotional aspect to death as everyone else. To many, death is regarded as a failure within an environment geared for returning people to health. Many are not taught about death and its effects on loved ones. In conjunction with this there is a general expectation that, due to medical and technological advances, a cure will be available that something can be done…heading on from this we, as parents, do not expect children or younger people to die, whereas this is an acceptable fact in Third World countries.

The reality of death is constantly ignored but the unreality is too pronounced. Death is witnessed in films, plays, news and documentaries on television. 'A child may see 15,000 deaths before reaching puberty', says Michael Simpson. The awareness of what death actually means to the families is ignored or glossed over so few have any idea what to expect when they find themselves bereaved.

Philippe Aries calls this 'Forbidden Death'.

Margaret Hayworth
The Compassionate Friends

References

Aries. P. (1976) *Western Attitudes towards Death*. Boyours.

Simpson, M.A. *The Facts of Death*.

Toynbee, A. (ed) (1968) *Man's Concern with Death*. Hodder and Stoughton.

Stages of Grief

Grief is a normal, essential response to the death of a loved one. It can be short lived or last a long time depending on the personality involved, the closeness of the relationship, the circumstances of the death and previous losses suffered. Death of a husband, wife or child is likely to be the most difficult.

In many cases, this grief can take the form of several clearly defined stages. Very often a bereaved person can only resume a normal emotional life after working through these stages.

(1) SHOCK AND DISBELIEF

This happens when our model of the world is upset. One not only loses the person but life also can feel that it has lost its meaning. Shock can take the form of physical pain or numbness, but more often consists of complete apathy and withdrawal or abnormal calm, in some cases even anger. Numbness can act as a defence so we are able to cope with the immediate jobs and needs.

(2) DENIAL

This generally occurs within the first 14 days and can last minutes, hours or weeks. In this stage the bereaved person behaves as if the dead person is still there, no loss is acknowledged. The dead person's place is still laid at meal times, for example, or a husband may make arrangements for both he and his wife to go somewhere together.

(3) GROWING AWARENESS

Many feel at this stage that they are abnormal because they have never before experienced the waves of savage feelings that surge through them and over which they temporarily have no control, such as tears, anger, guilt, sadness and loneliness. Some or all of the following emotions may be experienced:

(a) Yearning and pining – urge to search, go over death, trying to find a reason for the death, visiting where it happened.

(b) Anger – against any or all of the following: the medical services, the person who caused the death, in case of accident, God for letting it happen, the deceased for leaving them.

(c) Depression – the bereaved person begins to feel the despair, the emptiness, the pain of the loss. It is often accompanied by feelings of redundancy, lack of self worth, and point to anything. If a person can cry, it usually helps to relieve the stress.

(d) Guilt – this emotion is felt for the real or imagined negligence or harm inflicted on the person who has just died. People often say 'if only I had called the

Doctor – not gone out' etc. There is a tendency to idealize the person who has died and feel they could have loved them better. The bereaved can also feel guilty about their own feelings and inability to enjoy life.

(e) Anxiety – in extreme cases anxiety can even become panic, as the full realization of the loss begins to come through. There is anxiety about the changes and new responsibilities that are taking place and the loneliness looming ahead. There may even be thoughts of suicide.

(4) ACCEPTANCE

This generally occurs in the second year after the death has been relived at the first anniversary. The bereaved person is then able to relearn the world and new situations with its possibilities and changes without the deceased person.

Difficulties in Grieving

Many people do not pass through the 'stages of grief' without some hold-ups. Once these have been recognized and worked through the person is able to move forward through the grief process. Listed below are some of the hold-ups that are common to many bereaved people:

- opposition to letting go – refusal to accept the death

- lack of support – family/friends/community/spiritual

- not prepared to allow themselves to grieve

- marital or family discord

- doubt about the reality of the loss e.g. no body

- violent death or suicide

- mixed feelings towards the deceased

- difficulties in communicating and expressing feelings

- the social or religious customs that demand self-control often cause delayed grief, e.g. some Christian groups emphasize the certain resurrection of the loved one which is to be celebrated with joy and no space is allowed for the natural grief to be expressed

- low self-esteem/image

- not being allowed or able to attend the funeral (e.g. a child)

- financial problems

- when things have been left unsaid, a visit not made, or any other unfinished business

- dependent family members, allowing no time to grieve

- succession of losses – no time allowed to be able to grieve.

There are three ways commonly used for coping with bereavement (including divorce and other losses) which are not helpful over a long period of time and need to be faced by the bereaved person.

For Young People

(1) **Substitution**. The child may want to find a substitute mother or father.

(2) **Aggression.** The child may be always fighting, or avoiding School. A variety of discipline problems both inside and outside of school. e.g. drug abuse and general anti-social behaviour.

(3) **Helplessness.** This leads to a lack of curiosity and so impairs learning. The child may opt out of life – even become deaf in extreme cases.

For Adults

(1) **Substitution.** This might take the form of another marriage or focusing all attention on the children. The problem with a speedy remarriage is that it frequently fails because the grief work from the first marriage has not been done. The problem of the parent focusing all their attention on the children is that the children may feel smothered.

(2) **Aggression.** Anger is another way of coping. The anger may be against God, or against the doctor for not giving the right treatment. Sometimes the anger is directed against themselves.

(3) **Helplessness.** Another common way of coping is to be 'helpless' and get all the friends and neighbours running around. The problem is that this 'helplessness' has to stop if they are to adjust to their new situation.

Grief in Children

Perceptions and Explanations of Death

'The most meaningful help that we can give any relative – child or adult – is to share his feelings before the event of death and allow him to work through his feelings, whether they are rational or irrational'

(Elisabeth Kübler-Ross)

THERE ARE PARTICULAR ASPECTS ABOUT CHILDREN'S PERCEPTION OF DEATH THAT NEED SPECIAL CONSIDERATION:

(1) We all feel 'deprived' when a loved one dies but this emotion goes very deep in the young and it goes hand in hand with much 'fear'. Parents experience a fear and vulnerability about the safety of other loved ones but are more consciously aware of a world beyond their family network. Younger children's lives revolve completely around their mother, father, sisters and brothers. So not only do they feel 'deprived' of the family member who has died but the 'fear of death' for the rest of the family and themselves is heightened and becomes a paramount emotion.

(2) The actual thoughts that this age group have on 'death' is, in all probability, a distorted view. Those living in rural areas will have more of an idea about the cyclical rhythms of nature and will have witnessed the death of creatures in the wild. The town child will not have had these experiences and the main portrayal of death for the twentieth-century child is through the media – especially television – which gives an unreal picture of the event. The nineteenth-century child would have witnessed at first hand a death or deaths within its own immediate circle from an early age but it is a sad occurrence that now the death of loved ones usually happens away from most, if not all, of the family. This induces an anxiety and fear springing from a fertile imagination about an unknown event and the false pictures fed by the media. It has been noted that children often use the word 'kill' when describing death.

(3) Pre-adolescent children have great difficulty in grasping 'abstract' concepts about death. They are at the 'concrete' thinking stage in their development. Hence the difficulty in trying to explain the death of a loved one in a spiritual context.

So how do we explain death? For many of us, living in an age where any view, if not scientifically provable is automatically considered suspect, the difficulty in understanding death for ourselves is great. Let alone explaining it to young people! This uncertainty within parents and teachers usually means the subject is ignored or explained without real conviction, i.e. 'Granny's gone to heaven', but we are unable to follow on from this except in further vague,

33

unconvincing abstract remarks which many of us query ourselves! No wonder our children experience 'deprivation and fear'.

Marjorie Mitchell says that 'neither dogmas of immortality nor that of death being the final end are likely to create positive attitudes in the child and adolescent'. Neither is 'I don't know' very helpful, but to say 'NO ONE YET KNOWS' is in keeping with the natural urge of the exploring child, who from babyhood is bent on finding out what life is all about. She suggests saying 'People are still trying to find out, just as they are trying to find out what is in space. Probably when you are grown up you'll go on trying to find out too, but the brain is limited and can't find out everything.'

There are two aspects of death. One, the lifeless body and two, the spiritual aspect.

(1) **The Body.** What happens to the body is an aspect on which primary school children tend to concentrate. Jenny Kander explains it in this way:

'Tommy does not feel as you do because he is dead and that means that he does not have feelings anymore; he cannot feel hot or cold, that he is hurting or sick or well. He cannot think anymore either; not about nice things or scary things or good or bad things… And he does not need to be held or hugged or fed or played with anymore either because being dead means that his body is no use to him now. Remember how the tree's leaves die and then fall off the tree onto the ground? They are still beautiful but they are not alive and green after they have died. We will always remember and love Tommy even though we cannot see him or play with him anymore.

There are two things we can choose between to do with Tommy's body. We can have it put in a special box called a coffin and bury it in the ground in a place called a cemetery which is just for that purpose, or we can have it turned into ashes and that is called cremation. That is what we have chosen to do and so we will ask/have asked a man called a funeral director to take Tommy's body and put it in the special box, which is then put in a very small room – not like any room that we have in our home, all that is in it is a very hot fire, which changes that body into ashes. Then, when we are ready, we can bury them in the ground at the cemetery or we can scatter them in a place that we choose…'

For the 'concrete thinking' younger child, Marjorie Mitchell talks about a lesson with 9-year-olds in which atoms and electrons were being explained as the basis of all matter. It was pointed out that electrons are still moving in the chemicals of the ashes of the cremated and they go on 'circling like tiny planets'. These children found this objective observance meaningful. One child, who had expressed a fear of death, said, 'They (the tiny planets) *could* go on for ever; bits of me can go on for ever and ever and ever!!'

(2) **The Spiritual Aspect** can be subdivided into three viewpoints:

(a) There is no continuance of the individual spirit.

(b) That there is a continuation of life in some form. One mother quoted in Marjorie Mitchell's book said to her child, 'People usually die after they have done the work they had to do. As to what happens, nobody really knows, but many people believe that life continues in a different way.'

This different way is often likened to the butterfly emerging from its chrysalis. The small story book *Waterbugs and Dragonflies* by Doris Stickney puts over this concept of a living being's continuance in a completely different form delightfully.

(c) The religious aspect of soul/spirit. The explanation for this is a personal family matter but it is felt that children should be told that there are differing views.

Three observations about the spiritual aspect are:

(i) The religious content in the media presentation of death is minimal so children do not readily connect death with a spiritual meaning.

(ii) There is no evidence showing that religious attitudes make children feel more secure or console them. The abstract quality of them can frighten children.

(iii) Children tend to grasp theories on reincarnation and pantheism easier than those of Christianity, whose concepts are difficult.

Quoted below are three questions and answers taken from the book *A Child's Questions About Death* by Neville A. Kirkwood. They bring together some of the aspects spoken about. The first one deals with the difference between sleep and death. The difference needs to be made clear to a child, who could become anxious about sleeping.

IS A DEAD PERSON SLEEPING?

When we sleep we are resting our bodies. Our heart and other parts of our body do not work as hard. Sleep gives us strength for another day at school or play. When a person dies, his body stops working. There will be no waking up. The body's work is finished. So sleep and death are different.

WHAT HAPPENS TO DEAD PEOPLE?

We live in a house. The people living inside make a house a home. For our bodies to be a home, we have a spirit which lives in the house – our bodies. When a person dies, the body becomes an empty house. Most people believe that the spirit which was living within the body goes to heaven. Our spirit is not a part of the body. It is with our spirit that we are able to give love and receive love. The spirit or soul never wears out. We cannot see someone's spirit, nor can we see heaven. We believe that we have a spirit and that there is a heaven. This is what we call faith. People of all religions believe that we have a spirit that lives on after our bodies have died.

WHAT IS HEAVEN LIKE?

We do not know what heaven looks like. We cannot tell you where heaven is. We know our bodies on earth wear out and die. Because it is our spirits that live on, we believe that we shall not again experience the sadness, the troubles and difficulties we have on earth. We believe heaven is the place where God is. Because God is love, heaven will be a place full of love.

35

Teenagers, like adults, realize the permanence of death and so become involved in looking for a meaning – the eternal 'whys'. Grief superimposed on the normal adolescent search for personal identity whereby family and societal values and views are all being questioned must make a confusing situation almost unable to communicate their feelings!

The conclusions of a survey of 6–15 year olds about their perceptions of the meaning of death were:

(1) They wished to discuss death and have no 'unspoken barriers'.

(2) The best explanations especially for under-eight-year-olds were those that are 'simple, direct and draw as much as possible from the child's own experience'.

(3) It suggests that especially for those in the 'magical thinking' stage, it would be wise to ask the child to explain back again what he has been told so that gross distortion and misconceptions can be corrected.

A realistic, healthy understanding of death is required by society as a whole. This would remove much of the fear and anxiety that surrounds it and go a considerable way to easing the grief process for adults as well as the 'under twenties'.

References

'Explaining Death' is a section from the booklet 'Helping Younger Brothers and Sisters' by The Compassionate Friends.

Reactions of Younger Children

'At the time when they (children) need all the support of positive family experience...ironically it is the time when parents have least to offer as they struggle to survive their grief.'
Kathy La Tour

Children, like adults, are individuals. They go through stages of physical, mental, emotional and social development but the details for each child are unique. Grief and the variety of ways in which it can be expressed needs to be acknowledged.

REACTIONS WHICH MAY OCCUR

(1) Once realization of the death has begun, children, like adults, will enter a period of shock which will last for a few hours or up to a week. It can manifest itself by the child going through daily life mechanically, automatically smiling on cue, apprehensive; they may have periods of panic. Alternatively, they may become withdrawn and gaze into space for long periods.

(2) The death of a close relative heightens our sense of vulnerability and for children death and separation are synonymous. They may:

   (a) become very anxious about being separated from parents for any reason;

   (b) be reluctant to go to school;

   (c) be depressed;

   (d) be prone to infection such as colds, ear infections and tummy upsets;

   (e) bite nails or cuticles, pick themselves, twiddle with their hair;

   (f) develop a fear of the dark (which may last for years);

   (g) have difficulty in going to sleep;

   (h) possibly have nightmares;

   (i) develop a phobia about hospitals, nurses and doctors.

(3) Regression to an earlier stage of development is common.

(4) Loss of concentration for children at school is common.

(5) Food can become important. Some children will eat and eat to fill up the emptiness they feel inside. They may hoard food and secrete it away. Others though will lose interest in eating. This phase usually only lasts a comparatively short time.

(6) Sadness and anger need to be expressed but children are often afraid and confused about venting their feelings as they do not know what is allowed.

(7) Some may be frightened to ask questions and will only talk to 'outsiders', while other children only want to talk about the tragedy to the immediate family.

(8) The time put on the grief process for a child is the same as parents – approximately two years.

SPECIFIC AGE GROUP REACTIONS

Children process information differently from adults and this process changes as they grow.

Babies are affected by their parents' emotional state (although one twin is likely to miss the other). Reactions may include being very unsettled for a few weeks, losing weight and experiencing sleeping difficulties.

Toddlers (1–3 years) cannot understand the permanence of death and may ask repeatedly about the child coming back. They do not easily distinguish fact from fantasy and may believe they did something wrong which caused the death. They may regard their parents' apparent lack of interest in them as rejection. Separation anxiety is a key symptom.

Problems in toddlers are generally behavioural expressions of loss and insecurity and include reversion to baby talk, regression in toilet training, nightmares, insomnia and refusal to be left alone. Some search repeatedly for the child and others may act out the tragedy with their toys.

Magical Thinking Stage (3–7 years approx.) starts in an egocentric stage of growth when the child perceives that he is the centre of the universe and so believes his own thoughts, wishes and actions cause what happens to himself and to other people.

When told about the death they will probably react quite casually because they are used to playing 'bang, bang, you're dead' and getting up again. Most likely they will cry and ask about the death at a later time, perhaps at bedtime, as though you had not explained it before. This can be confusing for parents. The child may be frightened and remorseful that their jealous thoughts about the dead child made it go away. Their parents' preoccupation with the dead child may be seen as confirmation of their guilt, or they may try to comfort their parents in the way they have been previously comforted.

Children may experience a compelling urge to recover the lost loved one and will make every effort to search for them. This fits in with magical thinking which is reinforced by fairy and fold tales. Children will think that if they are always good and endure bad things and wait for a very long time the dead child will return and all will be 'happy ever after' (see Article 'How will Mummy breathe and who will feed her' in Section 3).

The child may re-enact the cause of death or an aspect of it such as the funeral. This should not be discouraged as play is the means by which children integrate and master life's experiences.

Some children become fearful that they may die themselves, or that they may disappear, or their parents might go away and so do not want to let parents out of their sight.

Concrete Thinking Stage (7–12 years) children at this age think in terms of either/or, i.e. good guys or bad guys. They have little ability to deal with subtleties, ambiguities or euphemisms. So care must be taken not to use figures of speech such as 'we lost your sister', etc.

The permanence of death starts to be recognized and by 9–10 years the irreversibility of it begins to be grasped and children realize they themselves will die one day. Over 11 years a child perceives the finality of death in an adult way.

Ideas for Parents on How to Help Children with Their Grief

*' A child can live through anything so long as he or she is told the truth
and is allowed to share with loved ones the natural feelings people have
when they are suffering.'*

(Eda Le Shan)

GENERAL IDEAS

(1) The first thing to communicate to a child is 'You are not alone: I am with you'.

(2) Share feelings with children. They want and need information and participation in the grief process. (Often parents wish to protect their children from reality, seeing childhood as a time of innocence.)

(3) Let children know that feelings take precedence – stop cooking, reading the paper, etc.

(4) Make sure children get the clear message that the death was not their fault. It was not because they were bad in any way or because they were unlovable. Neither was there anything they could have done or still do to alter the situation.

(5) Do not tell the child 'Don't worry' or 'Don't be sad' etc. As with parental grief, they are unable to control their responses. Also avoid messages that tell the child what he/she should or should not be feeling. Do not criticize or seem shocked by statements and feelings.

(6) Encourage the child to accept strong feelings, explaining that recovery to creative healthy living involves pain. Unfortunately there is no short cut.

(7) Be honest about the deceased and show that they were loved for themselves alone with all their strengths and weaknesses. Let children know their *value* has not changed, that they are *loved* and *special*.

(8) Do not deny your pain. It is all right to cry in front of your child.

(9) The child may speak of feeling the presence of the dead person. Do not dismiss this lightly because some children, like some adults, do have these experiences.

(10) Do not say the dead child 'fell asleep and did not wake up'.

(11) Do not say 'we lost our child' as children will fear becoming lost while out shopping etc.

(12) Take care of your marriage. It is easy to neglect other members of the family at times of loss.

(13) Parent–teacher co-operation should be sought. Teachers underestimate the time that a child will be disorganized. It usually lasts beyond the first anniversary of the death.

(14) Do not worry about 'regression'. Allow it until equilibrium and energies are renewed. The child usually emerges stronger and more competent. If the regressive behaviour causes problems away from the home, try asking the child if they could confine the behaviour to the home only, explaining your reasons for this request.

(15) To increase confidence, encourage the child in all his/her abilities.

PRACTICAL IDEAS

(1) Many children will respond to physical comfort. Suggestions are:

(a) Give special foods. Soft foods can be reassuring and are a reminder of earlier, easier times.

(b) Children respond to snuggling against a warm, soft rough surface. So let them sleep between flannelette sheets or have a blanket on top of them.

(c) Extra clothes in the daytime help to reduce the coldness of shock and instils a feeling of being lovingly wrapped and protected against possible harm.

(2) If difficulty in settling to sleep for relaxation, allow a radio or tape to play softly.

(3) For fear of the dark, use a night light.

(4) Children need physical play. Try not to cut this time down even if the child is getting behind with his school work due to lack of concentration. Seek teacher participation.

(5) Grief is tiring so alternate a child's passive and active occupations. Arrange a quiet time in the afternoon and plan an early bedtime.

(6) If they are having difficulty in following directions, make lists out. These can be done in the form of pictures for the very young.

(7) A special outing, treat, present or new colourful clothes can bring comfort and help to create a feeling of security.

(8) If the child is over-eating, serve the food on individual plates. You could say 'I wonder if you are really hungry, let's try a cuddle instead'.

(9) Offer small nourishing meals to those who lose interest in eating.

(10) For both over-eating and under-eating, teach the child to cook.

40

Sadness, Anger, Aggression and Guilt
(see also 'Dealing with Strong Feelings' in Section 2)

Children often have difficulty working through sadness and anger because past experiences have given them a fear of expressing these emotions. Tears are associated with injury, pain, being lost, separation and rejection; with feeling vulnerable. Neither are children sure about what is allowed. Tears can be met with disapproval from adults and other children. 'Don't cry, you are a big boy now', 'Cry baby', etc. Angry outbursts, due to their power and potential for destruction, can often lead to trouble with adults and are also frightening for the child. Children fear displeasing others and for some in the 'magical thinking' stage they have the anxiety that some other calamity may result if they express their anger. Some children will protect themselves from criticism and feelings of weakness by avoiding crying and anger.

ANGER is felt as a surge of energy in one of three areas of the body:

(1) the mouth .... bite, spit, scream or swear

(2) the hands .... punch, poke, yank, break

(3) legs and feet .... stamp, kick, trip, run

Anger can be expressed indirectly because it is pushed down inside but builds up, causing feelings of rage and guilt. The child may begin to antagonize and frustrate the adults around them to provoke punishment. This vents the anger and relieves the guilt feelings. Anger can show itself as dawdling, forgetting, day dreaming, bed wetting, losing or breaking things, or accidentally hurting others or themselves.

AGGRESSIVE BEHAVIOUR, which grows out of feelings of helplessness, is usually displayed in the early stages of grief. It shows itself by hostility to adults, aggressive behaviour to other children and snapping or lashing out at people untouched by the death. In many children this behaviour will modify as they progress through grief. It may persist with some children and may serve a purpose, meeting some need originating in the present or past.

GUILT. Children, like adults, will ask themselves 'What did I do to be punished like this – was I so bad?'; 'What's wrong with me – was I so unloving?'. Their self-esteem suffers and, like our own, it is slow to recover. Unconscious guilt can manifest itself in physical aches and pains, neglect of health and onset of real physical illness, accident prone-ness and self-defeating life choices at school and in personal relationships. If the child thinks the death was due to wrong feelings, they may deny all feelings and respond to life in an uncaring manner. 'I don't care', 'You can't make me'. They are often suffering loss of concentration and confusion, so learning, making decisions, setting goals or trusting their experiences is difficult. So these children decide not to think and say 'I can't', 'I'm confused', 'I don't know' or 'It's too hard'.

Suggestions to Help Children Express Their Grief

It is unwise to react to angry outbursts and aggressive behaviour with coaxing, punishments or threats of punishment. Children often need help to verbalize their feelings. Like many adults, they can feel uncomfortable about this. Following are some ideas to help children to express their grief.

(1) Tell a child that talking does not have to be so hard as five feelings that we all have are: being sad, mad, glad/happy, scared and lonely. Go through the list asking them what feelings they have. The body signals for 'any sad feelings' can be nodding, shaking of head, or shrugging of the shoulders. Shrugging can mean 'I do not want to talk about this'.

(2) Ask the child to indicate with his hands how much feeling they are experiencing.

(3) Have drawings of faces depicting feelings. Ask the child to point to the one he is experiencing.

(4) Have cards with a drawing showing all the feelings. Get the child to pick a card and tell
a story about that feeling or just talk about the feeling.

or

Have several cards the same, divide them out and place one at a time in a pile in the centre of the table. When two of the same come together, ask the child to talk about the card.

(5) Tell a story and pause when a description of a feeling is due. Ask the child what feeling they think is appropriate or get them to point at suitable drawings depicting emotions.

(6) The best way to deal with the physical release of anger is to respect the energy zone and devise a permitted expression for feelings. For example, 'When you have that hitting feeling, you may not hit Tom but you may hit your pillow or bang your fists on the table' or 'What you are doing is not safe for you. I want you to take care of yourself'. This approach avoids the conflict that will occur if the child is told 'Don't do that'. Suggested materials to have on hand to use as a means for release of anger are — newsprint, clay, reinforced cardboard blocks, foam bats, punching bags, inflated clowns, jointed play people and animals, hammer and nails.

(7) Aggressive behaviour: Talk to the child about the outcome of their actions and give them the freedom to choose how to deal with it. This overcomes the feeling of helplessness and gives them the feeling of being in control

(8) When the child seems to be losing control, support him by saying, 'It's getting hard for you to stop. I want you to sit down or go to your room to cool off'. If there is an argument with another child, the situation can be diffused by saying, 'How can we solve this fairly?'

(9) Always try to plan substitute behaviour.

Course of Grief and When to Seek Professional Help

For the first six to eight months, children are involved in their own particular mourning, which will involve much denial, sadness and/or anger. Once the first anniversary is reached the expressions of grief – sobbing, angry outbursts, etc. – are much fewer and gradually their psychological energy is put into the different tasks of growing up.

Around the first anniversary, look at the way the child reacts when distressing or frustrating events occur. Those children having difficulty respond in one of two ways:

(1) They do not express sadness or anger in situations where most children of their age would.

or

(2) They express much more sadness or anger more frequently in situations where other children are less upset.

For those children who deny their feelings and where the above suggestions have not proved helpful, then professional advice should be sought during the first year (see notes on Educational Psychologists).

References

Jewitt, C. (1984) *Helping Children to Cope with Separation and Loss.* Batsford.

Kander, J. *Explaining Cremation to Young Children.*

Kirkwood, N.A. *A Child's Questions About Death.*

Koocher, G.P. 'Talking With Children About Death' Report of a Survey.

Mitchell, M. *Bereaved Children.*

Mitchell, M.E. *The Child's Attitude to Death.*

Stickney, D. (1989) *Waterbugs and Dragonflies.* Mowbray.

Le Tour, K. *For Those That Live: Helping children cope with the death of a brother or sister.*
This article forms part of the booklet 'Helping Younger Brothers and Sisters' available from The Compassionate Friends.

Dying Children and Their Families

by Tessa Wilkinson, formerly of Helen House (see article in Section 3)
now the Family Support Officer for the Children's Liver Disease Foundation,
also author of 'The Death of a Child – A Book for Families'

We have realized at Helen House that it is extremely important that we include children in the time of death; the dying, the time immediately afterwards, and the funeral.

Obviously we would never tell a family how they should cope at this time. It is important that each family deals with this time in their own way, and in their own time. But if we are asked, we will always suggest that the children be involved.

It seems that the reality of death is often much gentler than an imagination left to roam. The films and cartoons that children have seen on TV and video may well have given them very unrealistic ideas about what death is like.

One child said that he did not want to see his dead sister, because when you die all your skin falls off and you become a skeleton. The relief that child felt when it was explained that this did not happen straight away, was immense.

Children need time spent with them so that they can ask questions, and get answers to them.

'How do you know that my sister is dead?' 'Might she not just be asleep, and she could be buried alive?' 'What will they do at the funeral/cremation?' We would let the child see for himself that his sister is really dead. If you hold a mirror up to your mouth it fogs up, if you hold a mirror up to the dead child's mouth, nothing happens.

Try to find the child's pulse; explain how the heart beats to pump the blood around the body, really let them see for themselves that the dead child's heart has stopped beating. These things may help the child to really believe that his sister is dead.

Children may well want an explanation about what happens when you die. One of the ways that can help to explain this is by using the analogy of the chrysalis and the butterfly. The body that left is like the empty chrysalis shell. The butterfly has flown free; if the dead child has been ill and trapped in a disabled body, the image of a butterfly flying free, can be a very beautiful one to give. Other resources can be used to explain this concept e.g. 'The Journey' and 'The Ship'.*

The child may need to be told about the registration of the death. He may like to be involved in the planning of the funeral, perhaps choose a song or hymn.

---

*   See Creative Activities

Time needs to be spent explaining about what happens at the funeral. One child thought that her sister's body would be taken out of the coffin before it was buried. She expressed much relief because it did not happen. But that worry could so easily have been removed if someone had just taken the time to explain what happened before the funeral.

One of the problems is that if the parents are very wrapped up in their own grief they may well not think to explain to their children what is going to happen. Someone who is close to the family may be able to help, and keep an eye on the children, explaining to them what is going on.

Preparation for a Child's Funeral

Suggestions for Parents

This has been written by members of The Compassionate Friends, an organization of bereaved parents. Some of us wish that we had known, at the time of our child's death, of the choices available to us; with hindsight, we might have done things differently. This is not a detailed list of such choices, but some pointers along the way which you can think over, and then discuss with family and friends, and with your funeral director.

Take as much time as you need over making these choices – there is no reason to feel hurried; the decisions you make now will have long-lasting effects. You may wish to talk to others in your family, to a minister of religion, or other people outside the religious field.

The first choice you will have to make is between burial and cremation. If you choose cremation, you do not have to make an immediate decision on the dispersal of the ashes.

Following that decision, you may then want to choose what your child will be dressed in, and whether this is something you want to do yourself (with help), or would prefer others to do. If the funeral director is doing this, it will be helpful to give him a photograph of your son or daughter. You can ask for a lock of hair, or to have a photograph taken.

There is too the question of whether you want to see your child's body again, and whether others wish to do so. This can be very helpful in coming to accept the reality of what has happened. You may, where appropriate, want to place a favourite toy in the coffin, or your other children may wish to do so.

If you have young children you will want to discuss – with them or with others – whether they are to be present at the funeral. Children of all ages can take part in the discussions and arrangements at their own level.

A religious service is not a requirement, you can plan and shape the funeral that you want for your child. You may want to invite people who have been important in your child's life to lead the funeral; this could be a teacher, a leader in a voluntary organization, a friend or an employer. Forms of service, both religious and non-religious, can be made available to you by your funeral director.

Music and readings can be of your own choice, and you may like to have photographs of your child in the chapel. You may wish to suggest members of the family, or friends, as coffin-bearers; you may wish to do this yourself. You can ask your funeral director to list the names of those attending the funeral, and those who sent flowers.

Consideration can also be given to questions such as flowers, or charitable donations instead, to memorial funds and other similar ideas. There can be the possibility of a memorial or thanksgiving service which could take place some weeks or months later.

Discussing the possible alternatives, and making the choices that are necessary, can reduce the feelings of helplessness and loss of control that arise at this time. Your involvement in these decisions, painful as it is, will ultimately help you to mourn the death of your daughter or son.

You may be offered drugs or alcohol 'to help you through'. If you can manage without these it will be better, because using them can impede your ability to make important decisions, and delay the grieving process too.

This has been written in a brief and simple way, to help you to consider carefully something that none of us ever wanted to consider. It is intended to widen your horizons about the different ways of preparing a funeral so that it will be meaningful for your child, yourselves and your family.

(Further copies of this leaflet are available from The Compassionate Friends.)

Children's Reaction to Death

1. Loss of a Grandparent

Setting   –   the school bookshop which happens Friday lunchtime, although supervised by a teacher is organized and run by children of Junior School; they can look, browse, and occasionally buy paperbacks.

Story   –   A second year boy (9) came up to me and said,

Ian   –   'My Grandfather died last week!'
'Oh, I'm sorry Ian. Do you miss him?'

Ian   –   'He'd been ill for a long time, and Mum and Dad kept leaving me to go and visit him. Mum's pretty bad. She keeps crying. She's gone to his funeral today. Dad has gone with her. I've got to go to my cousins tonight.'
'Did you want to go to the funeral, Ian?'

Ian   –   'Yes, I did, but Mum said it wasn't nice for me to go.'
'What did she say wasn't nice? Do you know what happens? Would you have liked to go?'

Ian   –   'I don't know, I'm not sure about it.'

The bell went and as Ian had to return to his class the opportunity to pursue the matter further was lost.

ACTION IN GENERAL

In my class I would have gone through the *Last Rites* Section of *Good Grief,* and would have talked with the children about what happens at funerals.

A fourth year child once wrote, 'Tears fall to the earth to give it strength.'

Ian has some very confused feelings which he needs to look at closely with a caring adult. He could: be taken to the cemetery to say 'good-bye' to Grandpa; plant a tree/bush in his garden to remember Grandpa.

2. Loss of a Pet

Setting   –   A nine-year-old boy came to school in tears. One evening Christopher's rabbit had escaped. It was found the next morning in his garden dead, following savaging by a dog. Christopher blamed himself for the rabbit' escape.

Action   –   Specifically for Christopher, at school.

I asked him for details about the rabbit – he was pleased to talk – soon the memories of the mutilated rabbit were replaced with memories of how it had been when alive.

ACTION AT HOME

A funeral was held for the rabbit, with Christopher and his parents; they allowed him to bury the body with a ceremony, and some solemnity.

NEXT DAY FURTHER ACTION AT SCHOOL

Christopher brought photographs to school, as requested. These were displayed for all to see. He talked about them, frequently looked at them, and shared new, remembered memories.

In the library he found a book with an origami rabbit, and he worked out how to make one. A whole line of origami rabbits, called Charcoal, appeared on the wall.

His parents decided that there should be no more rabbits. Another boy in the class asked for the hutch and Christopher cleaned it out for him. He was invited to 'share' the new rabbit.

Christopher's guilt at letting the rabbit escape was eased by an investigation into the behaviour of wild rabbits, the realization that the rabbit was following normal instincts. Each aspect of his loss was dealt with by positive input – good memories replaced the horror of the mutilated body. The burial was permission to 'let go'. The paper, origami rabbits, learned with difficulty, replaced Charcoal a hundred times. Children in the class instinctively offered great support.

3. Great-Granny

Jill, aged four years, after visiting a dying great granny, said to her mother: 'If I'm a mummy, will you be a granny?' 'Yes.' 'Oh no, I don't want you to be a granny because grannies aren't pretty, and when you're a granny you get very old, and when you're very old you die, and I don't want you to die. I want to stay with you.'

Jill was trying to make sense of the process of life and death, and ageing. Her mother explained to her that your feelings change as you get older. She said that when you get old, your body gets more tired and things wear out a bit, like your hearing, and your sight, and that great granny won't be upset when she dies because she's getting tired and her body is tired. She will be peaceful.

'Do you know what day she will die?' 'No, we don't usually know exactly when we will die.'

She reassured Jill that when she is grown up and a Mummy she probably won't feel exactly like she feels now and that while she is growing up, she will look after her and stay with her as long as she needs.

N.B. It is very important to explain, as Jill's mother did, to give information about the ageing process simply and clearly, and to reassure children that their needs, for love and security, will be met.

The Effects of Disasters on Children

William Yule[*] *Professor of Applied Child Psychology,*
University of London Institute of Psychiatry

Following major disasters, a high proportion of children experience a number of distressing reactions, including anxiety, fear, depression. It is now recognized that many show Post Traumatic Stress Disorder and without treatment such disorders can last for a considerable time.

Schools get directly and indirectly involved in the aftermath of many disasters. At Aberfan in 1966, 116 children and 28 adults died when a huge coal slip slid on to the school. One hundred and forty-three primary school children survived. Schools can be directly involved when there are life-threatening fires, fatal accidents in the playground, road traffic accidents involving children walking to and from school or during school journeys. Many of us recall our distress when learning of the party of children swept off the rocks in Cornwall, those who slid to their deaths on a skiing trip in Austria, or the 400 children and teachers who survived the sinking of the cruise ship Jupiter in 1988, 22 years to the day after Aberfan.

Children get caught up in other mass disasters outside school – in the stands at Bradford football stadium, watching the crush at the Hillsborough football ground, travelling on the Herald of Free Enterprise, living in towns like Lockerbie where major accidents happen. Sadly, they can also be the direct victims of malicious events such as the shootings in the school at Hungerford.

It is important that teaching staff prepare themselves to deal with the emotional aftermath of such disasters. The large, dramatic ones fortunately happen infrequently; smaller ones happen with great regularity.

Recent studies find that teachers report less psychopathology among child survivors than do parents, and that both report far less than the children themselves. One reason for the failure to recognize and report the severity of the effects of disasters on children is the understandable but misplaced reaction of adults who do not want to consider the horrors the children have faced. After some disasters, people in authority have prevented researchers interviewing children; schools have ignored the event or paid it cursory attention, arguing that children are getting over it and no good is done by bringing it all up again. The result is

---

[*]   William Yule is also author of *Wise Before the Event*. He helps schools to plan in advance how they will deal with a disaster (see 'Additional Resources' in Section 3).

that children quickly learn not to unburden themselves to teachers who then take a long time to link the drop off in standards of work and impaired concentration with the intrusive thoughts the children are experiencing.

Based on my own recent studies of child survivors (under sixteen years) from the Herald of Free Enterprise and 334 teenagers from the Jupiter, the following are some of the common reactions shown in the first few months after such life-threatening disasters:

SLEEP DISTURBANCE. Almost all children have major sleep problems in the first few weeks. They reported fears of the dark, fear of being alone, intrusive thoughts when things are quiet, bad dreams, nightmares, waking through the night. Problems persisted over many months. Use of music to divert thoughts helped.

SEPARATION DIFFICULTIES. Initially, most wanted to be physically close to their surviving parents, often sleeping in the parental bed over the first few weeks. Some distressed parents found their clinginess difficult to cope with.

CONCENTRATION DIFFICULTIES. During the day, children had major problems concentrating on school work. When it was silent in the classroom they had intrusive memories of what had happened to them.

MEMORY PROBLEMS. They also had problems remembering new material, or even some old skills such as reading music.

INTRUSIVE THOUGHTS. All were troubled by repetitive thoughts about the accident. These occurred at any time, although often triggered off by environmental stimuli – for example, movement on a bus, noise of glass smashing, sound of rushing water, sight of tables laid out like the ship's cafeteria. Thoughts intruded when they were otherwise quiet.

TALKING WITH PARENTS. Many did not want to talk about their feelings with their parents so as not to upset the adults. Thus, parents were often unaware of the details of the children's suffering, although they could see they were in difficulty. There was often a great sense of frustration between parents and children.

TALKING WITH PEERS. At some points, survivors felt a great need to talk over their experiences with peers. Unfortunately, the timing was often wrong. Peers held back from asking in case they upset the survivor further; the survivor often felt rejected.

HEIGHTENED ALERTNESS TO DANGERS. Most were wary of all forms of transport – not willing to put their safety into anyone else's hands. They were more aware of other dangers. They were affected by reports of other disasters.

FORESHORTENED FUTURE. Many felt they should live each day to the full and not plan far ahead. They lost trust in long-term planning.

FEARS. Most had fears of travelling by sea and air. Many had fears of swimming, of the sound of rushing water. Most of the new fears were specifically related to their recent bad experiences rather than being just a general increase in fearfulness.

It helps to say to children that they are experiencing normal reactions to an abnormal situation. Of course, one must also constantly remember that other disorders may also follow a disaster – particularly anxiety disorders and depression, the latter when bereavement has occurred.

Some Developmental Issues

Younger children may show all sorts of regressive or anti-social behaviour. There are many reports of children repeatedly drawing what they experienced or incorporating it in their play. Parents may avoid talking to the child about what happened, mistakenly thinking they will not remember or understand. However, even four-year-olds can sometimes describe vividly what they had experienced, much to their parents' surprise. Some pre-school children have very adult concepts of death and dying and it is important that we remember the range of individual differences in cognitive awareness when discussing (or not discussing) the effects of disasters with children.

Children over ten years of age have usually a very good understanding that their lives were threatened. Young teenagers often report a sense of foreshortened future – what is the point of planning anything when the fates can be so capricious? This realization is very difficult for parents to cope with.

Indeed, parents are often at a loss to know how best to react. If they were directly affected by the same disaster, they are having to cope with their own reactions at the same time as trying to support their children. Following the Australian bush fires, McFarlane (1987) found that, eight months on, the families showed increased levels of conflict, irritability, and withdrawal, with maternal overprotection quite common. The adjustment of the parents themselves was an important determinant of the adjustment of the children. In particular, he comments that '… families who did not share their immediate reactions to disaster may have had more trouble with their long-term adjustment…and experienced a greater degree of estrangement'. Equally important, the child's reaction to the fire affected the adjustment of the family, emphasizing the reciprocal interactions among members of a family system.

Teenagers who survived the Herald of Free Enterprise capsize often found it very hard to share their feelings with their parents. They would go out of the house a lot to avoid talking about it. Parents were often frustrated, in that they wanted to reach out to their children but did not know how to. Behaviourally, the children looked as if they had developed lots of interests outside the home; in reality, they were avoiding dealing with the effects of the trauma.

When children have returned from a traumatic school outing, they may well have enormous problems concentrating in class and in doing their homework. If they are not sleeping properly, all this is exacerbated. Children are sensitized to a wide variety of stimuli, mention of which may trigger an emotional reaction, as in the child who had to read about the evacuation from Dunkirk. Teachers need to make arrangements for child survivors to leave the classroom when such events occur.

For example, children returning to a very caring school after the sinking of the Jupiter entered a geography classroom where the walls were covered with projects on 'great disasters of the world'. Their upset was immediate and the connection obvious. Less obvious was the pressure put on a boy whose GCSE project had not survived the sinking of the Herald. Unable to concentrate on new learning, he was still pressurised to rewrite his missing project, until the problem was drawn to the school's attention. The teacher had, understandably, focused more on the impending exams than the current problems and these were then very quickly resolved. Overall, children who survived the Jupiter sinking performed significantly less well academically over the following two years, with the less able children taking longer to recover.

Teachers need to be aware, too, of the reactions of other pupils towards the survivors. One eight-year-old suffered silently for weeks after a classmate said, 'I wish you'd died in the ferry'. A 12-year-old girl had to cope with taunts about being orphaned. These episodes only came to light during a group run for the child survivors (Yule and Williams, 1990).

Treatment Needs

In the immediate aftermath, children usually need to be reunited with their parents and family. Even teenagers may go back to sleeping in the parents' bed. Tolerance and understanding are called for. Survivors need to talk over what happened so as to get the sequence of events clear in their minds as well as to master the feelings that recall engenders. Repetitive retelling is not enough alone. Professionals can help by creating a relatively safe environment in which such recounting can take place. Experiencing that the world does not come to an end when feelings are shared can be very facilitating. Learning that other survivors share similar, irrational guilt about surviving can help to get things in perspective. Learning how to deal with anxiety attacks, how to identify trigger stimuli, how to take each day as it comes – all are important therapeutic tasks.

However, these things should not be left to chance. Mental health professionals are rapidly learning that formal psychological debriefing can help victims of disaster. Ayalon (1988) emphasizes the need to help children make sense of what happened to them and to gain mastery over their feelings. To this end, many practitioners agree that children should be treated in small groups. They might be asked to write detailed accounts of their experience and to be helped to cope with the emotions that brings up. In addition, they may need specific treatment for fears, phobias and any other avoidant behaviours. They should get practical help with sleep disorders. Given that intrusive thoughts seemed worse at night just before dropping off to sleep, I advised many children to use portable tape-recorders to play music to distract them and blot out the thoughts. With better sleep, they were better able to face the thoughts in the safety of daylight.

Conclusions

Events of recent years have forced on us an awareness of the emotional effects of disasters on children. It is clear that children as young as eight years can suffer PTSD that is almost identical in form to that presented by adults. The effects can go on for one to two years, and cannot be considered transitory. Parents and teachers often underestimate the anxiety reactions that children report. Normal screening instruments will not pick up all the psychopathology.

There are developmental changes in children's reactions, but as so few young children have been studied, we cannot yet be clear of the nature of these changes. Children's reactions are intimately bound up with effects on the family, but some distress is directly caused by the trauma. Teachers, especially, need guidance on how to deal with the aftermath in schools.

There is a great need for good treatment studies. Because disasters occur unexpectedly, we need to plan in advance how to conduct and evaluate all forms of intervention.

References

Ayalon, O. (1988) *Rescue! Community Oriented Preventive Education for Coping with Stress.* Haifa: Nord Publications.

McFarlane, A.C. (1987) 'Family functioning and overprotection following a natural disaster: The longitudinal effects of post-traumatic morbidity.' *Australian and New Zealand Journal of Psychiatry 21,* 210.

McFarlane, A.C., Policansky, S. and Irwin, C.P. (1987) 'A longitudinal study of the psychological morbidity in children due to a natural disaster.' *Psychological Medicine* 17:727–738.

Raphael, B. (1986) *When Disaster Strikes: A Handbook for the Caring Professions.* London: Hutchinson.

Yule, W. (1991) 'Work with children following disasters.' In M. Herbert (ed) *Clinical Child Psychology: Theory and Practice.* Chichester: John Wiley.

Yule, W., Udwin, O. and Murdoch, K. (1990) 'The "Jupiter" sinking: effects on children's fears, depression and anxiety.' *Journal of Child Psychology and Psychiatry 31,* 1051–1061.

Yule, W. and Williams, R. (1990) 'Post traumatic stress reactions in children.' *Journal of Traumatic Stress 3,* 279–295.

Clinic for Children who have Suffered Acute Psychological Trauma. This new Clinic, the first of its kind in the United Kingdom, has been established in the Department of Child Psychiatry at the Royal Free Hospital, London, under the direction of Dr Dora Black.

It offers a national specialist service to children and adolescents who, without skilled intervention, are liable to suffer long-term psychiatric disorder and academic failure. In addition, it will undertake research and offer advice, teaching and training to professional workers.

Death of a Child – A School's Response

Natalie was in the first year of a Junior School when she was killed crossing the road, whilst abroad with her family for the summer half term. She had one sister who attended the Infant School.

School Involvement

(1) The Heads of the Junior and Infant School, and the class teachers, attended Natalie's funeral. The deputy head led a memorial service in school for children, parents and staff.

(2) Natalie's best subject was English. The children in her class held a collection for a trophy, 'The Natalie Turner Literary Prize', to be presented each year for the best first year story writer.

(3) A rose bush, purchased from money collected by the class, was planted in a special part of the school garden. A plaque with Natalie's name was put beside it.

(4) The children in Natalie's class were asked what she enjoyed doing most. Their answer was 'play'. The children were given ten minutes extra play in memory of her.

(5) A book of tributes to Natalie from her class was presented quietly to her parents in the Head's office. This included photographs, taken at various times at school, from her Pupil Record Folder.

Infant School

(6) Natalie's sister still attends the Infant School and each month a special assembly is held for children with birthdays during that time. Natalie would have been nine years old on 1 December. A 'Natalie Turner' award was given to the child who had been the most kind and helpful during the term. Mr Turner presented the prize at the December birthday assembly. It is hoped to present the award each year at the same time, although the criteria for the winner could change in the future.

N.B. Special care was taken to see that Natalie's sister also received attention. (She played 'Mary' in the School's Nativity Play, and received lots of praise).

Outside School

(7) It is important to inform the Director of Education/Education Department too, so they are able to write a letter of condolence to the parents.

(8) Child Guidance are also available for help and advice. The best help, however, is often from the people who had close contact and knew the family before the tragedy.

Hear our prayer, O Lord,
Hear our prayer,
Keep our friends, O Lord,
in Your care;
Keep our friends, O Lord,
in Your care.
O Lord, hear our prayer.

We planted a miniature

rose in our school garden

in memory of Natalie.

Loss of a Child – Helping the Parents

When a child dies the natural order of things is upturned. We expect old people to die one day, but no parent is ready to accept the death of a child cut off by an accident or illness from all their dreams and aspirations. Every year there are some 15,000 deaths of people under twenty years of age.

Certain types of loss such as stillbirths or that of a young baby can be particularly hard to grieve over. In these types of loss, there is apparently no one to remember or talk about.

The other main causes of death in children and young people are accidents, cancer, and suicide in the teen years.

What can we do to help the parents? Please see the list below.

A Reminder of Helpful Thoughts

- DO let your genuine concern and caring show.

- DO say you are sorry about what happened to their child and about their pain.

- DO allow them to express as much grief as they are feeling at the moment and are willing to share.

- DO encourage them to be patient with themselves, not to expect too much of themselves and not to impose any 'shoulds' on themselves.

- DO talk about the special endearing qualities of the child they've lost.

- DO reassure them that they did everything they could, that the medical care their child received was the best, or whatever else you know to be true and positive about the care given their child.

- DON'T let your own sense of helplessness keep you from reaching out to a bereaved parent.

- DON'T avoid them because you are uncomfortable (being avoided by friends adds pain to an already intolerable painful experience).

- DON'T change the subject when they mention their dead child.

- DON'T avoid mentioning their child's name out of fear of reminding them of their pain (they haven't forgotten it).

- DON'T point out that at least they have their other children (children are not interchangeable; they cannot replace each other).

- DON'T say that they can always have another child (even if they wanted to and could, another child would not replace the child they have lost).

When a Child in Your School is Bereaved

Teachers, counsellors and classmates make up a child's 'second family'. They, too, have strong feelings when a member experiences a death. These guidelines have been prepared by bereaved parents, surviving children, school personnel and professional caregivers in an effort to help those who want to help a child.

Children tend to express grief in their ways of behaving. They act their feelings and emotions. We cannot always know what they are thinking or feeling. Take cues from their behaviour.

All children react differently. Withdrawal, aggressiveness, panic, anxiety, anger, guilt, fear, regression and symptoms of bodily distress are all signs of grief. Be patient and understanding.

When children are grieving, they have shortened attention spans and may have trouble concentrating. School work may be affected. A child may attempt to deny feelings of anger, hurt and fear by repressing them. Eventually grief takes over and their feelings leak out. It may be months or even years before a child displays signs of the full impact of a family death.

Bereaved children must re-establish a self-identity. 'Who am I?' becomes a major concern. Help them in their search.

A child's perceptions of death change with age and experience. The pre-school and kindergarten age child may see death as temporary. The six-to-ten-year-old becomes aware of the reality and finality of death. He may be curious about death and burial rituals. By eleven, a child begins to perceive death on an adult level.

If a child seeks you out to talk, be available and **REALLY LISTEN**. Hear with your ears, your eyes and your heart. **TOUCH** – a warm hug says: 'I know what happened and I care. I am here if you need me'.

- Face your own feelings about death. Share your feelings with the child and with your class. It is all right to cry, be sad or angry. It is even all right to smile.

- Be open and honest with feelings. Create an atmosphere of open acceptance that invites questions and fosters confidence and love. Encourage children to express their grief in all its forms. Be supportive and available.

- Ensure that members of staff, especially in a large school, are fully aware of what has happened to a bereaved child, so that the child is not unnecessarily hurt by a chance remark made in ignorance by a staff member.

- Provide a quiet, private place to come to whenever the child needs to be alone. Almost anything can trigger tears. Help children realize that grief is a natural and normal reaction to loss.

- Do not isolate or insulate children from death. Expose children to death as a natural part of life. Use such opportunities as a fallen leaf, a wilted flower, the death of an insect, bird or class pet to discuss death as part of the life cycle. Talk together as a classroom family. By sharing a grief, we help eliminate the compounding problem of school and social isolation the bereaved often experience.

- Try not to single out the grieving child for special privileges or compensations. He still needs to feel a part of his peer group and should be expected to function accordingly. Temper your expectations with kindness and understanding but continue to expect him to function.

- If possible, talk to a few of the bereaved child's friends to help them cope and explore how to be supportive. Friends may be uncomfortable and awkward in their attempts to make contact.

- Where appropriate, help a child find a supportive peer group: perhaps there are other children in the school who are coping with similar losses. An invitation to share with each other might be welcome.

- Have resources available in the library about death and grief. You might offer to read a book with the child. Compassionate Friends operates an extensive postal library. Contact the librarian for details or advice.

- Establish lines of communication with the parents. Keep each other informed about the student's progress.

- It is important and appropriate for the school community to acknowledge the death of a child. Make a scrapbook; hold an assembly, plant a tree, have a small memorial service. Do something to acknowledge the death (thus giving children permission to do the same).

- As the child learns to cope, continue to be available; continue to reach out and CARE, just as you do now.

Created and written by: The Compassionate Friends, USA. (copies available from The Compassionate Friends, see useful addresses in Section 3.)

$\boxed{\textbf{1.17}}$

Bereavement in the Junior School

A Teacher's Experience

It was a year ago at a junior school that we put together our Health Curriculum. Many lunchtime sessions were spent deciding what should be included and what left out; when to teach and at what level – and how? Kidscape, Child Abuse, Aids were all agreed upon, but bereavement –? Well!?

Many of the younger staff had never personally experienced loss of any kind and were quite reluctant to venture into such a difficult area. Arguments waxed back and forth until it was pointed out that divorce was a form of bereavement we were seeing frequently, so surely we had better be prepared. Bereavement was to be included, it was finally decided. The third year (nine-to-ten-year-old) was considered the most appropriate age with the thought that if a teacher was aware of the need at an earlier stage of development, then it would be introduced wherever appropriate and necessary. I felt very clearly that for several teachers 'never' would be the appropriate time!

I had a fourth year class coming into the last year of the Health Scheme; they had many gaps in their previous work because they had not completed the full course. We planned to cover sex education – relationships and 'growing up'. To my surprise questions about abortion and miscarriages were asked. I answered them as fully and as frankly as possible without showing any personal prejudices, and found suddenly that I had a very close and frank relationship with a class of eleven-year-olds, who tried to shock me with four letter words – without success. Instead I told them the appropriate 'grown up' word.

We covered all the stages, from conception, the baby growing in the womb, to the birth, which we saw on video. They were not so interested in the baby growing into the toddler, but they were interested in how they become adults. Somewhere there must be a logical progression to bereavement, but where could I find it?

There was a display of toddler toys in the classroom in order to illustrate how the children had changed in interests as well as physically. To this display I added my own, very battered war-time teddy bear. The children laughed – he was so ugly – and a great surge of childhood memories came flooding back. I talked about the Christmas when I had first found him in my stocking – how the scarcity of consumer goods at all times made Christmas presents doubly precious, and my bear had been made out of the woollen lining of an old coat, with two small blue circles for eyes cut from a worn out pair of slippers. My mother had sat sewing him for me in the evenings, after I had gone to bed. Gradually the atmosphere relaxed as the children enjoyed the story and my bear didn't seem so ugly after all. Then I found myself telling the children how I used to take him everywhere with us and one terrible day he had fallen, unnoticed, from my pushchair, as we shopped in Uxbridge. At bedtime I missed him and cried myself into hysterics, refusing to sleep without him. My poor father got on to his bike and cycled to the police station to report a missing bear – he had not been brought to the police station. He then cycled every inch of the way my mother and I had covered earlier in the day, looking everywhere in the gathering darkness. He was just about to give up when he spotted the bear — pinned to a hedge by a sympathetic grown-up. My father cycled home as fast as he could to find me silent, angry and convinced we would never be reunited.

The children were utterly absorbed in the story — several hands reached out to take the bear and he was passed around the class with gentleness, several kisses were planted on his tired, old head. He was not ugly now and the flood gates opened. Several children had similar stories to tell: of lost toys, of being lost themselves, of losing a brother or a sister. They all wanted to talk at once; no one was prepared to listen any more, so now it was time to write. Everyone had something to write about but the writing was not good — it was purely factual and written very quickly. I put the stories away — there was a lot more to be done with them in order to unlock many of the emotions they were hiding away.

Shortly afterwards came a request to do some work on life-cycles, and the children's responses to bereavement,* for a BBC radio programme. The children had booklets, chose an animal, bird or plant and set to work. We enlisted the help of the local library. The children researched, discussed and planned their work, drew pictures, wrote poems, and eventually some very good booklets were finished.

---

*   See 'How Can We Help' for further details of the activities to use in the classroom.

Glossary of Words Associated with Death

BEQUEATH	–	to leave behind.
BEREAVEMENT	–	to be deprived by death, loss or parting.
CREMATORIUM	–	a place where cremations are held.
DEATH	–	the act of dying.
DECEASE	–	the end of life on this Earth.
EPITAPH	–	words inscribed on a tombstone or monument.
EULOGY	–	to speak or write well of someone.
EUTHANASIA	–	a way made easy for people to die.
FUNERAL	–	a ceremony.
GRIEF	–	distress – great unhappiness.
HEDONIST	–	someone who believes pleasure is the chief thing.
IMMORTAL	–	living forever.
LAMENT	–	to express grief passionately.
MAUSOLEUM	–	a magnificent monument.
MEMORIAL	–	that which serves to keep remembrance.
MOURNING	–	dark clothes worn as a sign of bereavement/to feel or express sorrow about something.
OBITUARY	–	the printed announcement of a person's death.
ORPHAN	–	a child whose parents are dead.
REINCARNATION	–	to live again in a different body.
RESURRECTION	–	to rise from the dead.
THANATOLOGY	–	the scientific study of death and the process of dying.
WIDOW	–	a woman whose husband is dead.
WIDOWER	–	a man whose wife is dead.
WILL	–	deed showing disposal of one's possessions – usually called a bequest – at death.

SECTION 2
ACTIVITIES

Creative Activities

Creative Activities

National Curriculum

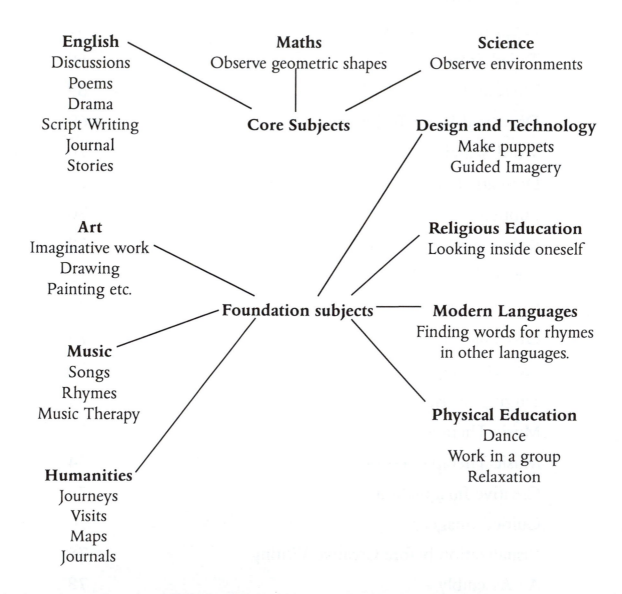

English
Discussions
Poems
Drama
Script Writing
Journal
Stories

Maths
Observe geometric shapes

Science
Observe environments

Core Subjects

Design and Technology
Make puppets
Guided Imagery

Art
Imaginative work
Drawing
Painting etc.

Religious Education
Looking inside oneself

Foundation subjects

Modern Languages
Finding words for rhymes
in other languages.

Music
Songs
Rhymes
Music Therapy

Physical Education
Dance
Work in a group
Relaxation

Humanities
Journeys
Visits
Maps
Journals

The lists above are only suggestions. Many more may be found in the text.

Creative Activities

'I know I cannot teach anyone anything. I can only provide an environ-
ment in which they can learn.'

(Carl Rogers)

Objectives

- To encourage discussion and exploration of feelings of loss and bereavement.

- To allow the unconscious to express itself freely.

- To develop creativity and choice.

Useful Resources

Background reading –   in Section 1   –   'Educator's Notes'
                                      –   'Teaching Methods'
                      in Section 3   –   'Additional Resources'
                                      –   'Book List'
                                          'Psychosynthesis in Education'
                                          'He Hit Me Back First'
                                          'Windows to Our Mind'
See selection of poems/articles   –   'Creative Activities'
                                      'Additional Resources'

Suggested Activities

- All teachers will be familiar with creative writing, drawing and the use of music or play.

Taped Stories

- Children can write and then record their stories.

Thesaurus

- An individual or class one can be made on different subjects.

Draw and Write Technique

(Evolved by Primary Project at Southampton University.)

- Children are asked after a simple relaxation and/or introduction, to focus their thinking on a word or subject chosen by the teacher, and not to talk about it to anyone else.

- They are then asked to draw as many pictures as they can and to write a phrase or sentence to accompany each picture.

- Alternatively they can be invited to whisper to the teacher, who can then write it for them.

- The pictures can be coloured.

Word Search

- This is illustrated in 'Feelings', and 'Living With Loss'.

- This can be used as an exercise to extend the children's use of language.

- Using 1cm. square paper, ask the children to write a word in the middle of the page – one letter for each square.

- Use the letters of this word to expand, in all directions, with other words expressing similar/related ideas or emotions.

   N.B. This can complement the above 'Draw and Write Technique' and facilitate access to feelings, and is particularly useful at times of loss and bereavement.

Dramatic Play

This involves the use of 'dressing-up' materials and/or the Wendy house for role play drama, and 'make-believe' activities.

Puppets

This involves the use of glove and finger puppets and can achieve the same functions as role play and other dramatics activities, for younger or more self-conscious children.

Role Play/Simulation

Used as a means of feeling/thinking/acting as another person might do, for example, 'getting into other people's shoes'.

```
                              P O W E R F U L 9
                              L         X     L
              W E L C O M E   E         S     A
              O       U       A         I     D
              n       r       S         T
              D       i       E         E
              E       o       D         D E L I G H T
              R       u                           A
              F       S A T I S F I E D           P
              U       |   |                       P
              L O V E   |   n                     Y
                        |   g
                        |   L I K E
                    n i C E     K
                            Y   I
                                N
                                D
```

WELCOME
POWERFUL
PLEASED
EXSITED
GLAD
WONDERFUL
CURIOUS
DELIGHT
SATISFIED
HAPPY
LOVE
TINGLEY
LIKE
NICE
KIND

```
                              h
                              u
                              r                r
            D e v a s t a t e d
            o        N          l
            o        G          i
G l o o m y          r          v
            e        y    u p s e t
            d        N          d
                     S I C K
                     O
      W O R R I E D         r
            R        D    f e a r f u l
      b o r e d      i    l          e
            N        e    i          f
            G        S a d v          t
                     p        l N v y o
            a        e    g l a d      u
            N        r        u        t
            X        a        n
      f r i G h t e n e d
            o        e        l
            U        J o y f u l l
            S
```

72

Scripted Role Play

To prepare dialogues/situations as an introduction to different experiences. It can serve as a model for 'free role play'.

   The importance of a careful introduction and debriefing cannot be emphasized too much.

N.B. Role Play needs careful handling and should only be used if the teacher/educator is experienced and confident in this method.

Rhymes – Songs

The use of both rhymes and songs help to build language skills, and also is a way of exploring a variety of human situations.

Observation

Is the art of noticing/seeing/perceiving what is happening, for example, when children: start school, fall in the playground, and how they behave.

N.B. Observation gives us clues as to how others are feeling and this develops sensitivity.

Free Drawing

This follows naturally after 'Guided Imagery' or 'Creative Imagination'. It is important to emphasize that it has nothing to do with 'Art'. (I often show my own very basic drawings to reassure the children before they start).

   This method is ideal for expressing troublesome feelings helping to free children for learning.

   Method A: Allow the children to play with paper and coloured pens/pencils. Encourage them to draw freely and spontaneously.

   Method B: Ask the children to draw the particular image(s), received during 'guided imagery'.

N.B. See also article: 'Value of Hospitalized Children's Art Work' in Section 3.

Singing/Music

Young children love singing and 'action' songs, and setting poems to music. The song 'The Streets of London' could be used to open a discussion on feelings.

Music Therapy

Music as therapy, and in relation to 'bereavement and loss', is a tool, and one which can be used to communicate with children at their own level – 'Music can be the only key that unlocks the inner child' (Lea 1984). Active participation with the controlled use of music, acts as a link between the inner world of the child with unresolved problems and difficulties, and the outward expression of those difficulties. The child is helped back to perceptive and emotional reality and becomes more able to express hidden feelings.

Percussion instruments are generally used by participants, with the therapist often at a piano, and sessions can be on an individual or group basis. Some therapists use music exclusively while others use a combination of music and discussion.

The use of rhythm, the beating of drums, tambourines, chime bars and so on, can be echoed on the piano; the use of the voice, of tonality, of pitch and timbre, can be improvised or echoed; there can be a 'dialogue' or duet in sound and rhythm.

Music can be happy or sad, descriptive of a situation, feeling or a scene. Therapy can be extended into drawing/word association or stories – the experienced therapist deciding how to guide each child.

Methods, styles and emphases of therapy vary, but the basic process of 'unlocking' the child's emotions, and building links from 'inside' to 'outside', is the aim of music therapy (see Music Therapy Session).

N.B. Further information can be obtained from the British Society of Music Therapy – see 'Useful Addresses' in Section 3.

Music Therapy Session

The following description is of a 45-minute therapy session with 12 mothers and their pre-school children as part of a two-day workshop on Music Therapy in Wrexham, September 1988 (see list of contributors).

- The mothers with their handicapped children (aged four months to four years) are sitting in a circle on mats on the floor; there is an outer circle of parents of older handicapped children, and professionals, seated on chairs. (I had no case histories, nor had I met anyone, beforehand.)

- I worked on my knees in the centre of the floor group. I had easy access to 50 musical instruments outside the two groups.

Method

As a Music Therapist I work on an understanding of music and its effect on mind, body and emotions. As a mother, I worked on an understanding of my relationship with my three children.

AIM

- Communication
- vocally, rhythmically, and melodically.

- Spontaneity
- exploration of 'me', themselves, sounds and instruments.

- Initiations and Responses

- Turn Taking

- Interactions
- between children and children, adults and adults, adults and children, and both with me.

- To play games and have fun

Instinctively I used my voice most of the time, plus the addition of drums, bells, autoharp, triangle, and guitar.

We sang songs about the body, pointing to each part, and played nonsense musical games. We all explored instruments, our voices, the floor space, ourselves and each other.

FEEDBACK

After the session from the mothers on the floor

- My little girl clings to me all the time, she never leaves my side. I was so surprised to see her on her feet the whole time, wandering around the centre of the group (around me), and the other mothers and children. She has never done that before (child aged four).

- It was wonderful to watch (the three-year-old severely handicapped, cerebral palsied boy), when we sang about finding our noses, eyes, and mouths. After all his excessive arm movements he finally found his nose – his eyes were all shining, and he was smiling – grinning actually.

- My little boy loved playing the strings on the guitar because he ran back to me for a cuddle afterwards. He only does that when happy.

- When can we do this again? It was such fun, I don't have much fun nowadays.

- When you sang to him his whole body relaxed in my arms, this rarely happens. He also opened his eyes wide, I hardly ever see this happen and it only does when he is happy. (This was a profoundly handicapped boy of three, unable to hold his head up or to sit up, his eyes were seven-eighths closed).

- I had such a shock when I saw you hold the beaker near G's hand and just let him take hold of it. I have always opened my seven-year-old's hand and shoved the spoon in it. I shan't now.

FEEDBACK

From professionals and other parents in the outer circle

- How can you cope with your own feelings in a situation like that?

- I could see myself in one of those mothers, all her pain. I remember feeling like that. I just wanted to take her in my arms and tell her it will be all right.

- I didn't expect the children to concentrate for so long.

- I am sorry, tears are just streaming down my face.

- I knew we needed a music therapist here in Wrexham, but being present, and experiencing this two-day workshop, makes one feel we must all fight to make a job available.

MY BRIEF COMMENTS

- I had no idea that a four-month-old, Down's syndrome baby could/would take turns on a drum with me, anticipating my turn (when I had purposely delayed it), and then smiling up at me when I eventually played.

- After the experience of this workshop I decided that I must try and set up a similar group in the Berkshire area.

Music Therapist

Creative Imagination

The purpose of this is to focus and energize, to enhance imagination and intuition, and to increase the flow of ideas around a particular subject, for example, loss or happiness.

Guided Imagery

Encourages creative imagination, choice and focuses attention. Invite the children to do the following:

- Close your eyes, and imagine an apple – see it as clearly as possible.

- Imagine the colour, shape, size.

- Move on to other objects and repeat the process.

- Then discuss it with the whole class or smaller groups.

N.B. This can be repeated imagining smell, taste, hearing or feeling. Also this simple activity familiarizes the children with closing their eyes and using their imagination.

Expanded Guided Imagery 1

Integrates the creative imagination into the learning process. Encourages a positive attitude towards a child's own creativity.

- ° The children start with their eyes closed and spend a few moments becoming still and relaxed.

- ° (See Sections on 'Relaxation' and 'How Can We Help'.)

DIRECTED

- Take the children on a specific journey, for example, to a house.

- You choose where they go, and constantly ask them what they see, hear, smell, and how they feel.

- Remind them to notice colours, shapes, people/animals.

- Bring them back to their starting place and ask them to write, draw or act out their experience.

UNDIRECTED

Ask the children to:

- Imagine inside yourself a very quiet place that is special to you, where you feel very good, and at home.

- From this place think about the story you are going to write.

- See the story beginning – watch it unfold – notice all the details, the colours, sounds, and feelings in it – imagine how it will end.

- When your story is finished – there is no need to hurry – come back into the classroom and begin writing.

N.B. This could also be adapted by using drama, drawing or other creative activities (see exercise following).

Expanded Guided Imagery 2

This visualization can be used as a transition from one activity to another, or following a playtime held indoors because of wet weather.

Ask the children to close their eyes and lead the children through a simple relaxation before suggesting that they:

- Go to that place in your mind where you can create or imagine.

- See yourself in your imagination, sitting at your desk/table, working comfortably and enjoying your work.

- Choose how you're going to be, what attitude* you're going to have.

- How will this attitude* help you?

- See yourself, your group and the rest of the class working well together.

- Feel this comfortable feeling.

- When you are ready open your eyes.

* **N.B.** You need to have discussed 'attitude' previously.

Visualization before Creative Writing

Builds creative imagination, self-discipline and focuses attention.
Ask the children to:

- Start with eyes closed as before.

- Find a place inside your imagination that is special to you. A part of your mind where you can imagine anything you want.

- This is a place where you feel good, and at home.

- You may get a picture for this special place.

- In this quiet place think about the story you are going to write … See the story beginning – the characters – what they are doing/saying – How they are feeling – watch the story unfold – notice all the details, for example the colours, sounds, feelings, in the story.

- Imagine how the story will end.

- When your story is finished – there is no need to hurry – come back to the room and begin writing.

N.B. Drama and Art can also be expressed following this approach.
A good initial introduction to this method is to stop at the 'special place' and to get the class to imagine it in detail. Then write a description of, draw, or make a model of it, and finally talk about their 'place'.

An Assembly

This assembly was designed to develop and foster children's creative imagination and was part of a series focusing on the implications for behaviour of a new set of rules.

'Try to be Kind to Others'

It was started by the children being asked for examples of a time when they would especially need people to be kind to them. The most popular answer was,

'when they are hurt in the playground.'

Taking this situation, the children were then asked,

'What does it mean to be kind to someone who is hurt?'

The answers were mainly,

> 'Bring them in and take them to the teacher.'

One of the children was then invited to the front and asked to pretend that they were hurt in the playground – the 'patient'. The other children were then invited to say how they would know if someone was hurt.

> 'They would be crying'.

> 'They would be on the ground.'

> 'They would be holding their arm/leg.'

The children were then reminded that they had said they would help the hurt child by 'taking them to the teacher'. This was then mimed with the 'patient'.

The children were then asked again if this was what they would do first. The answer came,

> 'No – I would talk to them.'

Further questioning revealed other suggestions such as:

- putting one's arm round the hurt person.

- holding the hurt person's hand, and asking what was wrong.

- smiling at the 'patient', and stroking their hair.

- offering a handkerchief to dry the tears.

This led to a discussion as to which of the suggestions would be the most appropriate, and how you would know this. When asked, 'How would you know whether the hurt person would like you to put your arm around them?' The answers came:

> 'You could ask.'

> 'They would smile if you put your arm around them.'

> 'They would look at you.'

> 'It would feel good to you.'

Further questioning as to how you would know that they didn't want your arm around them revealed:

> 'They would turn away.'

> 'They would wrinkle their face.'

> 'They would shrug their shoulders.'

This in turn led to an explanation that some people like to be touched and some don't. We all have to be very clever or sensitive (this word was described to the children), to find out what others like or dislike.

It was also suggested that the children think about how they know about other people's feelings, even without speaking.

Creative Writing

(1) Journal

Recording thoughts and feelings in a written or pictorial form have a valuable place in the learning process. Also it is psychologically important to 'ground' experiences in this way and/or by talking about them afterwards.

Encourage the children to design the cover for their own journal, either with their own drawings or pictures from magazines that have special meaning for them. Reassure them that they don't have to share the contents unless they wish to do so.

A loose leaf folder will enable children to remove work they may not wish to show to anyone else. They should also be given permission to destroy any part of their work, if they want, in a way that has most meaning for them.

There is a temptation for teachers to keep all the written work which children in the class produce, as tangible proof that the course has been covered.

Good Grief provides many learning experiences that cannot be recorded, evaluated or measured in this way. They will be recorded in the mind of the child, and will remain there to provide a firm foundation upon which to build their experiences of the future.

N.B. Children can make the journal up individually or in groups.

(2) Diary

Alternatively, a diary can be kept, to record events and/or experiences of personal significance. This can be particularly useful for children who have difficulty in talking about their feelings. It is important to emphasize to each child that the diary is for their own benefit and can be kept private. Ideally it should be loose-leaved so that children can remove information they don't want to share.

Expanded Creative Writing

OBJECTIVES

- To use poems or prose to facilitate discussion and explore feelings of loss and bereavement.
- To encourage creative writing.

RESOURCES

- Selection of poems and prose.
- Flip paper and pens. See also *Book Lists* and *Additional Resources*.

METHOD

- Read a poem or prose. This may be read by a volunteer.
- Ask the children to write without discussion the first two or three words which came to mind from the reading.
- List the words for the children.

- Read the poem/prose again with the words displayed.

- Form small groups to discuss the activity or discuss it with the whole group.

  N.B. This 'Method' may be omitted for younger children.

SUGGESTED DISCUSSION POINTS

(Depending on the chosen poem/prose)

Ask the children:

- What were the feelings of the people involved?

- How long did these feelings last?

- What happened to make them feel that way?

- What did they say or do?

- Can you think of anything, or anybody else, that could have been helpful at the time?

- Do you think the person or people involved gained anything from the experience?

- Do you remember a time when you felt like this?

EXTENSIONS

Ask the children to:

- Write a poem or short story using the words chosen in 'Methods' above. Write a poem or story about their own experience.

- Role play one of the poems or pieces of prose.

  N.B. Creative drawing/painting could also be used.

- Close their eyes and experience the feeling of the poem, then suggest that they draw a picture of the feelings that they have become aware of because of the poem.

- Alternatively, ask them to paint a picture of something the poem recalled to mind. Perhaps there was one word or sentence which struck some chord within.

Example of Poem

Violet Oaklander in *Window To Our Children* says: 'The poem, "There Is A Knot" in *Have You Seen A Comet?* never fails to bring forth some feelings usually kept hidden'.

Translation of a poem by an eight-year-old Turkish girl

There is a Knot

There is a knot inside of me
A knot which cannot be untied
Strong
It hurts
As if they have put a stone
Inside of me

I always remember the old days
Playing at our summer home
Going to grandmother
Staying at grandmother's

I want those days to return
Perhaps the knot will be untied
when they return
But there is a knot inside of me
So strong
And it hurts
As if there is a stone inside of me.

After hearing this poem, a ten-year-old girl drew a figure standing on top of a hill, a black dot in her middle, arms outstretched, with the words, 'I hate you, I hate you' written around the figure. She dictated to me: 'My knot is anger inside of me'. Prior to this she had defensively denied feelings of anger, in spite of her rebellious behaviour at school and home.

Teddy

He wasn't golden, he was blue,
He was so old – not nearly new.
I could poke a finger in
Beside his ear, beneath his chin,
My teddy

One day I gave my teddy away
To a girl, in the great big road she lay –
Never seen again
To this very day
My teddy.

Sally Crosher

First Day at School

A millionbillionwillion miles from home
Waiting for the bell to go. (To go where?)
Why are they all so big, other children?
So noisy? So much at home they
must have been born in uniform
Lived all their lives in playgrounds
Spent the years inventing games
that don't let me in. Games
that are rough, that swallow you up.

And the railings.
All around, the railings.
Are they to keep out wolves and monsters?
Things that carry off and eat children?
Things you don't take sweets from?
Perhaps they're to stop us getting out
Running away from the lessins. Lessin.
What does a lessin look like?
Sounds small and slimy.
They keep them in glassrooms.
Whole rooms made out of glass. Imagine.

I wish I could remember my name
Mummy said it would come in useful.
Like wellies. When there's puddles.
Lellowwellies. I wish she was here.
I think my name is sewn on somewhere
Perhaps the teacher will read it for me.
Tea-cher. The one who makes the tea.

RMcG

First Day At The Nursery

The so-seemed castle had opened.
Amazed by all those unknown faces,
My stomach tightened, but had no tears.
I knew mummy would go.
I saw Jenny, I felt gladness,
A power took us, made us all happy.
On the rocking horse I felt in charge of
a Cavalry, a leader, a master,
I went fast, I went faster.
Rolling in the mud I soon got muddy.
Heavy and uncomfortable like weights, as the
mud dried.
A dreamy smell of mash and sausages,
a cradle and lullabies.

Karen Fitzgerald

At School Today

At School today
They call me pinky ponky
You are a black honkey
I said white is paint, bread and butter.

At School today
I done sewing, writing and reading,
They said that's good
I said, thank you.

At School today
I said you cannot do the things I can do
I am Black Proud and Beautiful
They said, not true
I am going to test you.

At School today
My teacher hit me hard
She shook me til I was dead in my heart
Black Mother, save me from my troubles
And take me into your arms.

Accabre Huntley

Rain

Flying in the blue ice of the sky
a pearl in the winds
of the high places

Falling through air
mile after mile to the ground
a mile a minute
a mile a second
to hit the roof and
have to carry on
worming from slate to slate
a hundred droplets years one
brick at a time then
slowly
so slowly
down the window
till halfway in a sudden rush swept down and
lost
in the rainlake on the sill

My cheek against the warm
pink candlewick
bedspread
Watching
Waiting
for a sound
just one sound
to say I'm sorry, Mum, I'm sorry
My voice echoes back
'I hate you, I hate you'

Upstairs
wishing wishing
I could walk through a door
into a living room where
it never happened
and start again

Mick Gowar

Today Was Not

Today was not
very warm
not very cold
not very dry
not very wet.

No one round here
went to the moon
or launched a ship
or danced in the street.

No one won a great race
or a big fight.

The crowds weren't out
the bands didn't play.

There were no flags no songs
no cakes no drums.
I didn't see any processions.
No one gave a speech.

Everyone thought today was ordinary,
busy busy
in out in
hum drummer day
dinner hurry
grind away day.

Nobody knows that today
was the most special day
that has ever ever been.

Ranzo, Reuben Ranzo,
who a week and year ago was gone
lost
straying starving
under a bus? in the canal?
(the fireman didn't know)
was here, back,
sitting on the step
with his old tongue lolling,
his old eyes blinking.

I tell you –
I was so happy
So happy I tell you
I could have grown a tail –
and wagged it.

Michael Rosen

Poor Little Joe

Poor little Joe,
Stuck in your wheel-chair,
No one will talk to you
No one will care.
All day long
On your own
At school.
Poor little Joe,
Stuck out on your own!
Go join them, have some fun!
'They don't want to play, so what can I do?'
Just hand around
And wait;
Just talk to them
And hope;
Poor little Joe.

D. Norris

There's A Baby On The Way

My mummies got a bump,
And a baby's in that lump.
When will the baby come along,
Is it a baby or am I wrong?
My mummy left me for a day,
Daddy said, 'There's a baby on the way'.

Will it be a him or her?
I don't know which I'd prefer,
I don't really know if I want it now,
What if it's horrible, ugly and foul,
Tom, Kate, Clair or John,
Someone tell me what's going on.

Cathy Baker, aged ten

Hope

The handicapped child sits tied to his wheel
chair,
Gazing sorrowfully into the deep blue sky,
Watching the gusty wind move the clouds,
Across the watercolour turquoise heavens.
Children seem to shout and scream everywhere
In ignorance of the young cripple's plight.
Their rejoicing echoes the deep, cavernous
Thoughts of the boy.
'Come on, Michael, Eat up!'
His eyes return to the triangular head of the
nurse,
Each eyeball swelling with the bottomless pit
Of emotion he holds,
A deep, sinking hope.
She bangs his spoon against the mashed potato.
A primeval sign to eat.
The two wells of self-pity and deprivation
Cut through the nurse.
She winces,
Emotion like a germ has been
Passed on,
A fleeting glance has said all.
The self anguish has been released from its cage;
The bell and mirror can be left to rot and decay,
There must still be hope.

D. Grant

85

I Thought A Lot Of You

I thought you were my friend,
I thought you said you'd help;

I thought I could trust you,
I thought I could count on you;

I thought you were loyal.
I thought you would understand;

I thought I made it sound-straight forward,
I thought I had someone to talk to;
I thought you had an answer,

I thought you were a good listener;
I thought I was telling in confidence,

I thought I wasn't being stupid;
I thought you wouldn't make a fool of me,

I thought you weren't going to tell a soul;
I thought wrong!

P.S. Blackman (Jnr)

The Lesson

'Your father's gone', my bald headmaster said.
His shiny dome and brown tobacco jar
Splintered at once in tears. It wasn't grief.
I cried for knowledge which was bitterer
Than any grief. For there and then I knew
That grief has uses – that a father dead
Could bind the bully's fist a week or two;
And then I cried for shame, then for relief.

I was a month past ten when I learnt this:
I still remember how the noise was stilled
In school-assembly when my grief came in.
Some goldfish in a bowl quietly sculled
Around their shining prison on its shelf.
They were indifferent. All the other eyes
Were turned towards me. Somewhere in myself
Pride like a goldfish flashed a sudden fin.

Edward Lucie-Smith
© 1964

Happy Birthday, Dilroy

My name is Dilroy.
I'm a little black boy
and I'm eight today.

My birthday cards say
it's great to be eight
and they sure right
coz I got a pair of skates
I want for a long long time.

My birthday cards say,
Happy Birthday, Dilroy!
But, Mummy, tell me why
they don't put a little boy
that looks a bit like me.
Why the boy on the card so white?

Dilroy, aged eight

Daddy

Daddy lives in Tate Street now
he's got a flat
with patchy orange walls
and grey armchairs that
smell of someone else
And every Saturday we sleep there
Jo and me

Daddy lives in Tate Street now
he's got a flat
it's up a winding flight of stairs
it's cold and
dark at night it feels as though there's
no one there
not even Daddy Jo and me

Daddy lives in Tate Street now
he's got a flat
he grows tomatoes in a pot outside
and in a week or two
we'll help him put them on
a windowsill to ripen
Daddy says

Mick Gowar

86

Going Through the Old Photos

Me, my dad
and my brother
we were looking through the old photos.
Pictures of my dad with a broken leg
and my mum with big flappy shorts on
and me on a tricycle
when we got to one of my mum
with a baby on her knee,
and I go,
'Is that me or Brian?'
And my dad says,
'Let's have a look.
It isn't you or Brian,' he says.
'It's Alan.
He died.
He would have been
two years younger than Brian
and two years older than you.
He was a lovely baby.'

'How did he die?'
'Whooping cough.
I was away at the time.
He coughed himself to death in Connie's arms.
The terrible thing is,
it wouldn't happen today,
but it was during the war, you see,
and they didn't have the medicines.
That must be the only photo
of him we've got.'

Gone

She sat in the back of the van
and we waved to her there

we ran towards her
but the van moved off

we ran faster
she reached out for us

the van moved faster
we reached for her hand

she stretched out of the back of the van
we ran, reaching

the van got away
we stopped running

we never reached her
before she was gone.

Michael Rosen

Me and Brian
looked at the photo.
We couldn't say anything.
It was the first time we had ever heard about Alan.
For a moment I felt ashamed
like as if I had done something wrong.
I looked at the baby trying to work out
who he looked like.
I wanted to know what another brother
would have been like.
No way of saying.
And Mum looked so happy.
Of course she didn't know
when they took the photo
that he would die, did she?

Funny thing is,
though my father mentioned it every now and then
over the years,
Mum – never.
And he never said anything in front of her
about it
and we never let on that we knew.
What I've never figured out
was whether
her silence was because
she was more upset about it
than my dad –
or less.

Michael Rosen

He stayed for such a little while
So small, so complete but so frail
He stayed for so very short a time
That he hardly seemed quite real
But he stayed for just long enough
For you to know his touch, his warmth
He stayed just long enough
To know he was really yours
And when you felt you were getting
To know him
When you thought you were just making
friends
He heard the voice of a far greater friend
Calling him home from the struggle of living
To play in the sunshine of heavenly fields
There he can run without aids and crutches
There he can play and sing without tears
There he can wait in God's tender keeping
Until you can join him in coming years.

Anon.

Don't Interrupt!

Turn the television down!
None of your cheek!
Sit down!
Shut up!
Don't make a fool of yourself!
Respect your elders!
I can't put up with you anymore!
Go outside.
Don't walk so fast!
Don't run.
Don't forget to brush your teeth!
Don't forget to polish your shoes!
Don't slam the door!
Have manners!
Don't interrupt when I'm talking!
Put your hand over your mouth when you cough
Don't talk with your mouth full!
Go to the market with me.
You spend too much money!
No more pocket money for you dear.
Go to your room!
Don't stuff yourself with sweets!
Don't point!
Don't go too near the television!
You are not coming out until you have tidied your
room.
Don't interrupt when I'm talking!
Did you get any homework today?
Always carry a pen to school.
Eat your dinner up.
Wear your school uniform!
Turn the television over to watch 'Dallas'.
Bring any letters home from school.
Come straight home tomorrow.
Tidy your bed.
Don't shout!
Don't listen to my conversation.
Don't look at the sun it could blind you.
Don't bite your nails!
Don't suck your thumb!
Why don't you answer me!
You never listen to a word I say!
Don't interrupt when I'm talking!

Demetroulla Vasslil

Growing Up

In Infancy
He finds it very hard to play
like other little boys;
He'd rather wreck the Wendy house
or smash the classroom toys.
Poor mite, he's from a broken home
and hasn't got a dad;
It's social deprivation,
he isn't really bad.

In Boyhood
It seems he lies and often steals,
and tends to be a bully.
He swears and cheats, he's insolent
and thoroughly unruly.
But being underprivileged
should earn him absolution
And so we have to help him
escape from retribution.

In Adolescence
Completely antisocial,
a vandal and a thug.
He reckons every working lad
is nothing but a mug.
Because we feel he's still a case
for pity more than blame,
We try to ease his passage through
the Courts to spare his name.

Manhood
And now he's holding hostages
but claims it's not a crime,
That when his 'just' demands are met
they'll be released on time.
He swears that it's the System,
which causes all the pain
And if he has to kill them,
Society's to blame.

He cannot win by argument
much popular support
And so he's turned to Terror which
he thinks will be great sport
Now we've begun to wonder,
recall and try to trace;
Did we help to convince him
that he's a special case?

M.H.L.

In Defence of Hedgehogs

I am very fond of hedgehogs
Which makes me want to say
That I am struck with wonder
How there's any left today.
For each morning as I travel,
And no short distance that,
All I see are hedgehogs,
Squashed. And dead. And flat.

Now, hedgehogs are not clever,
No, hedgehogs are quite dim
And when he sees your headlamps
Well, it don't occur to him
That the very wisest thing to do
Is up and run away.
No! he curls up in a stupid ball
And no doubt starts to pray.

Well, motor cars do travel
At a most alarming rate,
And by the time you sees him,
It is very much too late.
And thus he gets a-squasho'd
Unrecorded but for me,
With me pen and paper,
Sittin' in a tree.

It is statistically proven,
In chapter and in verse,
That in a car-and-hedgehog fight,
The hedgehog comes off worse.
When whistlin' down your prop shaft,
And bouncin' off your diff,
His coat of nice brown prickles
Is not effect-iff.

A hedgehog cannot make you laugh,
Whistle, dance or sing,
And he ain't much to look at,
And he don't make anything,
And in amongst his prickles,
There's fleas and bugs and that,
But there ain't no need to leave him,
Squashed. And dead. And flat.

Oh, spare a thought for hedgehogs,
Spare a thought for me,
Spare a thought for hedgehogs,
As you drink your cup of tea,
Spare a thought for hedgehogs,
Hoverin' on the brinkt,
Spare a thought for hedgehogs,
Lest they become extinct.

Pam Ayres

Death

I had him and cared
He ran from man but not from me.
I played with him when I was in a good mood
And I even gave him his food.
I cried when he died.
He could have survived.
But the pain was with him.
He died.
I cried for five days
But he was not alive to play.

Sateki Faletau, Aged ten

Fluffy

Fluffy you are a lovely cat
All the time you play,
You made me laugh instead of cry.
You were the loveliest cat I knew,
And I'll say a prayer for you.

Love, David Haughton

My Gerbil

Once I had a gerbil –
Bought me by my Dad
I used to watch it in its cage,
Running round like mad
Or sleeping in a corner
Nesting in a hole
Made of shavings, bits of wool
And chewed up toilet roll.

I kept it in the kitchen
In the cage my cousin made.
It flicked all bits out on the floor
Mum grumbled – but it stayed.
I fed it; gave it water;
Was going to buy a wheel.
I used to take it out sometimes –
To stroke, I liked the feel –
All soft, with needle eyes,
A little throbbing chest.
I'd had a bird, a hamster too;
The gerbil I liked best.

I came downstairs one morning.
I always came down first,
In the cage there was no movement.

At once I knew the worst.
He lay there in the corner.
He'd never once been ill –
But now, fur frozen, spiky,
No throbbing, eye quite still.

I tell you – I just stood there
And quietly cried and cried,
And, when my Mum and Dad came down,
I said, 'my gerbil's died'.

And still I kept on crying,
Cried all the way to school,
But soon stopped when I got there
They'd all call me a fool.

I dawdled home that evening.
There, waiting, was my mother.
Said: 'Would you like another one?'
But I'll never want another.

John Kitching

If God had Wanted a Gerbil

If God had wanted a gerbil
He should have saved up like me
and gone to the pet shop and bought one
that's doing things 'properly'

If God had wanted a gerbil
then I think its awfully mean
to have made me drop mine and kill it
when I fed it and kept it so clean
If God had wanted a gerbil
He should have taken its cage and its straw
No. I won't have another gerbil
just in case God wants some more.

Susan Wallbank

To Emily

To Emily at four
death is grandma
a Christmas tea party
and then no more

death is a rabbit
an uninhabited hutch
and a garden rose
growing through its bones

death is a bird
so many birds die
death is a word
she follows with WHY

So I tell her OLD
and I tell her ILL
she's too young for CANCER
or MURDER or KILL

and heaven at best
is somewhere to rest
when we're tired.
Emily says yes

she can see heaven
clearly she can
with grandma and rabbit and bird
and the leg from the one-legged man

Susan Wallbank

3·2·87

Dear Grin-Gran,

Do you remember this writing set? Its the one you gave me for Christmas.

In the 'TARGET' leaflet from church it has st.Paul said "Help to carry one another's burdens." It comes from the Good News Bible, Galatians 6.2. I think we are all trying to do that for each other.

I hope this notelet cheers you

up. I like it because Care Bears are always cheerful. The sun is shining and there is a rainbow. Just two of them sitting there on the cloud makes me feel happy. I hope it does to you aswell I hope we see you again soon.

lots and lots of love
from Alison. x x x x

HONEY

Letter from a Grand-child   Alison aged eight

Alison wrote this letter to arrive on the morning of the Thanksgiving Service for the life of her beloved Grandpa.

My Grandpa

Mine was a lovely Grandpa,
Funny, jolly and kind,
I used to climb in bed with him
And talk nonsense talk.

My Grandpa's garden was beautiful,
Sweet-smelling and colourful,
The sun was always there,
On the flowers, bushes and trees.
I used to follow him asking him things
And he'd answer 'Yes dear, yes dear –'
As if he wasn't listening.

He made friends with a blackbird called 'Thingy'
A fearless little chap
Who tapped at the window for sultanas
Which we fed him every day –
It was all lovely …
But then, you see, my Grandpa died.

Now when I go to stay
Everything's the same but different;
The garden is sweet-smelling and colourful,
And the sun still shines there,
But now I walk in it on my own.

Thingy still comes to the window.

Kate

From Joyce: By Herself and her Friends

If I should go before the rest of you,
Break not a flower nor inscribe a stone,
Nor when I'm gone speak in a Sunday Voice,
But be the usual selves that I have known.
Weep if you must,
Parting is hell,
But life goes on,
So sing as well.

Joyce Grenfell

Why Me?

Grieve for the loss, the separation,
– Why me, why me? –
Grieve for the loneliness, the rejection,
–Why me, Oh why me? –
Feel the shock, the desperation,
–Why pick on me? –
So stamp, so scream and shout, destruction,
–My fault, my guilt? –

Feel the gloom and the depression,
–No talk, no talk! –
The most unutterable oppression.
–Don't speak, won't speak! –
Unspoken thoughts, so silent home. Home?
– Bursting, breaking –
Help me oh carer to mourn, to moan,
And in mourning, peace!

Sally Crosher

Death is nothing at all – I have only slipped away into the next room. I am I and you are you. Whatever we were to each other that we still are. Call me by my old familiar name, speak to me in the easy way which you always used. Wear no forced air of solemnity or sorrow. Laugh as we always laughed at the little jokes we enjoyed together. Play, smile, think of me, pray for me. Let my name be ever the household word that it always was. Let it be spoken without effect, without the ghost of a shadow on it. Life means all that it ever meant. It is the same as it ever was. There is absolutely unbroken continuity. What is this death but a negligible accident? Why should I be out of mind because I am out of sight? I am waiting for you – for an interval – somewhere near just around the corner. All is well.

Canon Scott Holland

Kate

What do you see nurses
What do you see?
Are you thinking
When you are looking at me,
A crabbit old woman
not very wise,
Uncertain of habit
with far-away eyes,
Who dribbles her food
and makes no reply,
When you say in a loud voice
'I do wish you'd try'
Who seems not to notice
the things that you do,
And forever is losing
a stocking or shoe,
Who unresisting or not
lets you do as you will
with bathing and feeding
the long day to fill,
Is that what you're thinking,
is that what you see?
Then open your eyes nurse,
You're not looking at me.
I'll tell you who I am
as I set here so still,
I'm a small child of ten,
with a father and mother,
Brothers and sisters who
love one another,
A young girl of sixteen
with wings on her feet,
Dreaming that soon now
a lover she'll meet;
A bride soon at twenty,
my heart gives a leap,
Remembering the vows
that I promised to keep;
At twenty-five now
I have young of my own
Who need me to build
a secure happy home.

A young woman of thirty
my young now grow fast,
Bound to each other
with ties that should last;
At forty my young ones
now grown will soon be gone,
But my man stays beside me
to see I don't mourn;
At fifty once more
babies play round my knee,
Again we know children
my loved one and me.
Dark days are upon me,
my husband is dead,
I look at the future
I shudder with dread,
For my young are all busy
rearing young of their own,
And I think of the years
and the love I have known.
I'm an old woman now
and nature is cruel,
'Tis her jest to make
old age look like a fool.
The body it crumbles,
Grave and vigour depart,
There now is a stone
where once I had a heart:
But inside this old carcas
a young girl still dwells,
And now and again
my battered heart swells,
I remember the joys
I remember the pain,
And I'm loving and living
life over again,
I think of the years
all too few – gone too fast,
And accept the stark fact
that nothing can last.
So open your eyes nurses
Open and see,
Not a crabbit old woman
look closer – see ME.

'Kate', the writer of this poem, was unable to speak, but was occasionally seen to write. After her death, her locker was emptied and this poem was found.

A Nurse's Reply

What do we see, you ask, what do we see?
Yes, we are thinking when looking at thee,
We may seem to be hard when we hurry and fuss
But there's many of you, and too few of us.
We would like far more time to sit by you and talk
To bath you and feed you and help you to walk.
To hear of your lives and the things you have done
your childhood, your husband, your daughter, your son.
But time is against us, there's too much to do
Patients too many, and nurses too few.
We grieve when we see you so sad and alone
With nobody near you, no friends of your own.
We feel all your pain , and know of your fear
That nobody cares now your end is so near.
But nurses are people with feelings as well
And when we're together you'll often hear tell
Of the dearest old gran in the very end bed,
And the lovely old Dad, and the things that he said,
We speak with compassion and love, and feel sad,
When we think of your lives and the joy that you've had.
When the time has arrived for you to depart
You leave us behind with an ache in our heart
When you sleep the long sleep, no more worry or care
There are other old people, and we must be there.
So please understand if we hurry and fuss –
There are many of you, and too few of us.

Liz Hogben

Kate: First printed in *The Sunday Post* in 1973, it has appeared in newspapers and magazines all over the world, and has been read on radio and TV. Over the years thousands of people have asked for copies of this and the poem written by a young nurse in reply.

Great-Gran

Great-Gran just sits
All day long there,
Beside the fire,
Propped in her chair.

Sometimes she mumbles
Or gives a shout,
But we can't tell
What it's about.

Great-Gran just sits
All day long there.
Her face is blank,
An empty stare.

When anyone speaks,
What does she hear?
When Great-Gran starts,
What does she fear?

How can we tell?
For we can't find
A key which can
Unlock her mind.

Great-Gran just sits,
Almost alone,
In some dream world
All of her own.

But when mum bends
Tucking her rug,
Perhaps she senses
That loving hug.

Derek Stuart

THE JOURNEY

They had been travelling together for some time – a little group on a special journey. They each had a tent in which to live – and their tents were of different shapes and sizes – each having its own unique character and individual beauty. Each day the group pitched their tents a little nearer to their destination – a place they could not see – but which was going to hold for them more than all the experiences of the journey put together.

The group had begun with two people – or perhaps I should say three – since when they had lived on their own in the open countryside, the two, at different times, had met the master of the Journey. He had pointed them in the direction of the destination, and from the day of this meeting he went with them on the journey. When on the way these two met each other, they decided to pitch their tents together. Three more soon joined their group and from then on five tents were pitched side by side.

A time came when the tent of one of the first two began to be a problem for her and the journey became difficult. Some work was done to try and mend her tent but there was little improvement, and the fabric of her tent seemed to be wearing out. The others in the group talked to the Master of the Journey about the situation. They knew that he was able to restore worn out tents and that he loved them all very much. The Master knew that it was best for the group not to tell them all his plans at once, so they continued their journey with him, wondering what the future would hold. As time passed the failing tent became more and more difficult to live in, and the one who lived there needed a new living-place free from the suffering of the tent. It was not that she minded the journey – in fact she loved travelling with the rest of the group – but she knew that what awaited them at the end of the journey was something to look forward to very much.

One morning something very special happened. The one whose tent had now got to the point when it was becoming impossible to live in, looked out – and saw that instead of being on open ground (as her tent had been throughout the journey) it was inside a magnificent house. The room was set out in a way that perfectly suited her and she felt every much at home. From inside her tent she saw standing in the room her greatest friend – the Master of the Journey. She could now see him in a way she never had before. She realised that now inside the house she did not need the tent any longer. The Master of the Journey reached out his hand to her and she went quietly from her tent into her own room in the Master's house. What joy to be there with him!

The one whose tent had been pitched next to hers since they joined together did not see the room, or the house, or the Master. These are all invisible to those who are still on the journey. All that was there to be seen was that the tent was now empty and the one whose tent it had been was no longer there. The group knew where she had gone – her journey was over – she had arrived at the Master's home. With her own special room she had no more need of the tent.

It was difficult for the group to know how to think about the tent now. In one way it was very special as it had been the tent in which the one they loved had always lived. Yet the tent was not the person – and now that she was no longer visible to them, the tent was only worn out fabric which was no longer needed. The tent was carefully packed away; and the group, along with many friends who were also heading for the same destination as they were, got together to say, 'Thank You' to the Master of the Journey for giving them such a lovely person, and to rejoice together that the Master of the Journey loved them all so much and that he was guiding them towards the enjoyment of his home.

The little group then continued their journey together. It was strange for them as they moved on with their tents no longer to have besides theirs the tent of the one who meant so much to them. But in some ways it was as if she was with them as she had always been, because there was so much that was lovely in each of them, and in the life of their group, which came from the love she had given each of them and the special way she had cared for them all.

Graeme C. Young

Footprints in the Sand

The following was receiving from Canada, where it was broadcast by a sixteen-year-old girl dying of cancer,

One night a man had a dream
He dreamt he was walking along the beach with the Lord.
Across the sky flashed scenes from his life.

For each scene he noticed two sets of footprints in the sand.
One belonging to him – the other to the Lord.

When the last scene of his life flashed before him,
He looked back at the footprints in the sand
And he noticed that many times along the path of his life
There was only one set of footprints.
He also noticed that it happened at the very lowest and saddest times in his life.

This really bothered him and he questioned the Lord about it.

'Lord, you said that once I decided to follow you, you'd
walk with me all the way
But I have noticed that during the most difficult times in
my life,
There is only one set of footprints.
I don't understand why in times when I needed you most,
you would leave me.'

The Lord replied:

'My precious, precious child,
I love you and I would never, never leave you
during your trials and suffering.
When you see only one set of footprints,
it was then that I carried you!'

Anon

The Ship

I am standing on the sea shore. A ship
sails and spreads her white sails to the
morning breeze and starts for the ocean.
She is an object of beauty and I stand
watching her till at last she fades on
the horizon, and someone at my side says,
'She is gone'. Gone where? Gone from my
sight, that is all; she is just as large
in the masts, hulls and spars as she was
when I saw her, and just as able to
bear her load of living freight to its
destination.

The diminished size and total loss of
sight is in me, not in her; and just at
the moment when someone at my side says,
'She is gone', there are others who are
watching her coming, and other voices
take up a glad shout, 'There she comes',
and that is DYING.

Bishop Brent

Feelings

Feelings

National Curriculum

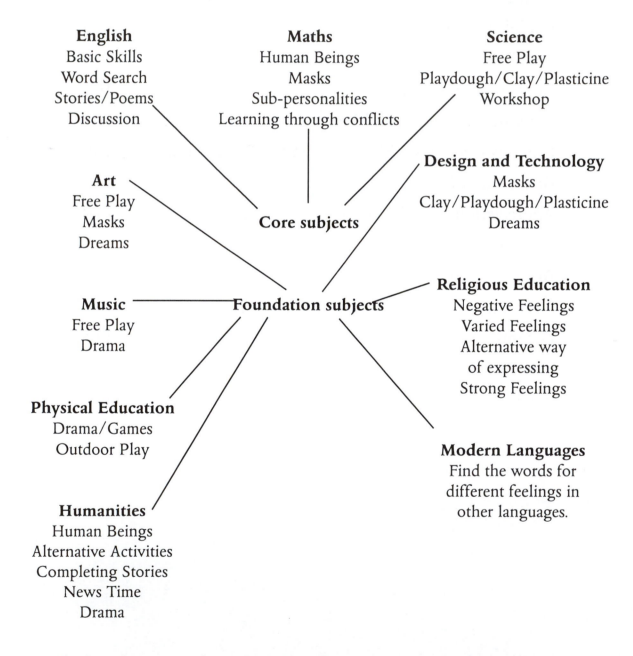

English
Basic Skills
Word Search
Stories/Poems
Discussion

Maths
Human Beings
Masks
Sub-personalities
Learning through conflicts

Science
Free Play
Playdough/Clay/Plasticine
Workshop

Art
Free Play
Masks
Dreams

Core subjects

Design and Technology
Masks
Clay/Playdough/Plasticine
Dreams

Music
Free Play
Drama

Foundation subjects

Religious Education
Negative Feelings
Varied Feelings
Alternative way
of expressing
Strong Feelings

Physical Education
Drama/Games
Outdoor Play

Humanities
Human Beings
Alternative Activities
Completing Stories
News Time
Drama

Modern Languages
Find the words for
different feelings in
other languages.

The lists above are only suggestions. Many more may be found in the text.

Feelings

*'Man was made for joy and woe and when that we rightly know
Thro' the world we safely go.'*

(Auguries of Innocence. William Blake)

Objectives

- to encourage children to understand and accept the wide range of feelings that exist in themselves and other people.

- to enable them to feel comfortable with those feelings and accept them as natural/normal.

- to contribute to their self-esteem.

- to provide a background to exploring loss and death.

- to help combat the British 'stiff upper lip', and recognize that boys as well as girls need to express feelings.

Useful Resources

- Background reading   — in Section 1
                          — in Section 2 — 'Creative Activities'
                                           'Creative Listening'
                                           'Developing Self-Esteem'.
                          — in Section 3 — 'Book List'.

- Stories/poems/pictures expressing feelings.
  (See 'There Is a Knot Inside Me'; 'Creative Activities').

- Vocabulary of 'feeling' words.

- Materials for different activities.

NB. Activities can be used to explore positive and negative feelings, whichever are most appropriate to the situation. It is important to strike a balance and see that children aren't left with negative feelings. Sharing something good or something they are looking forward to is a good way of ending a lesson. Give small examples, for example, play time — my lunch etc.

Some children are not familiar with what feelings are. Very young children do not have the language to communicate them. They need to know that everyone has feelings, what kinds there are, and how to express, share, and talk about them.

Free Play Activities

The imaginative play activities listed below provide opportunities for young children to explore and express feelings, and need to be available at all times. They give young children the chance to deal with whatever is affecting them or causing conflict, or simply giving them 'food for thought'.

The educator needs to be aware of the children's needs and to decide when to intervene and participate in the play or to extend it.

(1) **Home Corner:** include, for example: a bed, a table, chairs, cupboards, dolls and teddies, crockery and cutlery, play food, TV, telephone.

(2) **Dressing-Up Area:** possibly include mirrors, hats, shoes, clothes and jewellery, from different cultures.

(3) **Small World Area:** include dolls houses, small models of animals/or people, cars, trains, planes.

(4) **Music Area:** include instruments to bang, shake, scrape (see 'Music Therapy').

(5) **Material to Manipulate:** such as dough, clay, plasticine, cornflour.

(6) **Painting and Drawing:** include selection of pens, pencils, crayons, poster paints, finger paints, and paper (see 'Art Therapy').

(7) **Workshop:** for example, include junk, glue, scissors, paper, sticky tape, string, collage materials.

(8) **Drama:** for example, puppets, theatre. More details see expanded Section in 'Creative Activities'.

(9) **Cuddle Corner:** soft cushioned area with soft toys and a rug for the children to cover themselves with.

Further Suggestions

(10) **Book Corner:**

(11) **Outdoor Play:** small and large construction sand play

(12) **Water Play:**

Group Activities

These activities can be done in pairs/small groups or for the whole class, depending on the age and ability of the children.

Directed group activities allow information and experiences to be shared. Children will soon become familiar and comfortable with the vocabulary of feelings by talking about them.

Spontaneous Activities

Wonderful opportunities can occur during the course of a day for teaching children spontaneously how to express, and act on, their feelings in more creative, less aggressive ways. Where young children may have a very limited range of behaviour they may benefit from learning other ways of expressing their feelings.

Recognizing Feelings

Generate discussion about feelings by asking children questions about their everyday experiences and/or their observations of animals or people, for example:

- How do you feel when it's your birthday?

- How do you feel when you can't do your maths?

- Make a note of feeling words and add any other that are suitable for the age range.

N.B. These 'feeling words' can be made into a display/collage/frieze.

Basic Skills Necessary for Communicating Feelings

- Encourage children to make eye contact without actually staring.

- Encourage them to listen carefully to each other.

N.B. See also 'Creative Listening'.

Animals

Ask the children the following questions before encouraging them to talk about, write, draw or mime their own pets or other animals:

- How does a dog show that it is pleased to see you?

- How does a cat show when it is angry?

- What sounds does a cat make when it is angry/happy?

- What sound does a dog make when it is happy/angry?

Most animal feelings are related to survival needs, and are somewhat distorted by our providing for them.

These are:

- food, shelter

- protection, and leadership in pack situations

- continuation of the species.

Human Beings

Use pictures or photographs of people's faces expressing different feelings to encourage children to answer the following questions:

- How does the person feel?

- Can you make a similar face to the picture?

- Can you make a face that is… (*go through the different feelings*)?

Then:

- Repeat as above, but ask them to make sounds.

- Repeat as above, but ask them to put their body in a position that expresses that feeling.

- Ask them when they have these different feelings?

N.B. Explain that some people laugh to hide pain. Ask the children if they think it's a good idea to do so and why they think it happens.

EXAMPLES OF DIFFERENT FEELINGS

Happiness: smiling, laughing, open-ness.

Excitement: voice high, trembling knees, tummy rumbling.

Anger: shouting, clenching teeth, howling, frowning, stamping feet.

Fright: knees shaking, palms sweating, voice trembling, heart beating faster, screaming, tummy rumbling.

Discuss how different cultures express feelings; for example, Asian children are taught to look away when being reprimanded.

Alternative Activities

- The teacher mimes expressions/sounds/body postures and asks the children to guess what they are.

- Older children could do a similar activity in pairs, taking it in turns to mime feelings and to guess what they are.

- Let children make and wear masks of different feelings, and act out the different feelings (see also 'Drama').

- Photographs from home or of school events can be used to encourage children to talk about feelings that they had at the time.

- Pictures cut out from magazines can be used to make individual/class booklets or class collages expressing different or similar feelings. Facial expressions, gestures and other body language can be discussed.

- Make collage/picture with title, for example, 'Happiness Is', 'Sadness Is'.

- Ask children which things make them feel sad/frightened/happy/curious/amused, etc. Ask them to share their feelings and see if they are similar.

- Examine the feelings of members of their own family and compare them with those of other people they know. Explore whether boys and girls have different feelings. Include examples from other countries/cultures.

- Discuss whether there are differences between adults' and children's feelings. (Children can check these out by asking other children or adults involved with the school, or their own families).

- Complete the activity by making a collage, collection or book, to include pictures and/or writing. This could be on an individual or class basis.

- Hold an assembly on different feelings (see 'Creative Activities').

N.B. These activities could also include 'feeling' words from different languages/cultures.

Word Search

This can be used as an exercise to extend the children's use of vocabulary/language which express feelings.

- Using 1cm. square paper, ask the children to write a strong feeling word in the middle of the page – one letter for each square.

- Use the letters of this word to expand, in all directions, with other words expressing similar/related feelings (see figure).

N.B. See also 'Creative Activities'.

Stories and Poems

Stories provide many opportunities to familiarize young children with feelings. These could include stories about different ethnic groups – to allow for the expression of feelings connected with race and racism. Following the story ask any or all of the following:

- What are you feeling?

- What happened to make you feel that way?

- Do you ever feel like that and if so, when?

- Do you like feeling that way?

Completing Stories

Tell a story, letting the children fill in details as it goes along, for example:

Once upon a time there was a ....?

It was very sad!

Why was it sad do you think?

The .... was walking down the road when it met a ....?

Discussion

Invite children to share something that makes them feel happy/loved/sad/jealous/angry/something that wasn't fair etc.

N.B. It is important for the educator to share their own experience first, before asking children to share theirs (see article by Junior School teacher).

News Time

Invite children to share what they did at the weekend/in the holidays, etc. Ask them how they felt; for example, were they worried, pleased, excited, curious, lonely? Note similarities or differences between the experiences of different children. Perhaps produce a creative journal.

Magic Box

Have an empty box and tell the children that it is magical. In it they will find something that will make them very happy and/or they really want.

Invite them to come and look in the box and tell you about what they find inside.

> **Any of the following activities can be used to extend the above suggestions, or can be used in their own right.**

Drawing and Painting

Ask the children to draw or paint different feelings, for example, happiness, sadness, security, puzzlement, as follows:

- Faces with different expressions.

- A place where they have these feelings.

- Something which makes them feel like this.

- Shapes or patterns or choose colours to represent different feelings.

Make a book of feeling pictures, either individually or for the whole class.

Use the children's pictures, or those from magazines to make a collage expressing different feelings.

N.B. See article 'Value of Hospitalized Children's Art Work' in Section 3.

Playdough – Plasticine – Clay

These can be used to allow children to model humans or animals with different feelings. Start by exploring how clay feels and the different ways it can be used.

Puppets

Use these to tell a story, then discuss what the puppets felt like, how the children felt watching them.

Children can use the puppets to express feelings, for example, fear, anger, sadness. Ask them what made them feel that way.

Drama

Children gain increasing insights into different aspects of themselves and others by role play. It can be used to act out stories from books that have been read, or as a follow up to other activities. Encourage them to take roles they don't normally play in real life, for example ask a noisy child to be the baby Billy Goat in 'Three Billy Goats Gruff'. Discuss afterwards what it was like for them.

N.B. Remember the importance of debriefing, for example, the child says, 'I'm not Baby Billy Goat, I'm John' (see 'Teaching Approaches' in Section 1).

Masks

Children can make masks to express different feelings, and wear simple costumes to add to the drama. The costumes and masks can be left in the dressing-up area for children to use on their own.

Music

Play music expressing different feelings and ask children to identify each feeling.

Let children choose instruments to express different feelings. (See Music Therapy in 'Creative Activities'.)

Expanded Drama

Ideally this activity would take place in the hall, but could be modified for the classroom, and can be arranged as follows:

- Do the activities with your eyes open or closed.

- Stand in a space and begin to swing and move your body, allowing your arms and legs to move freely.

- What do you feel, right at this moment? (Give suggestions, for example happy, a little sad, tired, angry, relaxed.)

- Think about that feeling and, as you move slowly, show the feeling through the whole of your body.

- Now freeze with that feeling.

N.B. See also 'Relaxation'.

Further Suggestions

Varied Feelings

Ask the children to explore other feelings that they have had today, different from the previous one:

- How did you feel this morning?

- How did you feel earlier in the playground?

- How did you feel at lunch time?

Ask the children to let all these feelings come out and move around, as before, to these new, different feelings.

- Make the sounds of these feelings.

- Again use the 'freeze' signal, for each feeling.

N.B. These feelings could be talked about, drawn, or written down. (See also 'Relaxation Activities').

Negative Feelings

Talk about the negative feelings that we all can have from time to time, for example, anger, irritation, sadness, resentment, and ask:

- What negative feelings do you have?

- Do you like them?

- Can you talk about these feelings, ones that you probably don't like to have?

- Move around and express the feelings, make exaggerated movements, and make a sound for them.

- Next, with your body, shake these feelings out, and then 'freeze'.

- When you have experienced negative feelings remember ones that you love to have, for example, smiling, laughing, singing, dancing.

- Move to these happy feelings, expressing sounds to go with them.

N.B. Complete the lesson by sharing experiences, or extend it further with drawing and writing.

Activities for Older Children

Drama Game – 'Situations'

Divide the children into groups of four or five and give each three cards with the following written on each:

- A 'situation' or time when you felt misunderstood, excluded or blamed for something you felt was unfair.

- A 'situation' or time when you felt really angry with another person.

- A 'situation' or time when you felt really good about yourself, for example excited about something, appreciated by someone, a time when you felt really happy.

Ask each child to choose one situation and spend time telling the group about it:

- Where did it happen?

- Who was involved?

- How did you feel?

- How did it end?

N.B. The children will need help to organize the 'sharing' of this activity.

A child from each group chooses to go first and will be the director of the 'situation'. They choose another member in the same group and ask:

- Who will you be playing?

- How do you feel/move?

- What are you saying?

The group then re-enacts the situation with the director organizing the drama. Remind the director, as they will not be taking part, that someone will need to play them.

Each group spends time practising this before showing all the other groups. As each group finishes, ask the directors:

- Did you learn anything new about that time of your life?

- Is there anything you would like to change if a similar situation occurred?

- What different choices could you have made in that situation?

- What did you need?

Art Work

Begin with a discussion on feelings, for example, What are they? when are they strong/weak, etc? Make a list of feelings and ask the children to choose one from the list. Then ask them to:

- Close your eyes and remember a time when you have felt/experienced the feeling you have chosen.

- Remember why you felt that way, and what happened.

- Who was with you?

- See that time in your imagination and feel again how it felt.

- See it as clearly as you can.

- What does your picture/symbol tell?

- Don't worry if it's not clear or if you see patterns or shapes and not pictures; that's fine.

- Open your eyes, and without speaking, draw what you say, for example, the picture, the symbols, the patterns, etc.

N.B. This activity can be extended by sharing with a partner/a group or the whole class, and with written work.

Keep the time for drawing fairly short, say 15 minutes, and repeat the process twice more; in other words, three feelings can be covered in less depth – one then to be chosen to share or for further work.

Feelings – Suggested Lesson Plan for Top Juniors

This can only be taken when a great degree of trust has been built up in a class, and when children are used to sharing concepts and ideas which they know will be listened to and not laughed at (see previous work on 'Feelings').

Recall some or all of the following situations with the children. This can be built into stories as you go. Allow them a moment after each 'story' to write down the feelings they could experience in the following circumstances:

- The day before Christmas/Birthday.

- Going to the doctor/dentist/hospital.

- Losing something very special/finding something special broken.

- Going to buy something you have waited a very long time for.

- Going to buy something special as a surprise for someone else.

- Going home, finding the house empty and not knowing where Mum or Dad are.

108

- Waking up in the night and hearing a strange noise downstairs.

- A wet Sunday afternoon with all your family and friends being together and a good programme on the television.

- Having the main part in the school play and waiting for the curtain to go up.

- Breaking Mum's best/favourite ornament and being afraid to own up.

- Having a quarrel with your best friend and seeing them go off with someone else, leaving you on your own.

- Finding that a secret you trusted to someone has been told to others.

- Being sent for by the Head.

- Having an examination.

- Having a tummy ache and not being able to go on an outing.

- Getting an unexpected letter/parcel in the post.

- Getting a present you didn't want when you thought you would be getting what you did want.

- Getting teased about your new hairstyle.

N.B. There are endless possibilities, and each teacher should use examples which are personal to the class.

Activities

Divide children into groups of about four with an elected leader.

- Ask the leader to make a complete list of the feelings they have 'found'. (In this way a very sensitive child can 'let go' of a painful feeling, and not have to 'own' it before the rest of the class.)

- Collect these lists either orally or on paper and produce a shared class list. This can be used for discussion/art work and creative writing at a later date.

- Invite children to return their individual lists and draw a picture of themselves around which they arrange their own 'feelings'; using colour, letter size and shape as seems appropriate.

These activities can generate useful discussion as the children realize that some feelings can be both positive and negative; in other words, we can be nervous about both 'good' and 'bad' things.

Additional Activities

- The children can be asked to group their feelings in order to help them explore them more fully.

- A display/gallery can be made.

- Suggest making three columns for:
  - good feelings
  - bad feelings
  - don't know feelings

- The children could then, if they wished, go on to make 'Smiley' books with stories from their own experiences which illustrate those feelings.

N.B. See end of section.

Behavioural Problems

- When a child has behavioural problems, for example, hitting others, have a discussion with the class about the problem; for example, Ann keeps hitting her class-mates.

- Ask each child individually to let Ann know how they feel and how they can help her.

N.B. Before using the following suggestions see also 'Appreciations and Resentments'.

It may be necessary to reassure children that everyone has these feelings at different times. Give illustrations from stories/poems, or from your own or other people's experiences (see 'Recognizing Feelings').

- Follow up with creative activities to express feelings more fully if necessary.

- These can be linked with the following exercises for older children with teachers who are experienced with these techniques.

Appreciations and Resentments

- The children sit in a circle.

- Each individual is free to share whatever feelings, appreciations, resentments or requests they wish, with each other or with the teacher.

It will work best the first time if the teacher gives an appreciation to every member of the class, for example, I really liked the way you helped clear up today. When appreciations have been given and trust built up it will then be possible to deal with resentments and negative behaviour in the same way.

N.B. The person receiving the comment is not allowed to reply in any way. They can only nod their head, and take in the information. There are no justifications or denials.

Disputes Between Children

- ° Clarify the issue(s) and sort out the facts.

- ° Disputes are opportunities for children to find creative alternatives in their relationships, and to make choices about their behaviour.

- ° Let them experience their feelings, express them and come to a more satisfactory outcome.

- ° Sometimes this is not possible, but often, with good eye contact and listening, children become aware spontaneously that the other child is not their adversary, but another person with feelings.

- ° Ask them to 'hug',[*] as it sometimes solves the whole issue.

- ° One school has a 'cuddle' corner, with soft toys, cushions, etc., where children can go when upset.

Aggressive Acts

- ° Bring the children involved together and point out the effects of their actions, for example, 'look – he/she is crying, he/she is very upset – can you see the tears?'

- ° Encourage the hurt child to express their feelings about what happened, for example, 'you frightened me, I felt angry with you.'

- ° Encourage the aggressor to be caring; for example, wipe the tears, give them a hug, wash the wound.

- ° Encourage the victim to say positively, and with eye contact, 'don't do that again – I don't like it'. This response is self-empowering and enables the aggressor to see the affects of their actions.

Questions to ask the aggressor

- • What did you want?

- • Can you ask another way and/or take turns and/or share?

- • Can you suggest more acceptable behaviour that gets your needs met?

---

[*] Young children will generally 'hug' very easily, but top juniors may feel less confortable. **N.B**. (See *Books of Hugs* in 'Additional Resources').

Transforming Negative Feelings

Discuss activity with children and tell them that they are free to choose any situation or feeling. Remind them that all feelings are normal and that crying is OK.

EXERCISE

Start with a relaxation exercise and invite each child to do the following:

- Bring into your awareness a problem or difficult feeling.

- Think about and feel that particular experience/feeling. Remember when it occurred, who you were with and what happened.

- Allow an image/symbol to appear, one that is related to the feeling.

- Talk with the 'image' and ask what it needs.

- Tell the 'image' what you need from it.

- Ask it how you can move through and beyond your feelings/problems.

- Discuss the answer with the 'image', thank it for its help and then say goodbye to it.

Let the children draw and write about their experiences before inviting sharing. (See 'Creative Journal' in 'Creative Activities'.)

N.B. Some children may not want to share and shouldn't be pressed to do so.

Alternative Ways of Expressing Strong Feelings

'We can't stop things happening to us. We can decide how we let them affect our lives.'

- It is important to show that you accept the validity of the children's feelings, do not brush them aside but give them alternative ways of acting; that is be arbiter and not judge.

- It is helpful to read the notes at the beginning of 'Directed Group Activities' before continuing.

In the following activities only negative feelings have been chosen. Teachers might like to ask themselves and the children how they express other strong feelings, for example, excitement, happiness, joy, before using any of the following activities:

Anger

Anger expressed as aggression. These suggestions are for the creative, rather than the destructive, use of aggression. (Michelangelo was said to get into such rages that he was able to chip marble quicker than any one else!)

- Use words not hands to say what is needed.

- Draw or paint an angry picture.

- Write a poem/prose about a person/situation.

- Use hands to bang clay. Knead bread dough.

- Use mallet to bang, a hammer to hit nails into wood, hit a cushion.

- Stamp up and down or round the room and/or make sounds – animal ones are particularly good, for example, growl like a dog, or roar like a lion.

N.B. Behind anger is often sadness.

(See also 'Relaxation Activities')

Fear

Children often avoid what they fear, for example, another child, activity or situation.

- Encourage children to express their fears and go beyond them.

- Reassure children that fears are normal, and can help us keep safe from danger, but also can limit us.

- Point out that being brave is not the same as lacking fear. Give examples of people who have done brave deeds while scared, for example, David and Goliath, George and the Dragon.

- Fear of another child. Stand with the child and tell them to say to the other child, 'stop chasing/frightening/hitting me', – whatever is the problem. Say it with them at first. Encourage them to make eye contact and speak loudly, (as in Kidscape). Make sure the other child hears and responds (see 'Appreciations and Resentments').

- Sing songs; for example, 'Whenever I Feel Afraid'.

- Assemblies – tell children stories about brave people; for example, Florence Nightingale, Jesus sailing the storm.

Sadness

Sadness is often behind anger.

- Encourage children to say what is making them sad and ask what they want, for example, a hug, quiet time, reassurance, etc.

- Follow up with creative activities to express feelings, if necessary.

- Let children go to the 'Cuddle Corner'.

Loneliness

Discuss loneliness/rejection with the children. Reassure them that everyone feels like this at times. Sometimes we need to be on our own and some people choose to be alone.

- Show lonely children how to ask another child to play – explaining that we may want to play with someone who doesn't want to play with us. Sometimes we have to play alone and/or wait until someone is ready to play with us. We may need to find another friend.

- Get children to invent an imaginary friend, (who is all the things they would like). They can draw them and give a name.

- The song 'Streets of London' could be used to open a discussion on loneliness.

N.B. This last activity should not be a permanent substitute for real friends.

Withdrawn or Angry Children

- If children are stuck in one emotion, help them move through it.

- Explain that it is OK to be withdrawn/angry, etc.; it is their choice.

- Tell them that they can choose to be that way or choose to enjoy their time at school.

It is quite possible for young children to become conscious of what they are doing and choose to do something else. Once children see that they are not at the mercy of the world but have some choice about their reactions to it, they can change. When actions are changed, feelings can change too.

Problems Outside School

If children come to school distressed or upset, ask them what has happened. Often this, together with acceptance of their feelings, is enough. If not, encourage them to use creative activities to express their feelings:

- Paint/draw/write about feelings.

- Play with water.

- Role play the situation, becoming the mum/dad/big brother etc., whoever had upset the child. This is very energizing.

- Find a story that mirrors their experience or tell one of your own.

N.B. Always inform head teacher/person in charge at an early stage of a situation where outside agencies may be involved, rather than later, as happens all too often.

Further Suggestions

The next stage, which can be a separate lesson, is to ask the class to draw one, two or three of their sub-personalities. It is a good idea for the teacher to share pictures of their own. Depending on the level of the class, various activities can follow:

- If you are a particular sub-personality in a group, who are you with?

- How does it help you in your life?

- Does it hurt or limit you in your life?

- Write a detailed description of your sub-personalities, including the answers to the above questions.

- Add also such items as: what is your favourite food, colour, TV programme, activity, any other traits.

- Act out the sub-personalities with or without made facial masks.

- Develop each part into a detailed character and include it in a piece of creative writing.

Learning Through Conflicts

- Choose a conflict that happens inside the classroom or outside the school.

- Choose six children to be observers.

- Choose another group to create a 'still' photograph or image of part or the whole conflict.

Ask the children to hold the 'still' image/symbol of the conflict. Then go round and touch each child, in the group, in turn. Ask them to say what they feel about the conflict.

The group observing can then ask questions of the players, who answer from the role they are playing. (This helps to look at hidden feelings).

Then the two groups together decide how the situation can be changed or transformed, then the active group moves into the 'new' image.

N.B. This activity needs to be directed by the teacher to ensure the following points are discussed:

- Identify the conflict.

- Determine the underlying cause/misunderstanding, for example, lack of communication, provocation, insecurity.

- Discuss what can be done.

- Finally ask the rest of the class for comments and ideas.

Dreams

- Dreams express children's fears and hopes, needs and concerns.

- Talking about dreams helps integrate feelings and experiences.

- Children often talk spontaneously about their dreams, particularly the frightening ones.

- Encourage them to say more about what happened and listen to them respectfully.

N.B. It is important not to try to interpret or analyze dreams.

Additional Activities — Ways to Reduce the Power of Feelings

- Draw, paint or write about it.

- Make a model of the character that is most disturbing by creating it in paper/wood/clay, etc.

Extensions for Trained Therapists or Teachers with More Experience

If there is something frightening in the dream:

- Ask the child to imagine that they are the frightening part.

- Encourage them to say whatever they want. Then ask the child to return to being themselves and to set up a dialogue, talking to the scary part. (Giving the character a voice, and a dialogue, lessens its power over the child.)

- Tell the child if they have the dream again they can look into the eyes of the character and tell it clearly to go away unless it is going to be friendly (see 'Fear' in 'Alternative Ways of Expressing Feelings').

Sub-Personalities

Introduce the class to the idea of sub-personalities by getting them to sit in a circle, or a reasonably intimate group. One way of explaining, is to say have you noticed:

- How differently you behave at home from school?

- How differently you behave in the playground from the classroom?

- How you behave with your friends or your family?

Get the class to respond and give examples. This could take some time depending upon the willingness of the children to become involved. Give examples as needed, for instance:

- When you are in the playground, lose a game and get angry, you are being your 'poor sport'.

- When the head teacher is talking in assembly and you are very polite and quiet, you are 'Goody Two Shoes'.

Does anyone recognize these examples?
Ask the children for examples, also give some that are personal.

N.B. It is essential that the teacher is non-judgemental and encourages the same attitude in the children. (For more information read *Psychosynthesis In Education*. See 'Additional Resources'.)

by Sarah Hodder

Body

cross

unloved
upset
happy
excited
Anxious
miserable
relieved
Devastated
hurt
scared
down in the mouth
angry

Jealous
glad
envy.
worried
fearful
gloomy
depressed
silly
frightened
lonely
Joyfull
scared

unloved

nervous

happy   bored

curious

Curious

unsure

frightened

exciting

sadened

anxious

Glad

joyful

rejected

S
a
d

devastated

Good

uncomfortable

unloved

angry

deprived

lonely

worried

scared

fearful

jealous

strange

118

Anxious
envious
curious
tingley
Bored

angry
unloved
rejected
cross

Sad
gloomy
painful
scared
hurt
down
Hate
Devastated
miserable
worried
guilty
Dread
letdown

Happy
Joyful
Excited
love
glad

Frightened

I get frightened when
a big dog comes up to me
with out a lead on or with a
owner. I get frightened when
it comes up to me because
it might bite me.

Excited

I get excited when it is
my birthday and at christmas
I get excited because I get presents
and I get to see my grandad and
the rest of the family.

Sad

On Sunday I came down for breakfast. During Breakfast the dog died
he made a noise then died. When he died
I cried I felt sad miserable and gloomful
Because he won't be around any More and
he was used to me. We use to walk down
the B.M.x track and in the wood

NICE FEELINGS

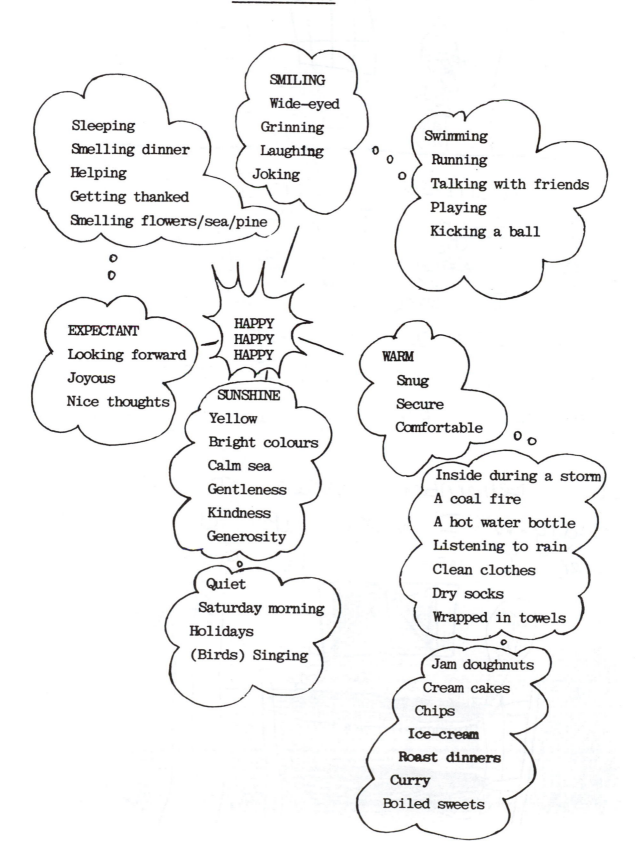

SMILING
Wide-eyed
Grinning
Laughing
Joking

Sleeping
Smelling dinner
Helping
Getting thanked
Smelling flowers/sea/pine

Swimming
Running
Talking with friends
Playing
Kicking a ball

EXPECTANT
Looking forward
Joyous
Nice thoughts

HAPPY
HAPPY
HAPPY

WARM
Snug
Secure
Comfortable

SUNSHINE
Yellow
Bright colours
Calm sea
Gentleness
Kindness
Generosity

Inside during a storm
A coal fire
A hot water bottle
Listening to rain
Clean clothes
Dry socks
Wrapped in towels

Quiet
Saturday morning
Holidays
(Birds) Singing

Jam doughnuts
Cream cakes
Chips
Ice-cream
Roast dinners
Curry
Boiled sweets

I remember when I
felt angry... I felt very
angry when my dady
didd. I cried Eaf half an
avar, aftr I did not cry.
Eaf weks be Eaf I code
let it go.   You are very brave.

crying

I Remember when I felt
angry... I woke up; crting   P
when I let my old friends.

Living with Loss

Living with Loss

National Curriculum

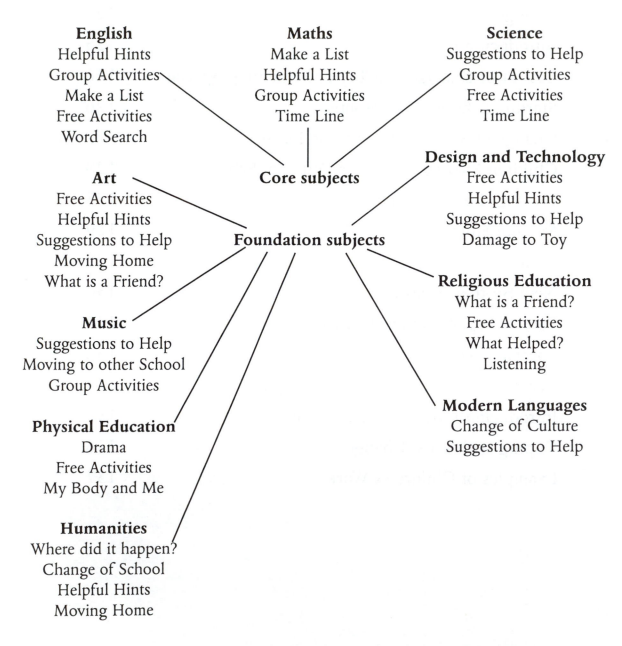

English
Helpful Hints
Group Activities
Make a List
Free Activities
Word Search

Maths
Make a List
Helpful Hints
Group Activities
Time Line

Science
Suggestions to Help
Group Activities
Free Activities
Time Line

Core subjects

Art
Free Activities
Helpful Hints
Suggestions to Help
Moving Home
What is a Friend?

Foundation subjects

Design and Technology
Free Activities
Helpful Hints
Suggestions to Help
Damage to Toy

Religious Education
What is a Friend?
Free Activities
What Helped?
Listening

Music
Suggestions to Help
Moving to other School
Group Activities

Modern Languages
Change of Culture
Suggestions to Help

Physical Education
Drama
Free Activities
My Body and Me

Humanities
Where did it happen?
Change of School
Helpful Hints
Moving Home

The lists above are only suggestions. Many more may be found in the text.

Living with Loss

'We can't prevent the birds of sorrow from landing on our shoulder.
We can prevent them from nesting in our hair.'   *(Old Chinese Proverb)*

Objectives

- To help children understand that loss touches everyone throughout life.

- To understand the feelings that accompany loss.

- To recognize that these feelings are a necessary and important response to loss.

- To be aware that all change has potential for loss as well as gain.

Useful Resources

- Background reading…in Section 1.

                 in Section 2. 'Creative Listening', also 'Feelings'.

- Appropriate Articles…Additional Resources in Section 3.
- Stories/poems/pictures/case studies of loss situations. Materials for different activities.

Directed Group Activities

These activities can be done in pairs/small groups or with the whole class, depending on the age and ability of the children.

Changes

Changes always involve a loss of the familiar and have the potential for loss or gain. Any change therefore should be prepared for by giving simple, clear information. Questions need answering before, during and after the event, and opportunities need to be given to express feelings. Children may have feelings we do not expect or think are not appropriate. Feelings are not rational, so we need to accept them as valid whatever they are.

Introducing Loss

Activities

- Books or poems on different aspects of loss can be read first – see 'Book List' and 'Creative Activities'.

- Ask the children what it means to lose something.

- Remind them of the 'Feeling' exercise and ask them what it feels like to lose something.

- Make a list on the board of different things children have lost – give examples from your own experience and those of other children, for example, toys, friend, grandparent.

- Discuss which things they miss and which they were glad to lose, and the feelings that arose.

- Ask them if they have ever been lost? How did it feel? – What happened?

- Use stories/drawings to illustrate.

Loss of or Damage to a Toy or Something Special

Be aware, this may be the first loss a child has experienced, and reactions to this could set the scene for the future.

Questions to Ask

- Have you ever lost/broken a toy or special article? For example, teddy chewed by dog.

- Where and how did it happen?

- What did you do without it?

- Will you/did you replace it?

- How did you feel when it was lost/damaged?

Starting School – Playgroup

As this sets the foundations for future transitions through the school system it is important that this should be a positive experience.

Helpful Hints

- Allow parent(s) one or more visit before their child starts.

- Allow the parents to see the various activities. Where possible arrange a home visit.

- Stagger the entry of children to avoid confusion and anxiety. Establish a relationship with the parents and their child will then trust you to build a relationship with them.

- Make sure time is given to each child when they arrive, based on the individual needs and circumstances.

- To ease the separation from parents, start children for a short time each day and gradually extend.

- Initially ask parents to leave for five minutes, then return so children feel they are not being abandoned. Always insist that parent(s) don't just disappear or children may think adults are not to be trusted.

- Encourage children to talk about their families and homes.

- Make rules and routines explicit, for example, always put on an apron for water play.

- Give each child something that is theirs alone, for example, a coat peg, a photograph displayed.

- Give very young children a book of photographs of activities, for example, sand play, home corner play, the interior of school, (toilets, garden, coat area). These can be taken home and read with the parent(s) before starting school.

- Include books on starting 'school' in the book corner

- Suggest ways children already in 'school' can help newcomers. They can act as role models as well as giving individual children help and friendship.

Change of School – Change of Teacher

Some children do not want to leave the security of their first school. It is helpful to let them know, they can always go back for a visit, that all the other children will be leaving too, and that as they grow bigger they will need different things, for example, larger chairs, larger toilets.

N.B. Similar feelings can occur on changing from Infant to Junior school.

Ideas to Ease the Transition from Nursery/Playgroup – Infant – Junior School

- Prepare them in advance. Tell them where they are going and let them discuss practical details, for example, whether there is a uniform, how they will travel, who will take them, what they will do. Where possible include parents in discussion.

- Go with them to visit their new school. Let them meet their new teacher and any children who may be in their class.

- Familiarize the children with the new school routine. Let them join in playtime, use the toilets, talk to older children, see where coats, books etc. are kept.

- Some schools produce a simple booklet for new pupils as well as parents.

- Keep the same class teacher for more than one year.

- Invite the non-teaching staff of the school to come and talk to the class about their jobs. This could include the lollipop person and local community police (see 'Use of a Visitor' in Teaching Approaches in Section 1).

° Encourage the children to make a collage of these people and/or have pictures, with their names and jobs underneath, in the school entrance. In this way children can quickly become familiar with them.

° Establish rituals to follow as each group of children leaves or moves up within a school, for example have an outing or entertainment for the children who are leaving. This gives them the sense of being special and being part of a group who are all moving onwards.

Children Moving Away to a Different School

° Have a goodbye ceremony. Let each child say goodbye and find out where their class mate/friend is going. It can be worrying for children to have friends who disappear over the holiday with no explanation for their going.

° Give everyone the opportunity to say goodbye and to show appreciation for having known them. At the ceremony each child who is leaving can say something, sing a song, or dance to the whole group. A last gift to be remembered by?

° A little gift can be given to act as a link and reminder, for example, a group photograph, a plant from the garden, a book of their own work, or a story book.

° Some children/parent(s) may like to give a gift to the school. This will help the children feel that they have not been forgotten or replaced.

N.B. See 'Life Summary' at the end of 'What is Death'.

Leaving/Losing Friends

Questions to Ask

- What is a friend?

- What does a friend do?

- How do you choose a friend?

- How can you make friends, what do you have to do?

- How do other people make friends with you, and what do they do?

- What do you feel like when your friend moves away/doesn't want to be your friend any more?

- What did you do together/what will you miss?

- How can you make another friend?

Moving Home

Questions to ask

- What did you like about your old home?

- What didn't you like about your old home?

- Who or what will you miss?

- How is your new home different?

- Is there anything that you liked in your old home that you like in your new/present home?

- If not, what could you do to make you like your new home more, for example, put up pictures?

Additional Activities

- Follow up work in pairs/groups, using drawing, writing or art work.

- Guided imagery or creative imagination work.

- Discuss what could have happened to make the experience better/less frightening.

Change of Culture

Children unable to speak English when attending school may have difficulties in adapting, also may suffer from culture shock. They may have come from a culture where different behavioural norms apply, for example, where it is polite and appropriate for a child to look away and down when spoken to by an adult, rather than to look at you. Not only may the child be unable to speak English, but every aspect of daily life could be different, for example:

- New surroundings.

- Different ways of eating, for example, with a knife and fork.

- Different types of food.

- Behaviour that is culturally acceptable at home being inappropriate at school, for example, no eye contact with adults.

Suggestions to Help

- Have someone who speaks the mother tongue available for the first few days; parents may need this service for meetings/interviews, for example, another child/parent/NNEB.

- Have some familiar things from their culture in the classroom, for example, toys, musical instruments, books, or a cassette in the mother tongue.

- Ask another child to be their 'special friend' for the first few weeks.

- Have a special notice on the door with 'welcome' written in the child's language.

- Display interesting pictures and items from around the world and discuss them.

- Have a notice board with examples of writing in many languages, for example, from food packets, magazines, menus, etc.

- Invite parents, or members of the English F.L. Team, to talk to children about their culture and/or prepare some food.

- Discuss similarities and differences of cultures.

- Tell stories from around the world, and the 'special' country.

- Share songs, stories, rhymes and games from different cultures and countries.

- Celebrate festivals and Holy Days from other cultures.

- Cook food from different cultures.

- Send out communications to parents in their language.

New Brother or Sister

Children often resent the arrival of a new baby, and the attention that this stranger receives. Changes will certainly happen in routines and parental expectations. The mis-match between what children may have been told and reality can make them confused and anxious.

They can feel ousted from their position if they are no longer the only, or the youngest child.

Encourage sharing of feelings: jealousy, love, annoyance, rage, curiosity, pleasure through activities as previously suggested in the section on 'Feelings'.

More Ways to Help Adaptation

- Give child/children extra attention.

- Encourage them to play being a baby, if this is what they need.

- Tell them how lucky the baby is to have them as a brother/sister.

- If the baby is brought by the parents to school for you to see, do make as much fuss of the child as the baby. (So often adults disregard a child when a baby arrives.)

- Encourage parent(s) to give the child a little job that only they can do to make them feel important, for example, greeting guests.

Group Activities

- Tell stories about babies.

- Read non-fiction books about babies, conception, pregnancy, and birth.

- Have animals in the school that mate and have babies, for example, guinea pigs, gerbils, rabbits.

- Visit a farm where there are new born/young animals. (Some cities have farms.)

- Invite 'mothers to be' into school at different stages of the pregnancy, to talk about it, and answer questions.

- Invite a mother with her baby into school, and ask her to bath and feed it … the children can watch and ask questions.

- Discuss with children, who have had/are about to have a new baby in the family, the practical details and their feelings, for example:

  - Who looked after them when their mother was in hospital?

  - What was it like when they visited her?

  - What does the new baby eat, like/dislike?

  - How long does he/she sleep? (Share how you felt if you had a sibling.)

- Discuss when they were babies, what they could/couldn't do; compare with their present size; look at photographs of them at different ages.

- Use songs, games and imaginative play where they can play being the baby and/or other members of the family.

- Encourage them to write stories/poems.

N.B. (See the poem 'There's a Baby on the Way' in 'Creative Activities').

Other Activities

FREE PLAY

(1)	**Home Corner:**	to include dolls of different ethnic groups. Other items such as a baby's bottle, dummy, nappies, potty, baby clothes, toys, articles for feeding and bathing, pictures of babies, pram. etc.
(2)	**Small World:**	to include play people, animals and baby animals.
(3)	**Puppets:**	of members of families, including babies, and big and small animals.
(4)	**Drawing and Painting:**	talk to children about their work and the inner world it represents. Be aware where baby is, in relation to other members of the family, for example, size and colour of the figures.
(5)	**Water Play:**	washing dolls, animals, babies' bottles, jugs, etc.
(6)	**Sand Play:**	families of animals, graded small and large containers.
(7)	**Dough:**	use graded bowls, spoons and cups.

(8) **Toys:**   Teddies … small, medium, large, like the story of 'The Three Bears', and dolls and animals of different sizes.

(9) **Junk:**   packaging and other waste materials.

Parents Separating or Divorcing

In many cases the child's routine could be completely different, parents/carers may change. It is important to keep a stable routine and a structured day at school.

∘ Encourage parents to inform you of any changes in the child's circumstances, this will help you to understand, and make allowances for, different behaviour.

∘ Take time, where appropriate, to talk to the child about these changes, and their feelings and give opportunities to act these out, for example, anger, sadness, disappointment, etc. … There may also be feelings of relief or happiness.

N.B. See 'Educator's Book List' and 'Background Reading' in Section 1.

Free Play Activities

∘ Water play can be very therapeutic. Children can bathe dolls acting as caring/non caring parents.

∘ Drawing or painting feelings/situations.

∘ Use of puppets to act out situations.

∘ Modelling with clay or other materials.

∘ Playing musical instruments, for example, drums.

∘ Banging on old saucepans/tins, for example, with mallets.

Other Activities

∘ Read old familiar stories, encourage children to bring favourite toys/dolls to school.

Special Needs

Most nursery and primary classes will have several children with different kinds of special needs. Children may also have brothers or sisters or parents at home with different conditions or illnesses. Relatively minor difficulties such as the need to wear a hearing aid/glasses, or the discovery of diabetes, can be just as traumatic for young children as more serious mental or physical ones, such as spina-bifida or cystic fibrosis.

∘ Talk about pets, and things they may have wrong with them, for example, some cats or dogs have epileptic fits. How do the children feel about it? Did they love them more or less when they first had something go wrong?

- Young children are often fascinated with the body and how it works. Get them to think about which bits of the body one can do without, and why? How do people feel when they have a part missing? What can help?

- Talk about parts of our own bodies that don't work properly/as well as they used to – no-one has a perfect body or mind, we all have some illness or condition to cope with at some time in our lives.

- Encourage discussion about what's special about having a member of the family or friend with a special need. Are there special things they can do for others without taking away their independence?

- Where appropriate, encourage children to experience/simulate different special needs; for example, wearing a blindfold or earplugs; having a go in a wheel chair; using crutches; wearing glasses. This work can be done in the context of body awareness, and our senses.

- Is there a special job that a child with a difficulty can be given to do?

- Talk about name calling and labelling. Why don't people like some nicknames? How do we feel – even if others didn't mean us to feel that way?

- Draw attention to similarities between children, rather than the differences.

- Are there things children used to be able to do, but can't now? This happens to us all! How do we cope with these kinds of changes?

- Have books for young children in the book corner (see Children's Booklist in Section 3).

N.B. The story of Helen Keller is an ideal introduction to the subject.

Accidents – Illnesses – Going to Hospital

Suggestions to Help

Hospital Corner: for imaginative play.

- Act out emergencies, accidents. For dressing-up include doctor, male and female nurse outfits: for situation play use bandage, sling, cotton wool, disposable glove, disposable syringe (minus needle), thermometer, stethoscope, oxygen masks, tubes, charts, bedding, bed-side table, books on hospital, and so on.

Small World;   Hospital play people, also finger and glove puppets.

Outdoor Play;   Make ambulances (put red cross on wheel barrow), cars, have area marked as hospital. Act out emergencies, accidents.

Group Activities

- Share children's experiences.

- Read, tell stories, rhymes about the topic.

- Extend work on 'My Body and Me' to include books and discussions on circulatory system/muscles/bones.

- Use magnifying glass to enable children to look at their own skin.

- Breathe on a mirror and watch what happens.

- Let them feel their bones, and see how their muscles work.

- Have jig-saws of children dressed and undressed.

- Have models of skeletons and torsos (available from Health Education Units).

- Discuss cuts and grazes, and what has happened. Include the welfare assistance/nurse where appropriate. Talk about the blood, the scab that will form, any dressing(s) etc.

- Outdoor play.

- Invite doctor/nurse, or play therapist/specialist to talk about their jobs. (This will often allay fear of visiting hospitals/clinics).

N.B. See Play Therapist/Specialist under 'Useful Addresses'.

Introducing Loss for Older Children

- Hand out squared paper and ask children to do a 'word search' with the word LOSS (see 'Creative Activities').

  or   invite the children to share all the types of loss they can think of. Write these on the board for the children to copy.

  or   ask for individual experiences of loss, or let each child share with a partner – in turn, one talking and one listening.

Further Suggestions

- Ask the group to write a story, or poem, or draw a picture, about a real or imaginary loss, using some of the words written on the squared paper.

- Explore colours which we somehow link with feelings, for example, black day, blue mood, rosy future.

- Each child to close their eyes and imagine a symbol, or image for loss. Draw it.

- Explore ways in which music can reflect feelings associated with loss (see 'Music Therapy').

Activities — Feelings Associated with Loss

Discuss and clarify the children's understanding of the word 'feeling'. Make a list of the common feelings they have experienced, for example, happy, sad, angry, excited.

- Ask the children to shut their eyes and think about an object which is important to them, for example, a cassette player.

- Ask them to remember where they keep it and to imagine going there to look for it.

- Tell them it has gone and let them become aware of the loss.

- Ask them to open their eyes and let volunteers share how they feel about the loss. Make a list of these feelings on a flip chart.

Ask the children to imagine that it is now half an hour later and they still have not found the missing object.

ASK THE FOLLOWING QUESTIONS:

- How do they feel now?

- Have they told anyone? (If not, why not?)

- Share responses of the children.

Repeat previous questions, but ask them to imagine that the object has now been missing for a day, then a week, then six months, and finally for a year.

- Ask them to share how they feel about the loss at these different intervals.

Creative Imagination

- Ask the children to write down the word or idea they want to explore, for example, 'loss'.

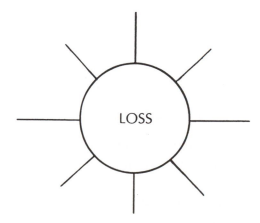

- Then reflect on the word for five minutes or so, depending on age, writing down every word, phrase or image that occurs to them.

- Then suggest they find a colour, a sound, a painting, a song/music that reminds them of loss.

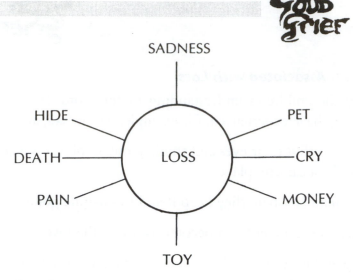

- Ask them to complete the sentence:

    'Loss is … '

Divide the class into small groups or pairs and let the children share their sentence with each other.

Some may, afterwards, want to share with the whole class, but should not be pressed to do so.

N.B. The activity could be extended by the use of poetry, art, or story writing.

Coping with Loss/Change

Activity

- Remind children of the different types of loss/change. Discuss this with them.

- Prepare or ask them to draw a 'Time Line' – (see over)

- Using the 'Time Line' invite them to write or draw in the different losses/changes they have experienced, first give examples, and then do the following activities:

    (1) Choose one of the situations and write briefly what happened in that situation.

    (2) Write briefly what helped, and what didn't help, in that situation.

    (3) Did you learn something about yourself and/or other people?

    (4) Would you have done anything differently?

    (5) How could you use this experience to help to prepare yourself and others to cope with losses/changes in the future?

- Invite children or ask for volunteers to share their answers, either in pairs/small groups, or within the large group.

- Read a poem, prose, or story, then ask the group to list the negative, and the positive aspects of loss (ending by focusing on positive aspects, for example, 'Good Grief').

N.B. Alternatively, the exercise may be done in pairs, as an interview, with the interviewer filling in the answers.

Tracey Toney
4ⁿ year

Wednesday 9ᵗʰ November

When my dog got was sent away

When I was I one my mum got a dog.
We named it Ben. One day my brother
paul took it out for a walk. When Ben
came back we found that she had cut
his foot on some glass and his foot
wouldn't stop bleeding the vet sent it to
a farm and it died. And it left a great big
gap in my life. I also had a cat named
Billy at the same time but he deid
as well and that left me very sad
because I grew to love it and care
for it and I cryed for three days
in a row.

Crawford Park Junior.

Monday 5th December 1988

Paul Sumpter Room Five Age 6

once I had a fish his name
is Sam. my mummy fed him every
Day. She called him a Little
Lamb he jamped out of the
fish tank and we were all
Sad. When I think about my
fish, I don't mind now,
because I've got another one.

---

monday 5th November 1988

Ben Beadle Room Five

I had a blankct. and took it everywhere with me. but when I went to
Portugal. I thew it in the sea but
when I was Seven I did miss my
blanket but I have still got
another one on my bed.

Tuesday 6th December 1988
when I was 3 I lost my blanket
My Mum hung it up and the
birds took it away

Monday 5th December 1988
Emma   hICKS

my sister got run
over a car came and
run her over

I was sad it was
my brothes fault
he pushed her
on the road

Emma

Emma is feeling sad about her sister.

What is Death?

What is Death?

National Curriculum

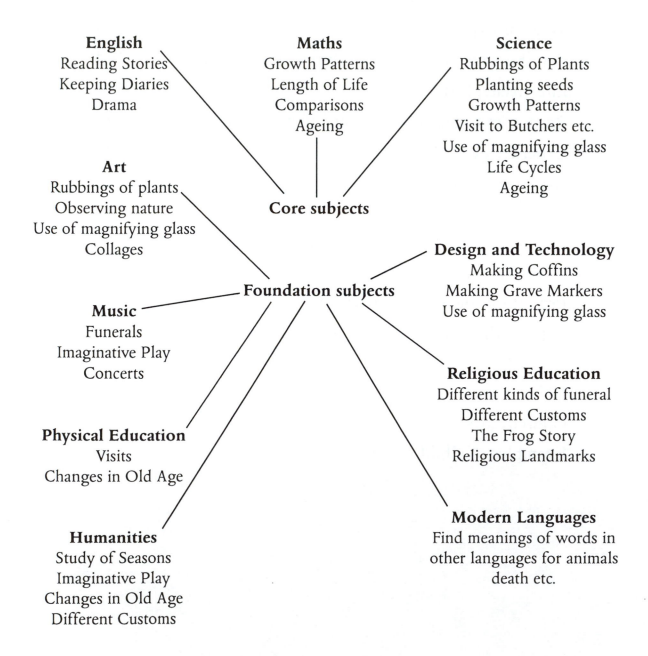

English
Reading Stories
Keeping Diaries
Drama

Maths
Growth Patterns
Length of Life
Comparisons
Ageing

Science
Rubbings of Plants
Planting seeds
Growth Patterns
Visit to Butchers etc.
Use of magnifying glass
Life Cycles
Ageing

Art
Rubbings of plants
Observing nature
Use of magnifying glass
Collages

Core subjects

Design and Technology
Making Coffins
Making Grave Markers
Use of magnifying glass

Foundation subjects

Music
Funerals
Imaginative Play
Concerts

Religious Education
Different kinds of funeral
Different Customs
The Frog Story
Religious Landmarks

Physical Education
Visits
Changes in Old Age

Modern Languages
Find meanings of words in
other languages for animals
death etc.

Humanities
Study of Seasons
Imaginative Play
Changes in Old Age
Different Customs

The lists above are only suggestions. Many more may be found in the text.

What is Death?

'To die must be an awfully big adventure.'

(Peter Pan, *J.M. Barrie*)

Objectives

- To enable children to explore what death means.

- To encourage discussion and sharing of experiences about death.

- To prepare children for death in their own families or of people close to them.

N.B. Because of the sensitive nature of this subject, trust and knowledge of the individual child's background, and emotional needs, are essential. It is also important to involve parents.

Useful Resources

Background Reading: Section 1. 'Understanding Death'.

Section 2. 'Feelings' … 'Living With Loss'.
'Creative Activities' … poems/prose.

Section 3. Information on funerals/rituals and customs.
Articles on: 'Life After Life';
'How Will Mummy Breathe And Who Will Feed Her'.

Books or materials for different activities – See 'Book List'.

Understanding Death

Small children may have learned to come to terms with a whole range of losses, for example, changing schools/friends. A child may have been aware of dead plants/animals, also could have visited a butcher's shop/a fishmonger's, and possibly could have attended a funeral. However, when death has occurred, all sorts of problems could have arisen, especially if adults have tried to avoid the subject altogether.

Many games played by children involve death, for example, 'Bang! You're dead'; Cowboys and Indians, space adventures, cops and robbers, playing hospitals, computer games. They could be influenced by television programmes, for example, seeing death in the news/in documentaries/in plays/films and cartoons. The difference between reality and fantasy may become a problem, for example, real or fictional death… There is no obvious difference between a reported murder in Northern Ireland or a fictional murder on TV.

In young children this could lead to all sorts of misunderstandings, for example, a four-year-old thought that everyone turned into a statue when they died because he'd seen Queen Victoria as a statue, in Kensington Gardens, and was told that she had been dead a long time.

Ways of Exploring Death

The subject of death needs to arise naturally out of everyday experiences, for example, if a pet or an animal in the classroom/nursery dies this gives a golden opportunity to discuss the fact of death as part of life, without dwelling on it or being morbid.

Other deaths experienced by individual children will need more careful handling, for example, loss of a grandparent/parent/sibling/friend or other relative … (see Section 1).

Activities

Four Seasons of the Year – Observation of Nature

- Watch trees, leaves developing/changing colour and falling off as they die. Follow up work to include: taking rubbings/leaf prints, noting different colours/textures, shapes and patterns of the leaves.

- Discussion of the four seasons of the year, then painting large friezes or making collages.

- Collecting and making scrap books of different plants/leaves/flowers, at different times of the year.

- Plant seeds and bulbs, watch them grow, flower/produce fruit or vegetables, and die – to see the cyclical nature of growth (seed – plant – flower – fruit – seed).

- Demonstrate by planting sunflowers/pumpkin seeds/beans, etc.

- Look at flowers that live for a short/long time, flower once/more than once in a season.

- Compare and observe individual growth patterns, for example, flowers/trees.

- Note differences in length of life of plants in pots/flowers in vases. Observe the changes in petals/leaves and stems – how long do flowers live when cut/uncut?

- The Harvest Festival service can be useful.

Life Cycle of Animals

- Study the life cycle of various animals. Observing classroom animals or children's pets.

- Observe insects and, if dead, put them under a magnifying glass or in a bug box, and note details of their appearance. Explain to children that they are dead and cannot see/hear/feel/smell/move. When the observations are finished put the insect back into the earth, in other words, where they came from, and in preparation for 'Funerals'.

- Collect frog spawn in spring and watch it grow, first into tadpoles then frogs. Observe how many survive. Take the frogs and put them in a pond where possible. Observe what happens, for example, a nursery teacher took some children to Holland Park to put a few frogs into the pond; no sooner had this happened than some ducks gobbled them up. (Although the teacher found it a difficult exercise, some useful discussion about life and death, and animals that eat each other ensued.)

- Plan a visit to a butcher's shop and a fishmonger's. Discuss animals being raised for food.

- Talk about the cooking of animals, fruit and vegetables, noting that we cook animals that are dead, but have 'live' fruit and vegetables.

- Use a magnifying glass to observe dead wood from park or garden and the many creatures/insects that shelter or find food there.

- Join the Royal Society for the Protection of Birds or the World Wild Life Fund. Adopt an animal at the zoo.

- Visit museums to see stuffed birds/animals or read about them; include extinct species, for example, dinosaurs. Discuss the length of an animal's life.

- Explore what happens when animals die – what happens to the body – the differences between insects/birds/animals and reptiles and their length of life in the wild/captivity.

- Think about death of pets/other animals. Read stories/poems, for example, 'My Gerbil' and 'In Defence of Hedgehogs' (see 'Creative Activities').

- Use children's experiences of death of their own pet or other animals deaths, for example, 'Animals Dead By the Side of the Road' or 'The Duck Who Drowned the Babies' (see under 'Experiences in a Junior School' following).

- If a pet dies in school, talk about why it died, how it no longer breathes, feels, eats, moves, for example, 'The Frog Story' (see under 'Experiences in a Nursery School' following).

- Discuss different kinds of funerals/cremations, and customs of different countries/groups. Arrange with the children for a funeral/burial for the 'pet', in a special place. Mark it with a suitable memorial. Let the children say 'goodbye' to the pet, either orally or with letters/drawings. Allow tears.

Responses to Death of an Animal at School

Experiences in a Nursery School

'THE FROG STORY'

One morning a teacher discovers that one of the two frogs she has recently acquired is dead. Before discarding the dead frog she leaves it in a bowl next to the enclosed, live one. She knows the children will miss the frog and will ask to see it. Johnny, aged three and a half, comes up to the frog and asks the teacher.

Johnny — Why is the frog here?

Teacher — The frog is dead.

Johnny — Who deaded him?

Teacher — Nobody did anything to him. He died by himself.

Johnny — Why did he die?

Teacher — He jumped out of the mud pan and we couldn't find him, so he had no mud or water, and he dried up and died.

Johnny — Is the frog dead?

Teacher — Yes.

Johnny — Put him in water.

Teacher — OK.

Johnny — Will he bite?

Teacher — No.

Johnny — Why is the frog dead?

Teacher — He dried up and died.

Johnny — Can I put him on the table? Isn't the frog dead?

Teacher — Yes.

Johnny — Can he turn over?

Teacher — The frog is dead so he can't do anything.

Johnny — Give him some food.

Teacher — No, the frog can't eat – he's dead.

Johnny — Why is he dead?

Teacher — He had no water or mud so he dried up.

Johnny — I'll turn him over.

As he does so, Johnny seems to realize that the frog is unable to move (certainly different from the jumpy live one he had finally made himself touch). But he pokes the dead frog and seems to be watching for a reaction.

He asks again, 'Is the frog dead?'

146

Further Experiences in a Nursery School

Death of Two Pets

- A four-year-old girl's gerbil and budgerigar both died. Her mother put the gerbil down the toilet and the bird in the dustbin.

- The little girl repeated the fact over and over again, to her class teacher and to whoever visited her class. When asked if she was sad when they died, she said, 'No, I never cried or nothing'.

- When asked if she missed them, she said, 'Yes'.

(It was obvious that events were causing her anxiety and she was having difficulty in coming to terms with them).

Death of a Mole

- A child found a dead mole that had probably had a heart attack. She kept it in the fridge at home before bringing it to school.

- She talked about how she found the mole, and it was put on display for a day or two, wrapped in cotton wool. One three-year-old boy kept going back to the mole. He held it close, stroked it and then returned to his table.

Group Activities

- Reading books, fact and/or fiction about moles.

- Observing the mole, for example, its soft fur, and hands useful for digging.

- Having a funeral. The lid was put on the box and a place chosen for the funeral/burial under a tree. Some earth was dug up, the box was put in the hole, the children said goodbye.

- A picture of the mole, drawn by one of them, was put on a stick to mark the grave.

- Several children visited it often.

N.B. About two months later, after the picture had fallen off, two children were heard talking by the grave, they said, 'Do you think it's got out yet'. 'Yes it must have. It's been a long time and it's good at digging'. They had not forgotten the mole or realized the permanence of death.

Experiences in a Junior School

(1) Animals Dead by the Side of the Road

Talking with the children after a journey by coach to 'Birdworld' led to several comments about the number of dead animals — birds, squirrels, hedgehogs, a cat, a fox, which they saw by the road.

The children were distressed and blamed people, for their fast cars, for pushing their way through land which had previously belonged to the animals, and for their apparent under-valuing of life.

This needed to be talked through, and anger helped by:

- looking at food chains, and the way in which the animal body becomes food for another animal, with very little waste.

- finding out what people had done to assist animals in motorway or fast road areas, for example, cattle grids, badger-runs under roads.

- a light hearted look at the poem by Pam Ayres, 'In Defence of Hedgehogs'.

(2) The Duck Who Drowned Her Babies

During a school outing to Bournemouth one May, the children were walking along the beach, back to our hotel. It was a very windy afternoon and the sea was running extremely high.

A young female mallard duck suddenly appeared from the scrub at the base of the cliff, closely followed by eight, newly hatched ducklings. She led them across the beach and launched herself on to the high waves. Two ducklings followed and were immediately rolled over by the waves, and drowned. The children were very distressed. Four more of the ducklings were drowned following their mother. The agitation of the children disturbed the mother duck and she flew away, leaving us with two survivors.

At this point the beach warden appeared and explained that this particular duck had nested in the cliff and had led her ducklings to the nearest sea as soon as they were hatched.

With some insensitivity he told the children, who by now were extremely distressed, that the two surviving ducklings would be abandoned by the mother who would 'smell' the intervention of humans. Showing a confidence I did not feel, I told the children to rub the ducklings with dock leaves, which were growing nearby, and then to replace them in the nest (the warden had pointed this out to us).

We surrounded the ducklings with food/sandwiches etc, from our packed lunches, as I hoped that the starving mother duck would be attracted by this food.

I praised the children for saving two ducklings when the mother would certainly have drowned them all.

Follow Up Activities — Back at the Hotel

- As we had no books to refer to, we had to discuss and share what we knew about the hatching of eggs and behaviour of mother and baby ducks.

- We drew comparisons between the instinctive risks taken by animals and those taken by humans, for example, risking their lives by drug abuse, smoking etc.

○ Finally several of the children wrote about the incident in their diaries.

I was left wondering if I could have dealt with the incident in a more satisfactory way.

Life Cycle of a Human Being

Allow discussion to follow from children's experiences of death, for example, of a grandparent/other relative/famous person, or experiences of a tragedy, for example, an earthquake.

- ○ Read stories/poems about people at different stages of life, from the birth of a baby to a death (see 'Creative Activities' and 'Book List').

- ○ Invite people in to school of different ages, for example, mothers to be, to talk about their lives.

- ○ Draw pictures/make collages of different age groups that the children know.

- ○ Look at family occasions, for example, birth, confirmation, engagement, marriage, retirement, death.

- ○ Ask the children to discuss extended family patterns in this and other countries.

- ○ Perhaps arrange to sing carols at a Senior Citizen's Home and/or invite them to a Carol Service or entertainment at school.

- ○ Discuss why people die, for example, illness, age, accident, suicide.

- ○ Talk about what happens to the body … it stops working, no feelings/senses (see article on 'Dying Children and Their Families' in Section 1).

- ○ What happens when people die – Where do they go?

N.B. Children are often fascinated by this topic (see articles, 'How Will Mummy Breathe and Who Will Feed Her', 'Book List' and 'Heavenly Bodies' all in Section 3).

Imaginative Play

- ○ Allow children to act out any situation in the Home Corner.

- ○ Many forms of dramatic play can be used to extend the above activities, for example, Cowboys and Indians, hospitals, accidents.

- ○ Also use role play of people at differing ages and stages.

Example of a Primary School Project on Ageing/The Life Cycle

This project was used to introduce the whole school to the concepts of age and ageing. Suggestions were made as to the topics to be covered, for example, plants, animals, buildings, history. Each year group was asked to choose from the following list:

Topics	Suggestions/examples
Farm visit	young animals.
Links with	the elderly.
Animals in school	tadpoles, fish, butterflies, young from the pet shop.
Ageing	in paper, food, rubber, other objects.
Plants	growth of alph-alpha, bean sprouts, cress, beans.
Buildings	churches, graveyards.
Life cycles	leaves, coming of spring.
People/	collection of family pictures to show:
(a) families	different ages.
(b) elderly	talk to older people about life when they were young.
(c) growing-up	think about and discuss life as a baby – hopes for the future.
History	sense of being different in the past, cave dwellers onwards. Visit the London Museum.
Animals	how young animals' behaviour can relate to people.
Collections	antiques.
Poems	give children positive attitudes to old age/cycle of life – from birth to death.
Families	family tree, birthdays; different stages of growth: babies, children, teenagers, young adults, parents, grandparents.
Changes in old age	diet, exercise, fashion, interests, retirement, need care in own home, living with relations, sheltered homes, and homes for the elderly.
Learning from	historical events, royal family, wars, Grandparents, hobbies, games, school life.
Religious landmarks	registration of birth, Christening, in the Life Cycle, coming of age, marriage and burial.
Multi-cultural	choose a stage to compare, for example, Society confirmation, barmitzvah, weddings.
Visits	to clubs, old people's houses, sheltered housing projects; of grandparents to school to talk/discuss/share skills.
Concert	for invited audience, possibly for grandparents; or given at old people's home/club.

N.B. (See examples of work from project following)

Project on the Subject of Death

A few years ago, as a result of my class's interest in the death of two famous people in the news, we quite naturally started a project on death.

The class was a mixed group of Infants and Juniors, ranging in age from six to eight years. The children showed a natural interest in death, though the parents weren't quite so sure (see 'Background to Pack' in Section 1). It was the start of the Autumn Term and so we had already started talking about autumn, as the time of dying leaves and so on. It was the time when Douglas Bader and Princess Grace had both died within a few weeks of each other, and newspaper cuttings were used to talk about their deaths.

Discussion covered what their lives had been like, and how their families must feel about the loss. Within a week a child's grandfather had also died and another child's cat was killed on the road.

During this period I visited Highgate Cemetery one weekend, and went back to school full of things I had seen. As a result of interest from the children we discussed, as a group, the idea of visiting the cemetery.

The day of the trip was a wet October day. We set off with paper to draw on, pads for writing, thin paper and crayons for rubbings, and our packed lunches. The day, in spite of the weather, was a huge success. The cemetery was overgrown and misty and as a number of parents came also, the class was split into groups of three to four children.

Graves had the most wonderful assortment of figures on top: angels, cherubs, animals etc. The children noticed, in particular, that many of the children's graves had cherubs on them. The tombstones had lichen growing on them and plants, especially ivy, growing around the stones.

Many items were taken back to school: the drawings of headstones, writings, poems, rubbings, and collections of plant life. Some of the children were fascinated by the angels atop the graves; these were 'writing' in little books.

Remembrance Day occurred during this period and, as Highgate had a lot of World War I graves, this prompted much interest. Especially as Douglas Bader had been a pilot during another war. Hallowe'en had also occurred, and much imaginative work was done around this festival.

The project culminated at an assembly involving the whole school and I can truthfully say that it was the most successful project that I have ever shared with a class. The children were totally motivated throughout, and were able to talk about many things for the first time. They could ask questions about a subject that is often taboo. They shared other cultures' perceptions of death, as there were Hindus, Sikhs, Muslims and Chinese in the class, as well as Christians.

Although, to some, it may seem morbid, I felt that it helped the children to come to terms with their own fears and grief; also they were able to talk more easily about their own experiences. I still meet children, many years later, who refer to the 'Death Project'.

Group Activities Included in the Project

HIGHGATE CEMETERY

- Copying epitaphs, noting the numbers of children in a family who died very young.

- Taking rubbings of epitaphs.

- Sorting graves into groups from same occupation or same country, for example, sailors, scientists, musicians, Poles. (A Polish grave was easily identified as it had a painting or photograph of the dead person beneath.)

FOLLOW UP ACTIVITIES AT SCHOOL

- Writing about the angels, seen on the gravestones, for example, what were they reading/writing, in their books, to the person in the grave?

- Paintings of the graves.

- Dressing-Up ... A little girl, with long red hair, was dressed up and posed as an angel for others to draw.

- Talking about how we feel when we lose something.

- How we feel inside when we are sad.

- How we show our grief.

- A series of paintings and drawings of animals who had died.

- Discussion of memories about animals and/or people the children had lost ... This developed quite naturally into children designing and writing epitaphs of what they wanted to be remembered for.

- Discussion about fear and what had frightened us.

- A set of skulls and a human skeleton was set up and this prompted much creative work.

- A short visit was made to a scrapyard close by (the last resting place for cars). Parts were collected, drawn and photographed.

ADDITIONS

- Design/paint/draw tombstones.

- Create an inscription for a gravestone, for example, 'Here lies the body of Stephen John, he was short but his tongue was long'.

Further Suggestions for Activities

○ Study the Church's Year, appreciating different colours for the different seasons, for example,

Christmas – new sun – birth of Jesus – white;

Easter – new life – planting, resurrection – red;

Harvest – thanksgiving, gathering in – yellow.

Explore the Theme of Death and Resurrection in History and Folklore

Different Groups Could Explore:

(1) Ancient Egyptian ritual – (Osiris Isis).

(2) Aztecs.

(3) Druid worship.

(4) Story of King Arthur.

(5) Symbolism of objects, for example, egg or rabbit (Egyptians have this).

(6) Christian meaning of Easter.

(7) Morris dancing and symbolism.

(8) Death and Resurrection in the Psalms of David.

(9) Customs and Rituals of other faiths, for example, Reincarnation of the Dali Lama.

(10) Tribal understanding of death and spirits.

(11) Epitaphs on gravestones – (see following 'Death Project', and 'Tributes to the Deceased' in 'How Can We Help' in Section 2).

(12) Arrange visits to churches. (See Figure at end of this Section 'Churchyards'.)

(13) Study the Hindu, Sikh, Buddhist, Islamic and Jewish religions with particular regard to Festivals. Look out for symbolism and similarities, for example, Festivals of life which symbolize birth/death, good/evil, darkness/light etc.

Hallowe'en Project

Hallowe'en could be a suitable time to think about death, its meaning, and children's related fears and feelings.

(1) Evolvement of Hallowe'en, for example, ancient ritual.

(2) Christianization, for example, All Saint's Day, All Soul's Day, St. George and the Dragon, (life of English Saint).

(3) Symbols of death and ghosts, for example, masks and lanterns can be made. Witches can be included.

(4) Hallowe'en today. This project could culminate with a Hallowe'en Party, including guests of different age groups.

N.B. These can emphasize celebration and thanksgiving, and the importance of remembering loved ones.

Churchyard showing suggestions for creative work

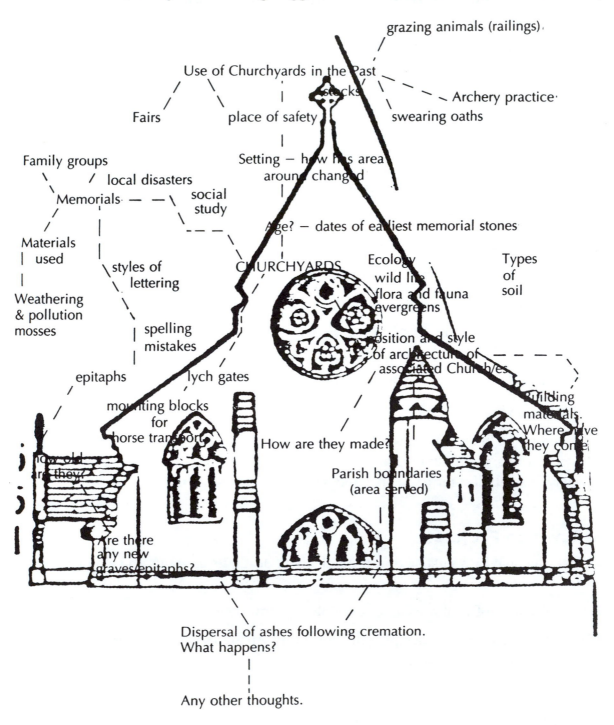

Use of Churchyards in the Past

grazing animals (railings)

stocks

Archery practice

Fairs   place of safety   swearing oaths

Family groups

local disasters

Memorials — — social study

Setting — how has area around changed

Age? — dates of earliest memorial stones

Materials used

styles of lettering

CHURCHYARDS

Ecology wild life flora and fauna evergreens

Types of soil

Weathering & pollution mosses

spelling mistakes

Position and style of architecture of associated Church/es

Building materials. Where have they come

epitaphs   lych gates

mounting blocks for horse transport

How are they made?

how old are they?

Parish boundaries (area served)

Are there any new graves/epitaphs?

Dispersal of ashes following cremation. What happens?

Any other thoughts.

154

Wednesday 9th November

The Fall of Freddie the Leaf

T.V.

On the tele the man or presenter was talking about a life of a leaf. It started wot with Summer when the leaves where strong and healthy. And Freddie the leaf had some friends called Daneiel. Well the story went on to Autumn. Freddie asked Daneiel why it was going colder Daneiel said " that " a different season was coming". After a coupel of days, Freddie saw some leaves falling from some neighboring trees. Well, when the programm finishing Danielle and Freddie fell from the tree too. The programm finished and I think the programm was all about life

The End.

Amrik Dhillion
4V
Cranford Park.

Life and Death

My dad got two budgies, and me and my sister chose one each. I had the blue budgie and my sister had the green one. My budgie was a good budgie. It never ever bit my fingers and it used to sit on my hand and let me stroke it. My sister's was a naughty one. It always bit my sister and never sat on anyones finger. I used to call it a chicken and my sister didn't like it. Then one day when I came home my sister was crying her eyes out. I asked her why and she said my budgies ran away. I was shocked. I looked at the empty cage and there was my budgie all alone pecking at the mirror. A tear rolled down my cheak. I started crying aswell I knew on the outside I didn't like him but deep inside I loved him very much. I still remember him because when ever I put the music on he used to cheep along.

gurvinder Sandhu

Life and Death.

Life.

Life is a new born baby.

Life is an ancient form of atmosphere.

Life is a gathering of human bodys.

Life is a time trap pulling the clouds round and round.

Death.

Death is the begining of a new life.

Death is the peace of sleep.

Death is a place to begin again.

And

Angela Cook.

Death

Life

Life and death.

LIFE Life! LIFE!

Life is a living person.

Life is loving and sharing.

Life is working for a living.

Life is having children and caring for others.

Life is something to hope for.

DEATH Death! DEATH!

Death is an end to a happy life

Death is a sadness of a disappearance.

Death is a place for rest.

Death is a flame of a vanishing soul.

Death is letting our spirits go free.

Sandeep Sahota

Life and Death.

Life is a never ending story.
That goes in circles.
Death means to let someone
to take your place.
Because your heart has stopped
beating.
Your spirit is left in the people woh
loved you.
All that is left of you is your bones,
in the grave.
Your spirit has just gone to heaven.
Where you start a new paradise
in heaven.
Where you are free!

Davinder

LiFE AND Death

One morning my mum was crying. Me and Emma asked mum whats up she said I don't feel very well I said no other wise dad would be hear I went down stairs and said to Emma. I recken that some-thing has happened to dad About 12.30 mum told us she said Daddy is in heaven Its a good place and its much better up there the angels are looking after him A tear began to roll down my cheeks and I was trying to hold my cry My dad is still in my heart and I feel missed Shocked and lonley.

Melanie Stone

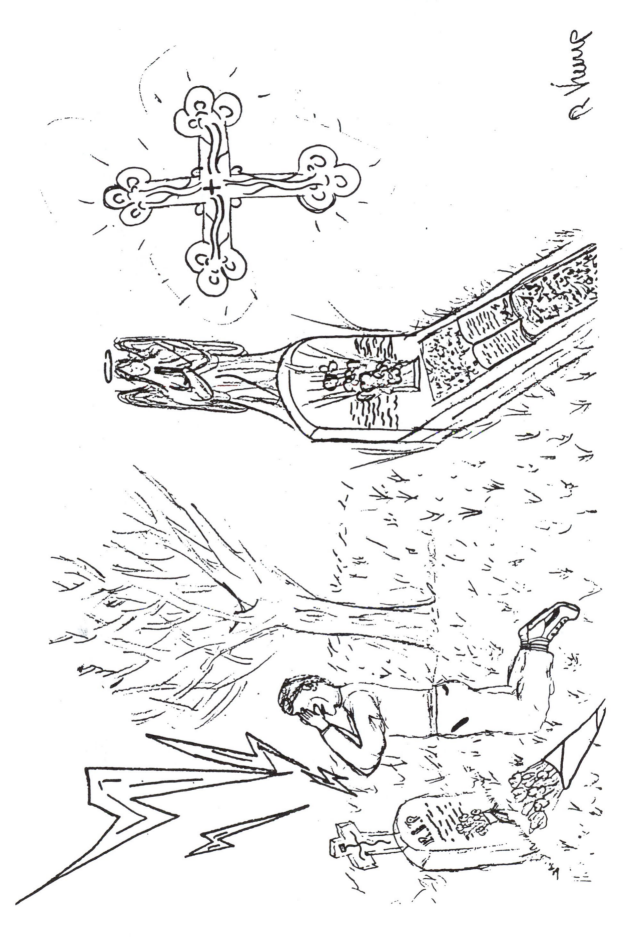

Sheenal Patel

Sheenal's mummy is cuddling her because her rabbit died.

162

2.5

How Can We Help?

How Can We Help?

National Curriculum

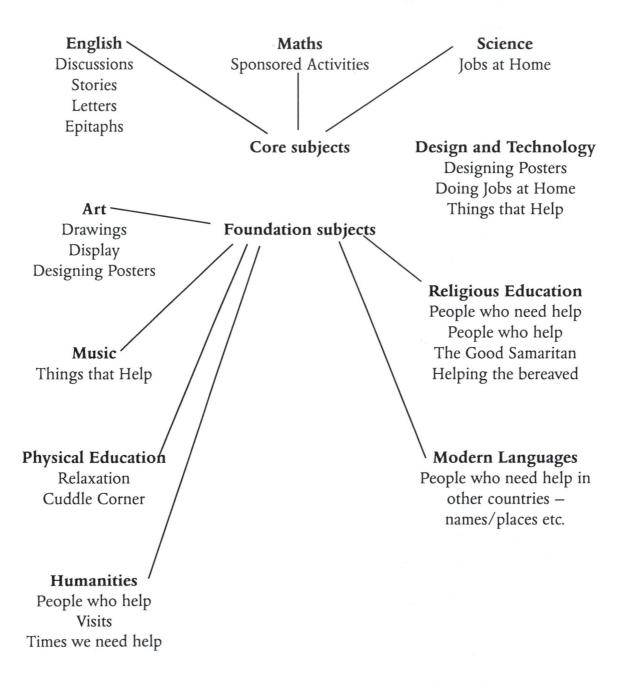

English
Discussions
Stories
Letters
Epitaphs

Maths
Sponsored Activities

Science
Jobs at Home

Core subjects

Design and Technology
Designing Posters
Doing Jobs at Home
Things that Help

Art
Drawings
Display
Designing Posters

Foundation subjects

Religious Education
People who need help
People who help
The Good Samaritan
Helping the bereaved

Music
Things that Help

Physical Education
Relaxation
Cuddle Corner

Modern Languages
People who need help in
other countries –
names/places etc.

Humanities
People who help
Visits
Times we need help

The lists above are only suggestions. Many more may be found in the text.

How Can We Help?

' A child can live through anything so long as he or she is told the truth and is allowed to share with loved ones the natural feelings people have when they are suffering.'
(The Compassionate Friends – Newsletter, Autumn 1987, Eda Le Shan)

Objectives

- To help children to develop sensitivity to others at times of loss and bereavement.

- To encourage children to explore their attitudes and experiences.

- To explore the resources and help available to themselves and others at times of loss and death.

Useful Resources

Background Reading– In Section 1

     – In Section 2– 'Feelings.' 'Living With Loss.'
           'What Is Death?'

     – In Section 3– Useful Articles and Addresses
           (see 'Book List' and 'Additional Resources')

Materials and books for different activities.

Directed Group Activities

These activities can be in pairs/small groups or for the whole class, depending on the age and ability of the children. Stories and/or poems can be read first to help discussion.

Introductory Activities

'We All Need Help'

Generate discussion about helping by asking children questions about their everyday experiences and/or their observations of animals and people. For example, use stories/poems to illustrate the following:

- How do animals show when they need help?

- How do babies show when they need help?

- How do we show when we need help?

- Read story of Grace Darling.

- Draw and write about the sounds and signals that can be made when we need help, for example, crying, screaming.

N.B. Include body language (see 'Creative Listening' in this Section).

FOR OLDER CHILDREN

- Use 'Word Search' or 'Creative Writing' (see 'Living With Loss' or 'Creative Activities').

People Who Need Help

Discuss who needs help, at home and at school:

AT HOME

- Parents/siblings/relatives and friends.

- Suggest children bring in photographs of those at home to show to others.

AT SCHOOL

- Friends/teachers/caretaker/secretary/welfare assistant/lollipop person/school meals assistants.

- Have photographs in the entrance hall, with their names and jobs underneath.

- Ask how new arrivals at school can be helped.

People Who Need Special Help

- Remind the children of some of the activities of the previous section and ask them who needs special help, for example, babies, the sick, the injured (in mind or body), people with 'Special Needs', senior citizens, poor, lonely, bereaved, shy.

- Invite older people to come to special assemblies or occasions, and/or to talk about their lives.

- Read stories/poems to illustrate, for example, Mother Teresa, Dr Barnado.

People Who Help in the Community

For example: – doctors/nurses/police/clergy/firemen.

- Invite a different person each week from the community, to visit school and to show the way in which they help people (see 'Use of a Visitor' exercise in Section 1).

- Visit the Library, include a talk on its uses.

- Visit from Health Visitor, with demonstration of baby care, for example, bathing.

FURTHER ACTIVITIES

- Do writings and/or drawings of people who help in the school or the community.

Societies Which Help

- Ask the children about different organizations that help, for example: Children in Need, Help the Aged, NSPCC, RSPCA, Oxfam, Save the Children Fund, CAB, Red Cross, NAWCH (see 'Useful Addresses' in Section 3)

- Invite visits from representatives.

- Display and/or design posters for the societies.

- Read examples from different religions, for example, 'The Good Samaritan'.

How We Can Help Others

Ask the children to share their experience. Some suggestions may be:

- Doing jobs at home.

- Running errands for relatives/older people/people in school/people with disabilities.

- Helping to feed or bath babies.

- Sponsored activities or collections for charities.

- Bringing gifts to schools for Festivals, for example, Harvest.

- Listening to others (see 'Creative Listening').

Writing a Letter to Someone Special who is Absent

Ask the children to suggest the reason(s) why they might write a letter.

- Pick out and emphasize reasons, for example, to keep in touch, to show that they care for someone, to share and remember things which have happened in the past. There will be many others.

- Ask them to write the name of someone or something on a piece of paper, for example, a pet, whom they love very much, and whom they don't see any more.

- Make this name special: by writing it all over the paper; by decorating it; by repeating it over and over again. This helps to emphasize the importance of this name.

N.B. It may be necessary here to point out that love is not taken away by death – tell the story of Queen Victoria; all the ways she showed her love for Albert after his death.

- Ask the children to close their eyes and remember what it felt like to be with that person/pet. Remember for example: going on an outing with them; being at home with them; being held close by them.

- Ask them to write down a funny story about that person, which makes them smile, for example, Grandad sticking the watering can with sellotape, and Grandma cheating at 'I Spy'.

- Write down a sad story about that person, for example, Grandma telling Grandpa off because he went down the garden in his slippers.

- Ask the children to write down the special places where they miss their 'person' the most, for example, in the greenhouse, the kitchen.

- Allow the children to share any of the things they have written down, if they wish.

- Suggest that they write these stories into a letter which says, 'I still love you ... I remember the good and the bad things which we shared ... You are still alive and with me, inside me'.

Encourage them to be positive to their absent friend; to emphasize what they have gained, as well as lost; to share joy as well as sadness, and to see how their lives have been enriched and rebuilt.

Additional Activities

Life Summary

Invite the children to:

- Write a short epitaph for themselves to go on their own gravestone.

- Write their own eulogy to include the following: ... Strong points of their personality ... Aspects of their personality that could develop or improve with time ... Deeds that they could have or would like to have done ... Things they would have done differently and why ... How they could have made their lives more positive ... Things they will be remembered for ... Things they would like to be remembered for ... Any other points they would like to include.

- Who are they closest to?

- Divide a picture of a shield into sections; in these illustrate any of the above values or qualities they regard as important to them.

N.B. This 'Activity' could be useful when children are changing school.

Your Own Personal Coat of Arms

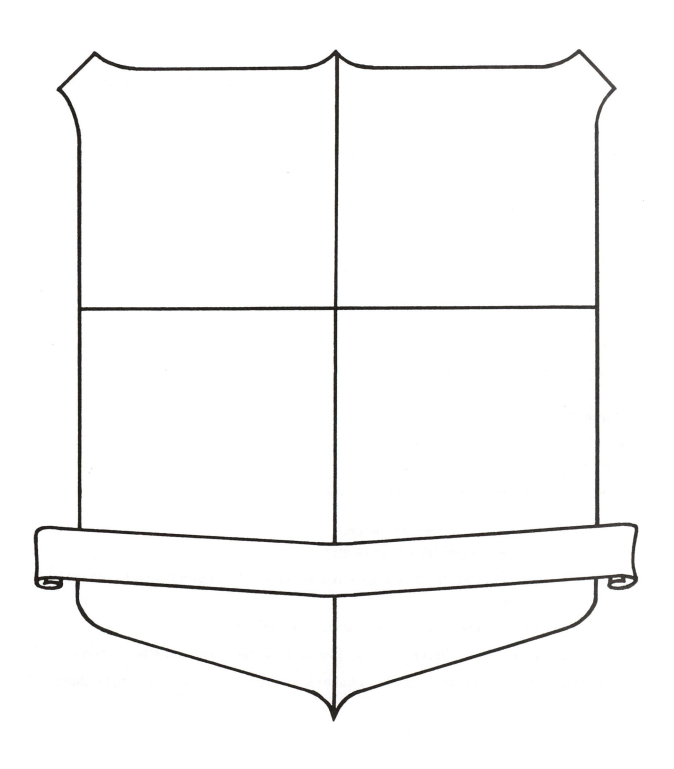

Times We Need Help

Discuss with children the differences between needs and wants**. Ask the children to share their experiences of:

- 'happy times'; for example, birthdays, holidays, celebrations, enjoyment of nature, success, being forgiven.

- 'unhappy times'; for example, loss, failure, guilt, accidents, sadness, death, being lost, regrets.

ADDITIONS

- Read stories/poems about people who need help.

**N.B. 'Needs' are essential to healthy life, for example, love, warmth, food and shelter, while 'wants' are nonessential, for example, unnecessary possessions.

Who Would Help Me?

Ask the children who would help them at home and/or school if:

- they felt ill
- they lost something
- a bigger child bullied them
- they fell over
- they were lost
- they were sad
- a relative/friend or pet died.

Things That Help

Ask the children to think about their experiences, and explore these with them, (illustrate with your own or other children's experiences first):

- In school
  - Do you hang up your coat?
  - Are you polite?
  - Do you care for others?
  - Do you take notes home?

- Have you had a pet that was sick? What did you do? Did you take it to the vet? What was done?

- Were you ever lost? How old were you? Who helped?

- Have you ever been hurt or in an accident? What happened and who helped?

- Have you ever had to go into hospital or know someone who has? What happened?

- How do people show they are in pain? (Explore if children think it is OK to cry. Also explain that people can laugh to hide pain and that laughter as well as tears can release tension.)
- How do people you know cope with painful feelings?
- How do you cope with painful feelings?
- What would you like to happen?

N.B. Some schools have 'Cuddle Corners' where children can go when they are unhappy. It can include soft toys, a rug to cover themselves with, and story books.

Responses to the Bereaved

The statements below represent the varied responses of people to the bereaved. Depending on the age of the children make a list of helpful/non-helpful responses to people who are sad for example, if a friend were bereaved I would:

- accept their behaviour no matter how odd
- ignore their loss, pretend it never happened
- tell them about my own woes
- let them cry and talk as much as they want to
- tell them they are luckier than some
- visit their home
- give them plenty of sympathy
- leave them well alone
- take my cue from them and be myself
- help them with practical problems
- tell them about everyone else's misfortunes
- encourage them to talk about their loss
- take some burden of everyday chores away
- tell them they'll get over it eventually
- provide food and encourage sleep
- talk about the weather
- try to make them laugh
- stick around when I'm needed
- tell them it could have been worse
- leave them out of my social circle
- tell them not to worry or think about it

- encourage them to go to the doctor for tablets.

FOLLOW UP ACTIVITIES

The above activities can be extended by any or all of the suggestions in sections: 'Listening Skills'; 'Self Esteem'; 'Relaxation'; and in 'Creative Activities', for example, write plays to act out/mime.

Further Activities for Older Children

Depending on the age of the children, invite them to discuss:

○ What happens when someone dies? (See following – 'A Letter to Someone Special Who Is Absent'.)

○ Talk about tributes, epitaphs and memorial services; give examples.

○ Let the children write and illustrate some humorous epitaphs.

○ Ask the children to share some of the things they would like to be remembered for.

Loss of a Pet

Christopher, a nine-year-old boy came to school in tears. The previous evening his rabbit had escaped. It was found the next morning in his garden, dead, having been savaged by a dog. Christopher blamed himself for the rabbit's escape.

ACTION SPECIFICALLY FOR CHRISTOPHER... AT SCHOOL

The teacher asked him for details about the rabbit – he was pleased to talk – soon the memories of the mutilated rabbit were replaced with memories of how it had been when alive.

ACTION AT HOME...

A funeral was held for the rabbit, with Christopher and his parents; they allowed him to bury the body with a ceremony, and some solemnity.

NEXT DAY FURTHER ACTION AT SCHOOL

Christopher brought photographs to school, as requested. These were displayed for all to see. He talked about them, frequently looked at them, and shared new, remembered stories.

In the library he found a book with an origami rabbit; he worked out how to make one. A whole line of origami rabbits, called Charcoal, appeared on the wall.

His parents decided that there should be no more rabbits. Another boy in the class asked for the hutch and Christopher cleaned it out for him. He was invited to 'share' the new rabbit.

Christopher's guilt at letting the rabbit escape was eased by an investigation into the behaviour of wild rabbits, and the realization that the rabbit was following normal instincts. Each aspect of his loss was dealt with by positive input – good memories replaced the horror of the mutilated body. The burial was permission to 'let go'. The paper, origami rabbits, learned with difficulty, replaced a hundred times, Charcoal. Children in the class instinctively offered great support.

Coping with Loss

My Time Line

Age
0 Years

for example 4–5 years,
started school

now

Dear Grandad,

 I used to run up to you and sit on your lap. I used to touch your face and feel your bristly chin and smooth cheeks. I remember the time when we went to the fair. Remember the twister? It was going so fast and the big wheel went so high.

I miss all the Museums, parks and fairs we went to. You took me to a circus to see all the clowns; remember?

I wish you could come back

With Love from

Deepak

To My gerbils

Wednesday 8th
June

Dear Gerbils

Do you remember the time I let you two out and you ran all around the lounge and My brother and I tried to get you? We got you two in the end by cornering you and picking you up. When I picked you up you felt soft and gentle.

The nicest thing about you was that you never bit us when we picked you up because you liked us alot as We gave you food.

The thing I miss about you is when you went in the wheel; you went very fast and you got tired out very quickly. I am sorry you died but I think you died in your sleep.

Love
from
Ben

9th June '88'

Dear   Mum

My favourite shared memory of you is smelling your purfume, it spelt lovely, your lap was slippery because of your sari. Do you remember when you used to say I was pretty? I miss you especially when you used to pick me up from nursery and then buy me Tooty Fruity sweets. I liked the pink sweets because they were nice and I liked the colour.

Do you remember that time I tried on a sari and I looked quite good in it but it kept slipping off? I am now adopted, I am very happy but I still miss you.

One day I will join you in heaven I hope you can wait that long.

With Love from
xxxxxxxxx ++ Karen xx xxxxx

178

<u>8/6/88</u>

<u>Dear Lady</u>

If you were dead this is what I would remember you by. I remember when you jumped up on me when I was crying. My mum had told me off because I had hit my Sister when she was being a nuisance. You came to comfort me because no one else liked me.

(We noticed) that when my mum knitted you always played with the wool so I made a silver ball for you.

You used to sit at one end of the room and I sat at the other. I used to pull it and you used to pounce on it. Did you think it was a mouse?

I miss you because I have no one to talk to and cuddle.

I miss you because I have no one to stick up for me I will still love you and I wish you were still here.

Lots of Love
Natalie xxx

This is what we need.

exercise.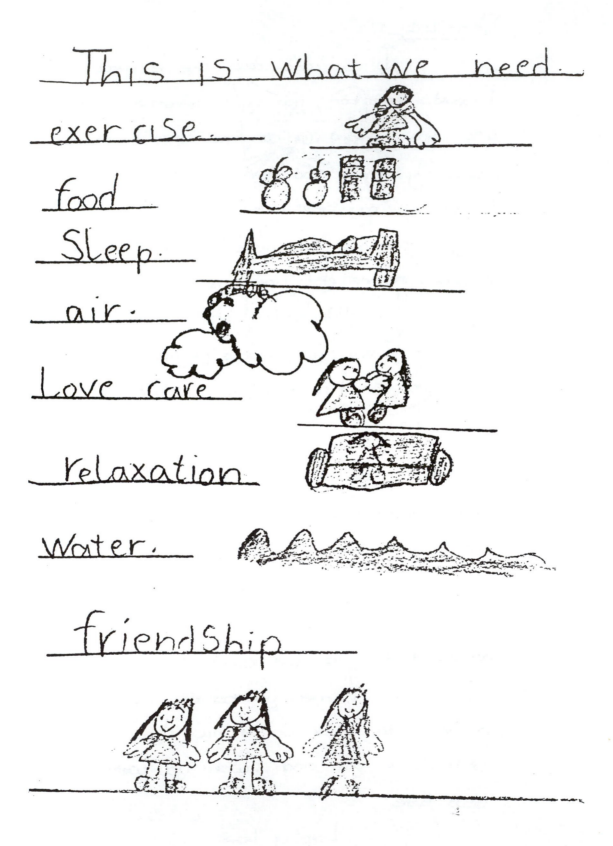

food

Sleep.

air.

Love care

relaxation

water.

friendship

This is what is in side you

Nicole

I remember when I felt sad
I felt very sad when my
Dad did not tell me
he was going to die

Creative Listening

'If we were supposed to talk more than listen, we would have been given two mouths and one ear.' (Mark Twain)

Objectives

- to introduce children to the idea that there is an 'art' to listening.

- to help children understand that we communicate with our tone of voice, facial expression and body language, as well as speech.

- to experience a variety of different responses, as a speaker, and as a listener.

Useful Resources

- Keys to Good Listening.

- Rhymes, stories and songs, for example, 'Simple Simon'.

- List of topics to talk about, for example, My favourite food or TV programme. (Avoid topics that could evoke strong emotion.)

- Ungame see Additional Resources.

Directed Group Activities

These activities can be in pairs/small groups or for the whole class.

- Generate discussion by asking children to share their experiences of being listened to.

- Use a cassette recorder to record the children saying something simple, like their name and age. Replay the tape so that they can hear their own voice.

- Let children record simple nursery rhymes/poems/stories.

- Encourage children to make up stories/poems/playlets, and record, then play back.

- Play 'Simon Says' … where various commands are made by the leader, but the children must not follow them unless they are preceded by the instruction 'Simon says'.

- Drawing a Picture … Children sit in pairs back to back, one describes a picture, for example, a triangle, and the other has to draw it from the description.

Group Discussion for Older Children

- Ask the children to think of a time they felt really listened to, and to share with you what was good about it.

183

- Repeat as above, but ask them to think of a time that they didn't feel listened to; share with you the reasons they think this happened.

- Repeat as above, but ask them to think of a time that they didn't feel listened to; share with you the reasons they think this happened.

- Ask the children to come up with a definition of listening … a child once described listening as 'wanting to hear'.

N.B. A recent programme on Radio 4 with eleven-year-olds sharing their views on different subjects, highlighted their difficulties in getting heard by adults.

Listening Activities

Tone of Voice

- Play a recording of different tones of voice expressing different feelings, for example, sadness, anger, happiness.

- Listen to a recorded story or a BBC radio programme, for example, 'Sad Feelings'. Stop the story at intervals and ask children to identify the feelings.

- Read a story/poem using different tones of voice.

- Ask children to express different tones of voice.

Body Language

- 'Circle Squeeze' or 'Telegraph' … Clasping hands in a circle send a message of squeezes around, for example, two long ones and one short one.

- This can also be played with nudges and winks.

- Ask children to assume body postures/facial expressions for different feelings, for example, furrowed brow, clenched fists/teeth (see 'Feeling' Section).

Facial Expressions

- Using a mirror ask the children to smile, then to look sad. Ask what it is that makes them look different.

- Working in pairs, let the children take turns in showing different feelings with facial expressions, which the other one has to guess.

Additional Activities

Exercise – Ask children to sit back to back: A to talk, B to listen, then to change places.

Debrief – How easy is it to listen to someone you can't see?

Exercise –	Ask children to sit facing each other, and both talk at once ... (too often we are waiting for a turn to 'put our spoke in').
Debrief –	If we didn't get 'listened to' by others, it is very hard to listen to them.
Exercise –	Ask one child to speak and the other to listen without speaking ... (non-verbal communication).
Debrief –	We can listen without speaking; silence can be valuable, especially if we have strong feelings.
Exercise –	Ask the children to have an ordinary conversation on a subject of their choice.
Debrief –	Conversation is fine most of the time but if we are upset or worried we need more listening to than usual.
Exercise –	Ask the children to share something that is on their mind.
Debrief –	Ask the children what they have learned from doing these exercises, draw up a list of helpful tips to help listen to someone who is sad/lonely/frightened or worried.

Follow Up Activities

- Ask children when they feel that it's most important to listen to people, for example, when hurt, lonely, if unhappy, worried or have a problem.

- Ask children what else happens at times like that, for example, hugs, treats, allowing tears, not having to pretend to be brave, just being there without talking.

N.B. Counselling/listening is about being with people in their pain, not providing answers.

Keys to Good Listening

Notes for Teachers – Guidance

WARMTH AND CARING
- being concerned, accepting, friendly.

EMPATHY
- trying to understand how it feels to be in someone else's shoes and showing that you want to understand.

NON-JUDGEMENTAL ACCEPTANCE
- not being shocked or judging someone. Accepting the person and their feelings.

RESPECT
- allowing someone the dignity of having the right to feel any emotion and the free choice to choose any action.

GENUINENESS
- being real, not just someone 'playing' a role.

LIMIT YOUR OWN TALKING
- you can't talk and listen at the same time.

CLARIFYING
- if you don't understand something, or feel you have missed a point, clear it up by asking a relevant question.

SUMMARIZING
- periodically check back with the person that you have heard them correctly by summarising the main points of what has been said. You may wish to encourage them to do the summary.

QUESTIONS
- always use open-ended questions, in other words, questions which cannot be answered by just 'yes' or 'no'. Be careful not to interrogate.

DON'T INTERRUPT
- a pause, even a long pause, doesn't mean the person has finished saying everything they want to say.

TURN OFF YOUR OWN WORDS
- personal fears, worries, problems not connected with the person easily distract from what they are saying.

LISTEN FOR FEELINGS
- don't just concentrate on the facts as these are often less important than the feelings.

DON'T ASSUME OR JUMP TO CONCLUSIONS
- don't complete sentences for the person either verbally or in your own mind.

LISTEN FOR OVERTONES
- you can learn a great deal from the way the person says things and what they do not say.

CONCENTRATE/ATTENTION
- focus your mind on what the person is saying. Practice shutting out distractions.

(Scott and Littlewood)

The Communication Cake

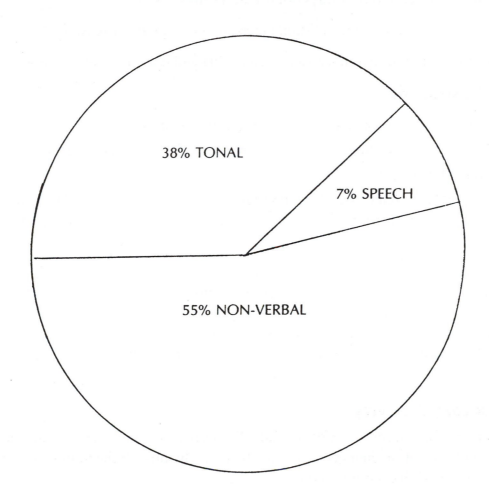

Source: Goom Helm 1986

'A Handbook of Communication Skills'

Take Time to Relax

'Sorrow that has no vent in tears makes other organs weep.'

Objectives

- To introduce children to ways of preventing stress.

- To encourage children to substitute relaxation responses for tension.

- To show children that touch can be enjoyable and does not have to be sexual.

Useful Resources

Background reading – Section 1   ...   'Creating the Climate'.

          – Section 2   ...   'Creative Activities' and 'Self Esteem'.

See 'Additional Resources'   ...

N.B. It is important to remember that relaxation is a skill and therefore will take time to learn. The earlier children start, the easier they will find it. It takes time to learn. and needs practise.

In the early stages of relaxation exercise, there may be giggles, tummy gurgles, and watering eyes, but these will soon go. When working with older children, who may be more self-conscious, it may help to say before starting, 'we are going to try an experiment'.

Relaxation can ease/or help children express the source of their tension. It can also assist a class to be calmed down/or centered after busy or noisy activities, for example, PE.

Introductory Activity

This activity can be introduced at the end of a PE, Dance, or Drama lesson. Ask the children to lie on their backs, close their eyes, and lead them slowly through the following instructions, which can be varied depending on the age group:

- Feel the floor under your body

- Allow your body to sink into the floor

- Notice if you are moving around a lot or whether you are quite still

- Let yourself become quieter, and ever more still, until you are hardly moving

- Now notice your breathing. Is it fast or slow? You don't need to change it

- Perhaps you can feel/notice your heart beating or you may feel aches and pains in your body

- Let your body become more and more relaxed, feel it sink more and more into the floor

- Now slowly stretch all of your body, then open your eyes and, finally, sit up slowly.

N.B. It is best to take only two to three minutes initially, building up to a longer time, depending on the age of the child. It is also important in the early stages to share experiences, for example, Did you find it easy or difficult? How did you feel?

Additional Activity

The relaxation can be deepened by asking children to imagine any of the following:

○ That they are in their own secret, quiet place, for example, they are a floating cloud; a strong tree rooted in the ground, with the sun shining down upon them; floating in warm, shallow water; lying on a warm beach etc.

Gentle music can be played, and ask them to visualize pictures. Creative writing/drawing could follow this.

○ Then the teacher or the children in pairs, gently lift each limb, one at a time, then the head, to see how relaxed the body has become.

General Relaxation

In the Sitting Position

○ Ask the children to sit with their feet flat on the floor, bottoms well back in the chair, hands loosely in their laps, with eyes closed. (If children feel uncomfortable with their eyes closed, suggest they look down at the floor.) Check that their spine, head, and neck are in a straight line.

Lying Down

Lead the children through the following instructions:

• Lie flat on your back, not touching anyone, with your eyes closed;

• Wriggle/move around until you feel comfortable;

• Tighten up your whole body until it feels stiff, like a board, and then relax it;

• Tell the different parts of your body to relax, starting with your feet, move on to your legs, stomach, bottom, chest, back, arms, hands, shoulders, neck, jaw, eyes, forehead.

N.B. Check that children know where their diaphragm, chest and stomach are positioned.

Breathing

Calm breathing has a rate of about six to ten breaths per minute. It can increase to as much as sixteen at times of disturbance. These activities encourage us to breathe more deeply and to relax our abdominal muscles, where a lot of tension can be held. Let children practise for one minute at first and then lengthen, depending on age and interest of the group.

Exercise 1

Ask the children to follow the 'Sitting Position' in 'General Relaxation Activity', then give them the following instructions:

- Put one hand on the upper part of your chest and feel your breathing slow down under it

- Put your other hand on top of your abdomen and feel yourself breathing into this hard

- When ready, drop both hands gently into your lap

- When ready, open your eyes and have a good stretch.

Exercise 2

Ask the children to sit as in the introduction to exercise 1, and continue as follows:

- Become aware of your breathing, feel it slowing down

- Make your out-breath slightly longer than your in-breath

- Have a pause at the end of your out-breath

- Let your breath come when it's ready

- Slowly stretch, open your eyes and 'come back' into the room.

Prevention of Headaches (often caused by stress)

Follow instructions for relaxing in a chair, as before then:

- Place hands loosely in lap, one on top of the other

- Picture warmth moving VERY SLOWLY down from your head, across your shoulders, down your arms, into your hands, and then to the tips of your fingers and thumbs

- When ready open your eyes and have a good stretch.

N.B. Children generally find it very easy to do this exercise and it is also a good exercise for general relaxation.

Meditation

Meditation can contribute to mental development, a clearer sense of identity and spiritual enfoldment. It also enables us to quieten busy thoughts and focus our minds. Like all skills it needs practise if it is to succeed. Children enjoy it and learn very quickly. Meditation can include a guided visualization, for example, a caterpillar turning into a butterfly. Otherwise focus on one object, for example, a flower or a feeling – joy/sadness – or the breath – or one word or number.

Silence

Allows for the stilling of thought, for openness, and to encourage insight. Montessori schools regularly use silence. Anita Courtman, one of the contributors to this teaching book, effectively encourages her junior age children to find 'their own secret, quiet place' – their 'creative part' – before many of their activities.

N.B. See also 'Relaxation'.

Aditional Activities

Imaginary Journey

Builds the creative imagination, self-discipline, and evokes the quality of serenity and calmness.

This is a good activity to use at the start of day or lesson. It can also help the transition from one very active, to a more static, lesson. It rests the body, feelings and mind, releasing energy to handle life a little more creatively.

N.B. Always make the imagery safe; for example, it's a friendly wood, you safely cross the stream and so on.

Start with the children sitting in a relaxed position, backs against the chair, so that they can breathe freely. Ask the children to take a few deep breathes, so silently that no-one can hear them.

Here is an example: *(any of the words can be changed to suit the age of the children, and the inclination of the teacher.)*

> 'Today we are going on a journey. We are going to use our imagination, that part of our mind that sees pictures. I'd like you to imagine now that you are walking down a path in the woods. It is a friendly wood. The sun is shining and you can feel it on your skin, and there is a gentle breeze blowing. You may see flowers, butterflies, birds, all kinds of beautiful leaves. You can feel the firm earth under your feet and see the sun sparkling through the trees. As the path curves, you will come to a stream. It's a shallow stream, and very clear. You can see the pebbles on the bottom. Find a safe place to sit down and look at the water. The water is so shallow you could paddle if you wished. Instead you may just like to sit and enjoy it. All is quiet and peaceful. You hear the birds singing and, deep down inside, you feel very good. There is nothing you have to do. You can stay there as long as you want …

> As you look around a beautiful animal comes out of the woods, on the other side of the stream. It pauses. You sit very quietly, watching. You sense that it trusts you and that you are its friend. Slowly it returns to the woods. You sit watching it go, feeling very good about yourself, about the animal, the woods, and just about everything. You know that you are all right.

> Now, in your own time, quietly return up the path and come back to this room. Become aware of your body sitting on the chair, hear the sounds in the room. When you are ready, open your eyes.'

Further Activities

These activities can be done with pairs/groups or for the whole class.

- Ask the children to share what they feel like when they are sad/lonely/frightened/angry.

- Use large sheets of paper and draw round a boy's and a girl's body. Get the children to mark where they get feelings of tightness, for example, in the tummy.

- Invite children to close their eyes and remember a time when they felt one of the feelings described above. Ask them to draw a picture of what it felt like or to 'free draw'.

N.B. The children might say that they felt tight and horrid inside and/or outside, and might for example draw a picture of a big finger clawing.

Depending on the age, some or all of the following activities can be used. Allow about five to ten minutes each, with time for discussion between. Music can be introduced to encourage different moods/feelings.

- Ask the children to stamp around the room, then stand still and/or close their eyes and imagine they are a tree, just moving backwards and forwards in a breeze.

- Ask them to tighten every part of their body, then to stay like that while they walk around the room and greet all the other children.

- Then suggest they 'flop' all parts of their bodies, going slower and slower until falling down in a heap.

- Teach them a simple meditation.

Massage

SIMPLE BACK MASSAGE

Demonstrate first on one of the children. Suggest to very young children that they take the tiredness away from the other person, rather than explaining complicated massage strokes. Also see they check with their partner whether they like a gentle or a strong massage.

SHOULDER MASSAGE

Either ask the children to work in pairs, with each taking turns to massage or receive or:

- Form a circle, turn to the right and place their hands on the shoulders of the person in front. Suggest they leave them there for a few moments to allow the other to get used to their touch.

- Towards the end of the time, suggest they end with a gentle stroking motion across shoulders, down arms to end of finger tips.

N.B. Massage can be an ideal way to introduce the subject of appropriate touch.

Additional Activities for Older Children

BACK SCRATCH

- Use finger tips and finger nails to give a 'gentle scratch'. Emphasize 'no tickling'.

HEEL OF THE HAND RUB

- Heels of the hand are used to ease tension and tiredness.

FLAT HAND BACK RUB

- The same as the previous exercise, but using the flat of hand.

TICKLE BACK

- Emphasize this is to be slow and gentle and is not meant to make their partner laugh or become uncomfortable.

KNUCKLE STROKING

- The knuckle edges of a clenched fist can be used gently, to run up and down the back, to take away any tension and tiredness.

SIDE OF THE HAND CHOP-CHOP

- The side of the hands are used to give gentle chops up and down the back.

N.B. Any of these methods can also be used with the recipient seated, either on a chair or on the floor, with their partner sitting or kneeling behind.

OTHER MASSAGES

HAND AND ARM

- Ask children to work in pairs, sitting on the floor, opposite each other. The recipient then gently places their arm on their partner's knee. Suggest they explore their partner's hand or just the thumb, using some of the strokes used on the back.

- These can be extended up the arm to the shoulder.

FOOT MASSAGE

- Feet are very sensitive, so the massage should only be undertaken with children who have used the other methods first.

- The giver takes the other person's foot onto their knee, gently squeezing it several times, before following the techniques described for the hand, being careful not to tickle.

FOREHEAD

- This can be done with the giver standing or sitting behind the receiver.

- Place hands gently on the receiver's forehead, so the finger tips touch in the middle. Leave for a moment, to allow partner to get used to the touch. Use gentle, smooth strokes to move outwards to the temples. Repeat several times.

N.B. Children can massage their own hands, feet and forehead.

Follow Up Activities

- Ask the children to share their experiences of massage.

- Ask them for suggestions of times when people would enjoy massage.

- Ask who they would like especially to massage them, and who they would like to massage.

N.B. Make suggestions, if necessary; for example, Mummy's/Daddy's shoulders when they are tired.

Self-Esteem and Self-Image

Self-Esteem and Self-Image

NATIONAL CURRICULUM

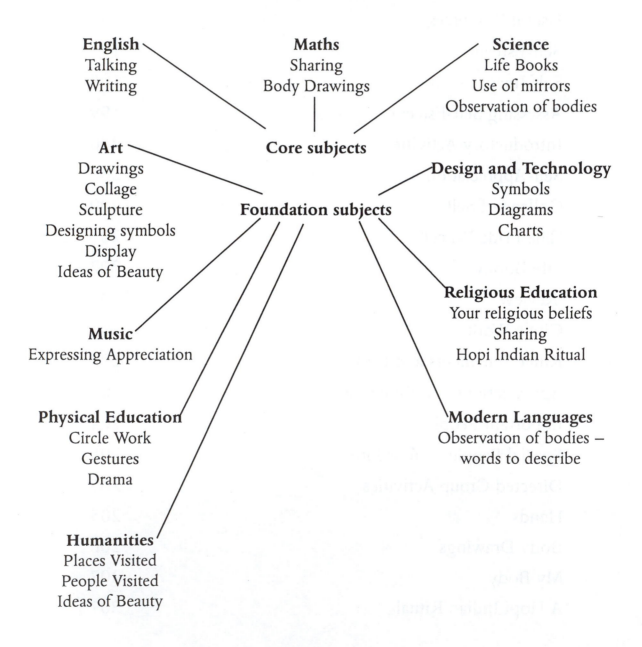

English
Talking
Writing

Maths
Sharing
Body Drawings

Science
Life Books
Use of mirrors
Observation of bodies

Core subjects

Art
Drawings
Collage
Sculpture
Designing symbols
Display
Ideas of Beauty

Foundation subjects

Design and Technology
Symbols
Diagrams
Charts

Religious Education
Your religious beliefs
Sharing
Hopi Indian Ritual

Music
Expressing Appreciation

Physical Education
Circle Work
Gestures
Drama

Modern Languages
Observation of bodies –
words to describe

Humanities
Places Visited
People Visited
Ideas of Beauty

The lists above are only suggestions. Many more may be found in the text.

Self-Esteem and Self-Image

'CHILDREN LEARN WHAT THEY LIVE

IF
a child lives with criticism, she learns to condemn.
IF
a child lives with hostility, he learns to fight.
IF
a child lives with ridicule, she learns to be shy.
IF
a child lives with shame, he learns to feel guilt.
IF
a child lives with tolerance, she learns to be patient.
IF
a child lives with encouragement, he learns confidence.
IF
a child lives with praise, she learns to be appreciated.
IF
a child lives with fairness, he learns justice.
IF
a child lives with security, she learns to have faith.
IF
a child lives with approval, he learns to like himself.
IF
a child lives with acceptance and friendship, he or she learns to find love in the world.'

(Scottish Health Education Group)

Self-Esteem and Self-Image

'Every second we live is a new and unique moment of the universe, a moment that never was before and never will be again. And what do we teach our children in school? We teach them that two and two make four and that Paris is the capital of France. We should say to each of them, "Do you know what you are? You are a marvel. You are unique. In the millions of years that have passed, there has never been another child like you".'

(Pablo Casals)

Objectives

- To encourage children to respect and value who they are and what they do

- To combat the low self-esteem and self-image that can occur at times of loss.

Useful Resources

Background Reading — see Section 1.
  — see Section 2.

See 'Book List' and 'Additional Resources' —
  — *100 Ways to Enhance Self-Esteem in the Classroom*
  — *Let's Co-operate*

Materials and Resources for different activities.

Self-Esteem

Self-esteem is how you value yourself. When your self-esteem is high you feel confident. You trust your judgement and you know what you are capable of. You respect yourself for what you do and who you are.

When you lack self-esteem you feel weak and helpless. You are uncertain of the value of anything you do. You don't trust yourself or other people's reassurances. You are unsure of who you are. This is a common experience which may result in difficulty in making satisfactory relationships.

A child that has grown up feeling loved and secure is more likely to have a high sense of self-esteem. They will have grown up with a true sense of who they are. They will have learnt to trust the reactions they receive from the outside world. They feel secure.

Many children grow up without a sense of who they are. They may have to struggle to be what someone else wants. They may have been given confusing messages about what they should and should not do; they may never have been praised for achievement nor given helpful criticism.

Self-Image

Self-image has two sides — the ideal self (the person I would like to be) and the actual self (the way I see myself). The ideal self is an image put together by identifying with models such as parents, friends, pop-stars or people we admire or wish to emulate. Television and other media are particularly powerful in presenting 'ideals' and stereotypes to us. We tend to 'measure' the perceived 'self' against this ideal.

Children need a clear idea of their own identity, a feeling of being a person distinct from others — separate and unique. The main components of self-image are:

- The 'Outer' Me — physique and body image

- The 'Inner' Me — feelings, emotions likes/dislikes

○ The perception of self as a learner

○ The roles the child is called upon to play.

Assessing Self-Esteem

Assessing self-esteem in the classroom is fairly difficult. Here is a useful checklist that might help, to ask of each child:

- Do they make self-disparaging remarks?

- Are they boastful?

- Are they hesitant and timid in new situations?

- Do they make excuses to avoid situations which may be stressful?

- Are they continually asking for help and/or reassurance?

- Do they hang back and remain on the fringe of the group?

- Are they apathetic in a learning situation?

- Do they daydream a lot?

- Do they avoid work even though risking your displeasure?

- Do they tend to blame others for their failures?

- Are they reluctant to assume responsibilities?

N.B. See 'Book List', *Enhancing Self-Esteem in the Classroom.*

Introductory Activities

Sharing

Builds trust, empathy and tolerance. This activity can be used throughout the year.

- Each child talks about themselves, their families, holidays, while the rest of the class listens. The teacher usually gives examples from their own experience. With younger children this can be done over a period of days, not necessarily in one lesson.

- Alternatively, this activity can be done using partners, each child having its chance to share. Then some may like to share in the class group.

N.B. The teacher takes the role of the creative listener. This involves receiving the information without judging it. This becomes a model for the children.

Self-Appreciation

Builds self-awareness, self-acceptance.

- Ask the children to write down a list of things that they can do ... say, three to six. Get them to start with 'I can ... '. It often helps to give examples of things that you can do. Ask the children to read them out to the class/partner or group.

- The next stage is slightly harder and can be done as a separate lesson or it can follow on from the last.

- Ask them to finish these sentences:

> 'One thing I like about myself is ...'
>
> 'One thing others like about me is ...'

- You may well need to give examples, for example, I'm kind, I'm a good sport, I always tell the truth.

- When they have completed the sentences in rough, give them some drawing paper and ask them to draw a picture/or symbol that goes with the sentence. Write the sentences at the bottom of the paper, that match the pictures/symbols.

- The pictures and statements can later be shared in a group or put on display and shared with the whole class.

Collage of Self

Builds self-awareness and tolerance.

Ask the class to cut out pictures, symbols and images that:

- Represent themselves
- Are things they like to do
- Are things they own

- Represent places they have visited

- Are people they admire

Ask the children not to sign their work, then display to the class/show in groups.

- Everyone tries to guess

  - Who it is

  - Whose work it is

- Discuss

  - How it was for them

  - How it felt to be on show.

'The Pride Wheel'

Builds confidence and a sense of self-worth.
Discuss with the class how difficult it can be to say:

- 'I am proud that I …'

Ask them to think about the following:

- Things you have done for parents

- Things you have done for a friend

- Your work in school

- How you spend your free time

- Your religious beliefs

- Something you've bought recently

- Habits that you have

- Something that you do often

- Something you have shared

- Something that you have tried hard for

N.B. The children may not be able to do them all.

- Ask the children to draw a circle with spokes, get them to write the sentence: 'I am proud that I …' on each spoke; and complete it.

- The centre can be decorated, and a border put around the edge; this would make a Mandala for each.

- The work can be displayed/discussed/shared.

- It could be extended into poetry/story writing.

Life Books

Make books with drawings or photos of the children at different ages; things that might be included:

- Things I could do ... (Skills)

- Activities I enjoy

- My favourite toys/possessions/games/hobbies

- I liked myself when ...

- I disliked myself when ...

- My best friend was ...

- Other important things in my life.

'Review'

Builds self-evaluation and self-appreciation.

- At the end of each day/week or term ask the children to share their successes, and what they have learned.

This can be done verbally or as a written piece.

N.B. If you were doing these regularly they could be kept in an individual folder, and if less regularly, in a class folder.

Circle Work

It is often a good idea to get the class to sit in a circle when sharing. This enables everyone to have eye contact, and can help create an atmosphere of trust.

Some activities are particularly suited to circle work.

Killer Statements and Gestures

Builds self-awareness and acceptance of feelings, honest and direct relationships, empathy with others.

Everybody begins by sitting in a circle.

QUESTIONS TO ASK

- Have you ever worked hard at something you felt was not understood or appreciated?

- What was it? (*Give time for responses.*)

- What was said or done that made you feel your effort was appreciated? (*Again allow time for responses.*)

- Have you ever wanted to share things, ideas, feelings, something you've written or made, but were afraid to do so?

- Were you afraid people might put you or it down?

- What kind of things might they say?

N.B. This could be one lesson depending on how much child response you want or get. The next part can follow on or be a separate lesson.

THIS TIME YOU WILL BE INTRODUCING 'KILLER STATEMENTS AND GESTURES'

All of us have many feelings, thoughts, and creative behaviour, that are 'killed off' by other people's put-down comments and physical gestures, for example:

- 'We don't have time for that now.'

- 'That's a stupid idea.'

- 'You know that's impossible.'

- 'Are you serious/looney/dumb?'

- 'Only boys/girls do that.'

Ask the children to keep a record of all the 'killer statements' they hear at home/school/at play. Have a lesson discussing them.

Additional Activities
DO THE SAME EXERCISE WITH 'GESTURES'

- Get the children to shout out all the 'killer statements' and 'gestures' at one go.

- Make a collage of 'killer statements'.

- To conclude, organize a discussion on how the 'statements' serve or help them.

QUESTIONS TO ASK

- What do 'killer statements' protect you from?

- Are there things that you would really like to say but are afraid, so you say a 'killer statement' instead?

Appreciations and Resentments
(This activity is also included, in a modified form, in Living With Loss)

This following activity can be very powerful. It helps create a harmonious and healthy group atmosphere, particularly when groups are spending significant amounts of time together, for example, a class, a staff, a family. There are always some unexpressed communications among those who are frequently together, for example, children and adults. Some of it will be positive and some negative. What is unspoken remains 'in the air', and influences the relationships in the class. This activity supports the previous ones above by encouraging honest and direct communication.

It shows children that it is acceptable to let our feelings and needs be known, but that it doesn't mean we get what we want every time.

- It's essential to sit in a circle and to have eye contact

- The children are asked to express appreciations to each other

- They need to say the child's name, and to look at them, then say the appreciation, for example, 'Peter, I really appreciate your letting me play football'. 'Jane, thank you for playing with me today, and looking after me when I fell over.'

- The other child doesn't reply except perhaps to say 'thank you'.

- The person getting the appreciation just receives and takes it in – very difficult for some children to do this.

The Next Stage is to Move into 'Resentments' and 'Requests':

- Sit as for the previous exercise and state the resentment, for example:

    > 'Sharon, I don't like it when you take my pens out of my desk without asking me.'

    > 'Paul, it upsets me when you laugh at me in the playground.'

    > 'Jill, I really wish you would stop hiding my shoes. It makes me really angry.'

- The receiver, as before, doesn't reply, but sits and listens, and hears/accepts, as best they can.

This activity clears the air and deals with a lot of minor squabbles. It increases caring and empathy, and creates a togetherness.

Important People

To encourage recognition that we are all unique, special, and important.

QUESTIONS TO ASK

- Why are you important/special?

- Look around the room and see that everyone has two eyes, two ears, a nose, a mouth, hair, etc.

- Is there anyone else who looks like you?

- You are the only person in the whole world like you – that means you are special/unique.

N.B. You may need to explain about twins.

Follow Up Activity

- Look at themselves in a mirror.

- Creative drawing/writing.

Special People in Your Life

A teacher needs to have a knowledge of children's home background before using this activity.

QUESTIONS TO ASK

- Who are the special people in your life?

- Why are they special to you?

- How can you let them know that they are special to you?

- How do they let you know that you are special?

- Is there anything that you would like to say/do to someone that you haven't said/done?

- Ask the class members to choose a partner, and pretend that your partner is that 'someone'.

- Practise doing/saying what you would like to do/say.

- Change partners so that both have a turn.

FEEDBACK

- Ask the class to share with their partner; how it felt for them, and how they think that their partner felt.

- Invite them to ask their partner if they guessed right.

Directed Group Activities

These activities can be done in pairs/groups or by the whole class.

'Hands'

Builds self-appreciation, increases awareness of body functions, observation and concentration.

This activity focuses on the hands, but may be used for any body part. The children choose a partner and then decide who is going to start. You lead them through the following:

- Look at your partner's hand, both sides

- Look at the colour/the lines

- Are your partner's hands long or short, thin or plump?

- Are there any interesting marks on them?

- Gently feel them all over. How do they feel?

- Now tell your partner what you found out about their hands. Repeat the process with the other partner

- Now look at your hands in the same way. (Guide them through as before.)

Then ask everyone to close their eyes and become very quiet, and continue as follows:

- See yourself in your imagination using your hands

- Remember all the things your hands do, for example, all the actions, all the jobs, kind things and unkind, interesting and boring, difficult and easy

- Now open your eyes and see if you can finish this sentence: 'My hands are …'

- Then get the children to draw round their hands and write their sentence underneath

- Ask them to decorate the hands, to go with the sentence

- These can be displayed, and shared in a variety of ways.

Body Drawings

Builds body awareness, body image, allows communication of likes and dislikes of body image, and helps them to come to terms with their body image.

- Ask the class to choose a partner

- Ask one of each pair to lie down on a large piece of paper and the other draws around them – thus creating a body outline

- Make sure that fingers, neck, hair, and shoes are on the paper

- Change over and repeat the process

- The children then cut out the body outline

- Ask them to colour and fill in their body cut-out, using any colours that they feel they would like to use

- Suggest that the colouring expresses how they feel about the various parts of their body. (It does not have to show how they are dressed at the moment or be totally realistic.)

- Suggest again that they are colouring in their feelings about their body.

Additional Activities

- Put the cut-outs on the wall and discuss them in a large group

- Give each person time to say how they feel seeing their drawing on the wall; how they feel about any part of their body that they are not comfortable with

N.B. You may feel it is better to do this in smaller groups over a longer period.

My Body

Builds body awareness, positive self-image, trust and empathy.

- Sit the class in a circle, so they can see each other. (They also need to have worked in a circle before with a less difficult subject).

QUESTIONS TO ASK

- Which parts of your body do you like best?

- Which parts of your body do you like least?

GO AROUND THE CIRCLE SHARING

- Where do you get your idea of beauty from?

- Do TV adverts or magazines influence you?

- How does your body influence or affect you?

- What are bodies for?

This could be followed by written work.

A Hopi Indian Ritual

Builds a positive environment, inter-personal relationships.

Ask each child to bring from home an object which is important to them, or if possible they are taken outside to find something from nature which has the same meaning.

- The class sit in a circle with the object, and close their eyes for a few moments to be silent

- Then they sense everyone else in the group and make silent contact with them

- They open their eyes, and anyone can start the 'ritual'

- Ask the first person to take their object into the middle of the circle, turning round so that everyone sees. This is done in SILENCE

- Then ask the child to tell the class what the object is, and why it is important to them

- Then put the object in the centre of the circle and return to their place

- This continues until everyone has done it, and created a sculpture of objects

- When that is complete, allow a moment of silent looking at the sculpture they have created, and which is a symbol of the class.

N.B. If a child forgets their object they can describe what they would have brought and its importance.

Section 3

APPENDICES

To separate or to stay together? What children really think of divorce

Tomorrow a children's television programme will tackle the subject of divorce. Will it make uncomfortable viewing for parents? **Sally Brompton** investigates

Abbi was five when her world fell apart. "My mum... went upstairs and packed her bag, she put her coat on... she opened the door and she said, 'I'm going away for a few days.' And then I said, 'Why are you going away for a few days?' and then she didn't answer and walked away. Then I started crying and I thought I'd never see her again."

Five years on, Abbi can look back calmly at that terrible moment when her whole life crumbled. At the time, however, convinced that she was somehow to blame for the break-up of her parents' marriage, she retreated into a cocoon of guilt and confusion.

As Britain's divorce figures soar, more and more children suffer the psychological backlash of broken marriages. Enmeshed in their own unhappiness, it is perhaps understandable that the adults unwittingly overlook — or cannot cope with — the profound effects their actions may have upon their children.

Two million youngsters are currently affected by divorce and another 160,000 join them each year. One child in five will watch parents split up before he or she is 16. These are the forgotten casualties of a conflict commonly cloaked in mysteries and half truths. But even quite small children often appreciate more about the situation than their parents realize.

"The instinct of the adults is to conceal the truth, whereas children are almost psychically aware of atmosphere," says Charlotte Black, director of tomorrow's children's television documentary, *Unhappy Families* (BBC2, 5.05pm), which studies the children of divorce.

The programme explores the effects of divorce on six children aged between 10 and 14 from a mixture of backgrounds in the Avon area. Anxious not to exploit the children or cause additional trauma within the family, Black selected youngsters who seemed able to look back on the experience objectively.

In the words of 13-year-old Sarah: "Before our parents actually split up, I used to think that if they did I'd never get through it. But now I've realized that if you persevere, you can."

The children in the documentary tell their own stories, providing a revealing insight into their individual reactions. "I used to think it was all my fault," admits 11-year-old Debbie, who was four when her parents separated. "I used to think that they were rowing because of me and that if I wasn't there it wouldn't happen..."

When his father left home, Demian, now 12, became aggressive towards his younger brother. "I used to thump him and cry and break things... he used to make Lego models and I used to stamp on them, kick them about the room... I used to think that everybody else has got a dad and I haven't and I don't deserve one."

Philip Darley, a social services training officer in the Bristol area, believes that

ABBI, 10, WHOSE MOTHER PACKED HER BAGS AND WALKED OUT FIVE YEARS AGO...

'I started crying and I thought I'd never see her again'

Unhappy ever after?

"children vary in their reactions according to how they have experienced their parents' marriage. If their needs were being really well met in the first place, they will have a lot of internal strength to cope with the divorce.

"Another factor is their age. Quite young children find it very hard to believe that the problem isn't of their making. It is important to reassure them that it isn't." While adolescents, according to counsellor Lynda Osborne, resent the fact that "just when they want their parents to be the wallpaper, they suddenly come off the wall and create problems of their own".

Because children often find it difficult to accept that they are not alone in their predicament, they tend to be reluctant to talk about it. Darley, who runs "Surviving Divorce" courses for both parents and children, has found that the main reaction of the children is relief — "at being able to talk to other children in the same boat and share ideas about how to cope.

"One of the saddest things is that a lot of children don't know what is going on, and they know they don't know. I've had three children tell me, 'My mum says my dad is living at the office', and each of them knew that dads don't live in offices. They knew they weren't being told the truth but somehow they couldn't demand it."

So few divorcing parents know how to respond to their children's needs that a small, independent organization called People Projects has produced leaflets* for both parents and children explaining how to cope with divorce. Parents are advised to tell their children the truth from the start and to emphasize that

SARAH, 13, AND HER BROTHER, DAVID...

'Dad didn't kiss mum when he came home'

though they no longer love each other, this in no way affects their feelings for the child. Practical arrangements and continuity are very important to children who want to know how their day-to-day lives are going to be affected. Their opinions should be asked about custody and access arrangements but they should never be expected to take sides or choose between their parents.

Children are warned that their parents may be very upset and may not understand how they can love their other parent.

"They are all obvious things but in some ways it is the most obvious things that need saying," says Mary Travis, a former marriage and relationship counsellor who formed People Projects and produced the leaflets.

In the television documentary, 11-year-old Liam believes that children should be given an explanation as to why their parents are separating so that "it won't come as a big, big shock". It came as a shock to Sarah and her younger brother, David, despite the fact that they had noticed that their parents "didn't seem to be getting on like they used to... just little things like dad didn't kiss mum when he came in from work". When their parents eventually told them that they were splitting up, "it was a shock because we didn't want to know, in a way."

The parents, who were not present during the filming, were amazed at how mature and articulate their children were about their experiences. "They were surprised at the power of the conclusions and feelings their children had come to, that they knew quite definitely who they wanted to live with and that, in many cases, the adults hadn't realized what they were going through," says Charlotte Black. She found that the children all had "a forced independence of emotions and had learned self-reliance early on" as a result of their emotional upheaval.

It was the children's decision to take part in the programme. "I think that most of the parents would have preferred to let sleeping dogs lie but because they felt it was the children's right to talk they let them do it," Black says.

She is hoping that parents will watch the documentary — as well as their children — in order to gain a clearer insight into the ways that youngsters react. It will not necessarily make the adults feel that they should never get divorced, but it will bring home to them the need to consider their children, whose views are often more circumspect than their parents realize.

In Debbie's words: "I don't think divorce is bad... it can be a good thing because it can stop the parents from being upset and sometimes the child can be happy as well."

*Available through The Children's Society, Edward Rudolf House, Margery Street, London WC1X OJL. Send 50p and a large SAE for the two leaflets.

CAUGHT IN THE MIDDLE

Finding that increasing numbers of children from broken homes are being referred to school psychological services, Kathleen Cox and Martin Desforge have made a special study of their difficulties and of the way teachers can avoid making things worse.

The final straw for many families is the failure of the annual vacation to live up to the promise of the holiday brochures. With the end of the summer holidays many children whose parents have recently separated will be returning to school.

Obviously children cannot learn efficiently if they are thinking of personal problems rather than classroom-based lessons. But does the school, its practices and curriculum also inadvertently add to the pupils, distress?

Schools, like children, find themselves caught in the middle of a situation not of their making but which they cannot ignore. There are few clear expectations and guidelines for either and limited experience to call upon to decide what to do. Teachers, parents and pupils are equally unsure what to expect of the school.

Some teachers regard themselves simply as educators. They feel they have been trained specially for this task and resent being asked to act as social workers even though they recognize that anxieties caused by parental separation and divorce may make pupils less receptive to teaching.

Some parents think their separation is a private matter and are reluctant to tell teachers of the home crisis. They may fear the teacher will be prejudiced against divorced parents and their children and often wish to keep such a personal matter private. Others, hoping for a reconciliation, do not wish to inform the school of what they hope will be temporary disruptions.

Some pupils habitually prefer their home life to have nothing to do with school. They like to separate their two lives, to leave their family concerns at home and their academic life in school whether or not there are problems in either place. These children resent what they see as prying teachers who may appear over-anxious to help.

However, with one in five children experiencing divorce before their sixteenth birthday and an unknown number affected by parental separation, schools can no longer ignore such events.

About two-thirds of children will show marked changes in school behaviour following parental separation. Common changes are a deterioration in work standards, restlessness, lack of concentration and a big increase in day dreaming. About one-fifth of these children exhibit sadness in school.

The changes often disrupt friendship patterns, with friends understanding even less than the pupils themselves and avoiding contact. The period of disturbance can last up to two years or more.

With a disturbed home life pupils can be lacking basic physical requirements such as sleep or regular meals. Under these circumstances the most basic requests from schools are difficult to meet and can be an additional burden to a pupil trying to maintain an interest in school. Homework, for example, may be impossible to complete if out of school facilities no longer exist.

Schools are in a unique position to help as all children are obliged to attend. The familiarity of school routine can in itself provide comfort and security to a child without any special efforts on the part of the school. Predictable routines can afford safety and stability at a time when home and family are undergoing change.

Schools and teachers contrast with clinics and counsellors in that they are not problem focused and can help by their mere normality. They can respond flexibly in a child-centred approach which allows children to talk when they wish to rather than when they have to in response to a clinic appointment. A sensitive teacher, by allowing children to express worries and fears in a calm atmosphere can certainly help them to re-establish their own sense of place and purpose in a changing situation.

Through routine daily contact pupils and teachers develop a relationship and trust which is available to help with personal problems. For this teachers need only basic counselling skills to encourage pupils to share their problems.

Many children whose parents separate have never had the opportunity to discuss their situation with anyone and say they would liked to have been able to talk with a neutral adult. Attentive listening can help resolve difficulties by allowing children time and space to define problems in their own way.

Some parents turn naturally to school to help them too. At the outset of such a parental interview it is essential to try to establish whether it is the parents' or the pupil's problems which are under discussion and to draw a clear distinction between the two.

Most teachers wisely choose not to involve themselves in parental difficulties directly and one way of helping parents in this situation is to know and suggest alternative sources of help: marriage guidance counselling; the DHSS, a solicitor or the Citizen's Advice Bureau for more practical problems; the Samaritans if the parent needs a sympathetic listener.

Parents and teachers should try to establish together what can be done to help the child who is their joint concern. It may become apparent that the school could complement existing parenting if the quality of parenting provided from home is temporarily diminished.

Extra attention may be required from a teacher who is prepared to bear children's news when their parents are too busy dealing with the essentials of living to give sufficient attention. Support of a more tangible nature is required to provide the materials the school requires for its curriculum, such as in home economics or PE.

The school's procedures should ensure that the facts about a pupil's life are recorded and updated as necessary and are accessible. Twenty-nine out of 30 parents in one survey in 1984 had informed the headteacher, but this did not mean that those who taught the child were aware of the situation.

Parents no longer living together but still maintaining an active role in child care may require separate copies of letters and reports. Offering this service rather than waiting to be asked is a positive way of helping both parents who may be too embarrassed to make such a request.

The school needs to know the basic arrangement of custody, care and control and access. This means that legal terms and their practical implications must be understood.

For the post-divorce family, schools can be one of the places where separated parents can work together for the well-being of their children. Parental cooperation following separation can be a valuable way to help the children to recover from the trauma of the split. Most parents are concerned about the education their children receive and school can be one neutral place to meet and discuss unemotively a topic of mutual concern, namely their children's education.

Until recently most school organizations assumed that their pupils were being brought up in a traditional nuclear family where father was the major breadwinner and out of the house during the day and mother was responsible for the daily lives of the children.

The practice of sending one letter to the child's home automatically addressed to Mr and Mrs all state clearly the assumptions on which the school is operating.

Failure to conform to the school's expectations with regard to family patterns affects the 200,000 or so children per year whose parents separate or divorce. The re-assessment of school practices and the innovation of others to take account of different situations accepts that not all children are brought up in stereotyped families.

The assumptions about family life are also reflected in the specific content of some subjects although not apparently directly relevant to the subject. In modern languages the vehicle for conversation is often the nuclear family in its stereotyped form.

In history, comments on the significance of certain marriages and their political implications reflect views on marriage today. In craft children may be encouraged to make things for homes and people which do not actually exist; a most obvious example being mother's or father's day cards. Christmas celebrations with the emphasis on the perfect family is stressful as parents and children privately compare their own situation with the ideal.

Personal and social education is now on the timetable in most schools in some form with a recent HMI report recommending it should be as much as one-sixth of the syllabus of a school. Although it does not yet enjoy the status of other subjects on the timetable, it is important both as a preparation for life after school and also may help pupils to see their own lives in a different perspective.

Another school practice which could help these children is the availability of books where separation and divorce occur. Including such books in the library accepts the occurrence and enables pupils to read, in relative privacy, books they may need. Friends may also gain a deeper understanding of their predicament which those directly involved are unable to express.

Schools should recognize that pupils' emotional and social development may be impeded as well as their academic work. Some will regress to an earlier stage of development and become more immature, while others do not regress but become fixed and cease to progress emotionally.

Friendship patterns can become disturbed as a consequence of changing lifestyles, and valuable peer support is lost in these ways. Pupils' social development might therefore need more active help from the school in order to overcome impediments to normal social maturation.

Teachers know the range of behaviour to expect in a certain age group and knowledge of children allow them to be aware of changes in individual behaviour. Teachers can assess reaction to stress and should consider referral to an outside agency if this reaction differs greatly from what is expected.

Initially, however, by knowing a significant number of children will be in this position, by expecting prolonged reaction and by being sensitive to the assumptions about the family which the school makes, teachers can go a long way to help.

Kathleen Cox and Martin Desforges work for Sheffield's School Psychological Service.

212

Helen House

Helen House is a small hospice which gives day-to-day love and care to gravely ill children and supports their families. The idea of Helen House started in 1980 and thanks to the wonderful generosity of thousands of people building began in 1981. Helen House opened in 1982, the first of its kind in the world. It relies entirely on voluntary contributions.

Why is it called Helen House?

Helen was a bright, lively, happy child, two and a half years old. In 1978 she suddenly became very ill. She had to have an emergency operation to remove a brain tumour. Although the tumour was successfully removed, Helen's brain suffered severe, irreversible damage. Now she remains totally helpless, unable to speak, sit up, or control her movements. She seems to be partly aware of her surroundings but it is impossible to know how much she understands. Shortly after the operation, Mother Frances, who is the Superior General of the Anglican Society of All Saints and is also a Registered Sick Children's Nurse met Helen and her parents and a close friendship developed. She visited Helen frequently during her six months' stay in hospital. After Helen returned home, Mother Frances looked after her from time to time at All Saints Convent in order to give her parents a short break. Helen House grew out of this friendship with Helen and her family.

Families who have a very sick child usually want to look after their child at home once hospital no longer seems appropriate. But the strain and the loneliness can be very great. Helen House is small and homely, a place where children and their families can come to stay from time to time – just as most of us have a holiday occasionally or go to stay with friends for the weekend. Friendship, support and practical skills are what we offer.

Who is Helen House for?

Most of the children who come to Helen House have chronic, life-threatening illnesses of one kind of another.* They live at home with their families and visit us every now and then for a short stay. Families are welcome to come too – parents, brothers and sisters, occasionally grandparents; we have even welcomed a dog, a terrapin and a pet terantula! Sometimes though the family will take the opportunity, while their child is cared for in Helen House, to have a holiday or do things at home which they could not normally do. The frequency of visits varies according to the individual needs of each family and we try, to the best of our ability, to meet these needs sensitively.

A few children come to Helen House at the end of their lives. Our aim is to provide a loving, supportive environment for them and their families, ensuring that pain and other unpleasant symptoms, which can cause acute distress and anxiety, are controlled or prevented.

We welcome children of any race or belief and of any age from birth to sixteen.

Illnesses such as muscular dystrophy, Batten's disease, mucopolysaccharidoses, malignant disease and many others.

We are sometimes able to continue to care for children after they have reached sixteen but we cannot normally take anyone for the first time beyond this age. There is no defined catchment area and children from many parts of the United Kingdom and the Channel Islands come to Helen House. We make no charge. We do not provide long-term care and would not attempt to look after those who would benefit more from treatment in an acute hospital ward. We cannot normally look after children with an illness or handicap which is not life-threatening.

What is Helen House like?

Helen House can take eight children at any one time and each child has his or her own bedroom. Parents may choose to sleep in the same room as their child, or alternatively, there is family accommodation with two double bedrooms, a sitting-room, kitchen and bathroom, providing comfort and complete privacy.

The living rooms are designed to be as homely as possible. A jacuzzi provides therapy and relaxation and fun for the grown-ups as well as the children. Outside, the garden of Helen House gives the feel of being in the country and is in constant use in fine weather. Just around the corner are busy little shops and all the activity of local town life and a little further away the beauty of the City and University of Oxford.

The routine is like that of any family and tends to vary depending on who is staying. Families who stay can choose to take an active part in looking after their children or they can leave this to the team.

Who works in Helen House?

Helen House is run by people whose common qualification is their love and concern for children. They include trained nurses, teachers, a nursery nurse, social worker, physiotherapist, a chaplin, and others, some of whom are parents themselves. A local Practitioner is the medical officer. An administrator, a secretary, two sisters from All Saints Convent and a few volunteers complete the team. Everyone shares the household chores as well as the care of the children and families, and no one wears uniform. If a child's home is near enough to Helen House, the doctor or other professionals who care for him or her at home are welcome to continue to be involved at Helen House.

What does Helen House try to do?

Our aim is quite simple – to offer friendship and practical help to very sick children and their families. We try to be sensitive to their individual needs, enabling the child and family to achieve the best possible quality of life for them. If and when the time comes for a child to die we try to ensure that this happens with dignity, the child surrounded by the people he or she knows and loves best, whether at home or in Helen House. The friendship and support does not end there but continues for as many months or years as the family wishes.

Helen House relies entirely on voluntary donations.

You can become a Friend of Helen House by making a minimum contribution of £5 a year, or a Friend for Life by giving £50. As such you will receive our newsletter twice a year.

Correspondence should be addressed to:-
HELEN HOUSE
37 Leopold Street
OXFORD OX4 1QT
Telephone (01865) 728251

What to Do When Someone Dies

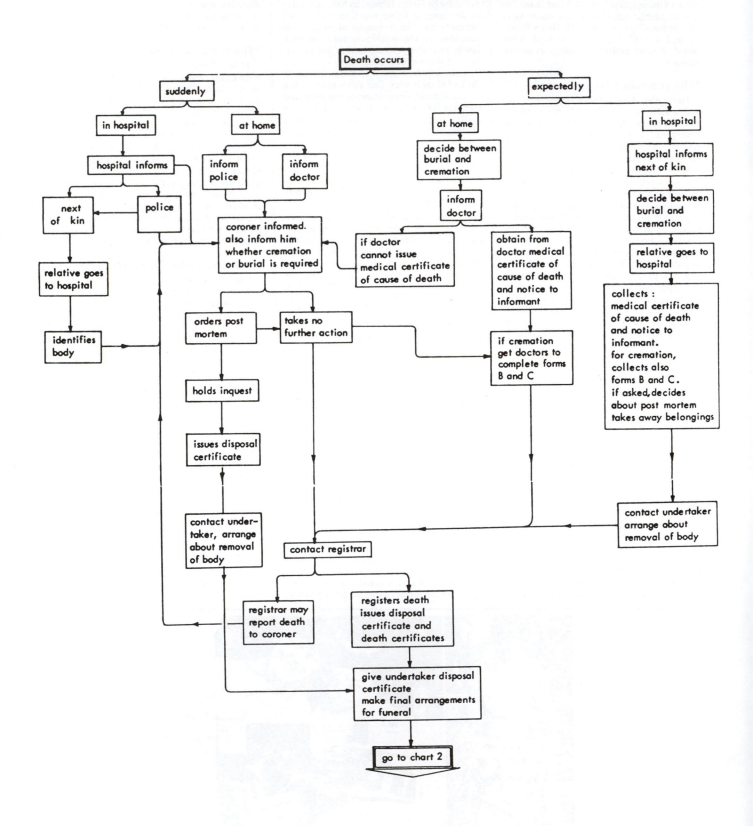

Chart 2

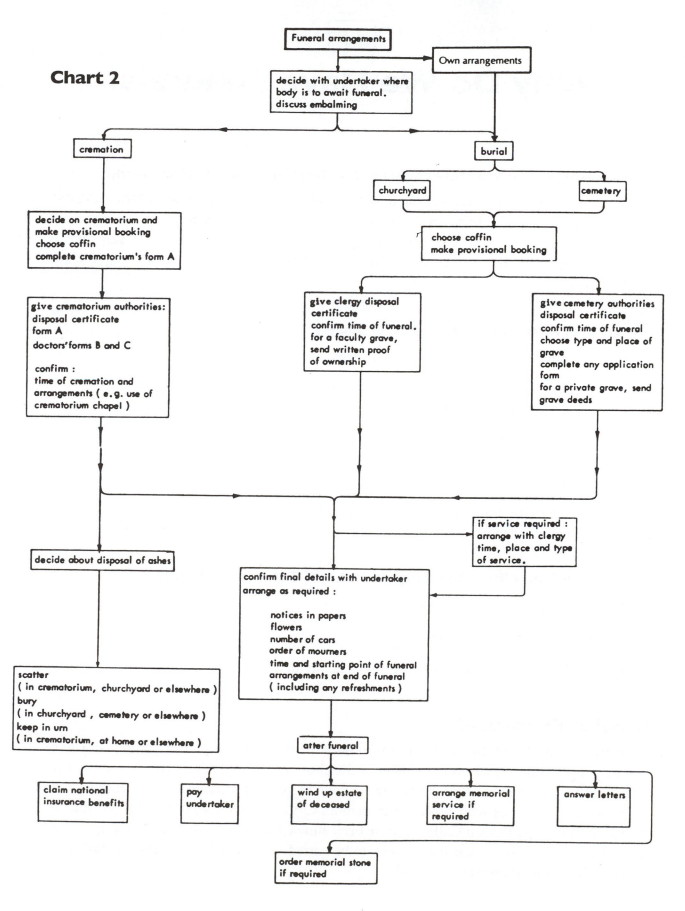

Funeral arrangements

Own arrangements

decide with undertaker where body is to await funeral. discuss embalming

cremation

burial

churchyard

cemetery

decide on crematorium and make provisional booking
choose coffin
complete crematorium's form A

choose coffin
make provisional booking

give crematorium authorities:
disposal certificate
form A
doctors' forms B and C

confirm :
time of cremation and arrangements (e.g. use of crematorium chapel)

give clergy disposal certificate
confirm time of funeral.
for a faculty grave, send written proof of ownership

give cemetery authorities
disposal certificate
confirm time of funeral
choose type and place of grave
complete any application form
for a private grave, send grave deeds

if service required :
arrange with clergy time, place and type of service.

decide about disposal of ashes

confirm final details with undertaker
arrange as required :

notices in papers
flowers
number of cars
order of mourners
time and starting point of funeral
arrangements at end of funeral
(including any refreshments)

scatter
(in crematorium, churchyard or elsewhere)
bury
(in churchyard , cemetery or elsewhere)
keep in urn
(in crematorium, at home or elsewhere)

after funeral

claim national insurance benefits

pay undertaker

wind up estate of deceased

arrange memorial service if required

answer letters

order memorial stone if required

Why Do We Have Funerals?

The Funeral Gives a Structure to Secure the Reverent Disposal of the Body

This greatly helps to keep the emotions under control and reduces the anxiety of the bereaved.

Customs and outward forms of observance vary greatly from place to place. What they do give is a framework for the bereaved to express their grief and sorrow in a way that is recognized and accepted by the wider community. (This is an important early stage of the grief process.)

The Funeral Makes Real the Death for Society

- It is a public recognition of what has happened.

- The more important the individual is in our society the more people will wish to share in the funeral act itself.

- Where people are well-known families often prefer to have a private funeral which is followed later by a 'memorial' service for all the friends and associates of the deceased.

- With the more important public figures society itself takes over most of the funeral arrangements from the family, for example, The Royal Family; leading politicians.

The Funeral Symbolizes the Change in Status of Those in the Family

- The wife becomes the widow

- the husband becomes the widower

- The child becomes part of a one parent family or an orphan.

Burial or Cremation?

Until recently in Britain the tradition was to bury the dead. However, today, the majority of British people choose cremation (in 1986, 68% chose cremation). The first crematoria were opened in England in the 1880s and there are now 233 crematoria throughout Britain. There are religious groupings who object to cremation. Orthodox Jews and Muslims will not be cremated. Although Roman Catholics have been allowed to be cremated since changes made in Rome in 1963 many of them still prefer to be buried. In other countries, such as India, the tradition has been to cremate the dead.

Burial

Advantages

- Family tradition (family grave)
- Graves can be visited and cared for after the funeral which can give much comfort to the bereaved
- A headstone can be erected
- More personal.

Disadvantages

- More expensive
- Burials can be more distressing for a family
- It can be difficult to get the elderly relatives and friends to the graveside
- Bad weather can make the funeral difficult for those attending
- Family and friends can be distressed years later when the grave becomes overgrown – perhaps because the relatives are elderly or live some distance from the grave.

Cremation

Advantages

- Cheaper
- More pleasant and comfortable surroundings which are not dependent on the weather
- Easier for the family and friends to participate in the service or ceremony
- Easier for the clergy, or whoever is leading the funeral, to be heard and to give an eulogy
- More hygienic
- Saves land
- The ashes can be buried or scattered sometime later.

Disadvantages

- Many people psychologically dislike the committal proceedings when the coffin slides away on rollers or a curtain falls across the front of the coffin. The coffin has disappeared but it is not a true committal to fire. The earth is cast on to the coffin in a burial.
- Many people find later that they would have preferred the chance to visit a grave with a headstone. Plaques on a wall, buried or scattered ashes, or a rose-bush don't seem adequate in themselves.

- The funerals can feel staged or rushed as the time is limited in the cremation chapels – one funeral every half hour is quite normal. This can make it feel more impersonal.

At funerals most officiating Ministers will welcome participation by the family in the service (obviously arranged in advance); for example a favourite reading or poem of the deceased might be read by a member of the family, or maybe they give the eulogy, or play and sing a special piece of music.

'If words do not come naturally to them other means of expression might. Why not encourage people to kiss the coffin, or put a candle by it, or stick a label on it – or anything else to serve as active tokens of their grief, no matter how vulgar or unorthodox?' (Christopher Martin)

A Non-Religious Funeral Service

People who have little or no conventional faith may choose to have a non-religious service. The Humanist Society helps many people arrange funerals and will lead them if requested.

'As far as funerals are concerned, we see the ceremony and the whole process of mourning as of considerable help to family and friends in adjusting to the fact that someone near and dear to them has died. It is healthy to mark this change in circumstances by public ceremony as long as it does not become extravagantly morbid.

We are not in favour of great pomp or displays of wealthy ostentation at funerals. The officiant is there to help the mourners have their own ceremony with words and music to meet their expectations. We are very happy to assist friends or members of the family to conduct the ceremony themselves, although most people don't have the courage to take it on.

As far as attitude to death is concerned, the Humanist accepts that death is the natural end of all of us. We do not believe in any tangible survival beyond death. It is an evident truth that you can't be dead: you can only be alive. Being is synonymous with living.

The Humanist funeral ceremony – or memorial meeting – is therefore not being held to help the departed soul on its way to the beyond. We don't think in terms of souls and we don't believe in the beyond. The ceremony is to help the living.

Humanist funerals need not be terribly sad. If somebody has had a good life and is remembered with affection, there is no great cause for grief. The music can be cheerful and respectful at the same time. The words that are spoken might even cause the mourners to laugh. There is a proper place for a certain degree of ritual and the point of committal is to be marked with due respect.

Finally, the occasion of the funeral allows us – society as a whole – to remind those of us still living that life is a good thing and we had better do something useful with it while we can. Some families ask for a non-religious funeral because it avoids awkward clashes of different religious faiths in a multi-cultural society. A Humanist funeral is not anti-religious: it celebrates the Human values we all share and cherish.'

Extract from a letter by David J. Williams – British Humanist Association ...

3.6

Rituals and Customs

The rituals and customs surrounding a funeral reflect the beliefs of the deceased and the society in which they live.

The major world religions give hope – that death is not seen as final but rather as a stage in the journey of life. People are naturally afraid of death and the way they will die, death itself and about what sort of life, if any, there is after death. The religious beliefs incorporated into the services give the bereaved hope and reassurance and helps them to grieve and to look forward.

Ever since the beginnings of religious beliefs people have paid great attention to the burial of the dead. This was seen to be a preparation of the departed for the next life.

For example, tribal people are frightened of the dead because they believe the power of the dead spirit can bring bad luck. The dead depend on the living to perform the death ceremony correctly so that they may rest peacefully. The living depend on the dead to link the family with the spiritual power which the ancestors possess. To ensure that this happens, the dead are buried with great care.

Examples of Funerals

(1) A Funeral of the Toraja People of Indonesia

For many, the death of a person is an unhappy time not only because they may be losing someone who has been close to them but also because they may be unsure of what comes after death. This uncertainty can often cause fear. Tribal people, too, are frightened of the dead because the power of the dead spirit can bring bad luck. For this reason the dead are buried with great care; a word or action out of place during the ceremony could result in the dead person bringing bad luck. The dead depend on the living to perform the death ceremony correctly so that they may rest peacefully. The living depend on the dead to link the family with the spiritual power which the ancestors possess. When the ceremony is performed correctly both the living and the dead are much happier.

If you were to visit a funeral ceremony of the Toraja people of Indonesia, you might think you have come upon a carnival rather than a funeral. The people who gather for the funeral are in very high spirits and they appear far from sad. Processions of people arrive at the funeral field with buffalo ready to be sacrificed in honour of the dead person. A large pavilion is built from bamboo and everyone awaits the procession which brings the body to the funeral. The dead must be given a good send off. The dead person is about to become an ancestor. The coffin containing the dead person is brought onto the field. In a special ceremony the bamboo pavilion is burnt and buffalo sacrificed. The Torajas believe that the pavilion and the buffalo will go ahead of the dead spirit and be there in the spirit world to await its arrival. The body is taken to the grave site where it is to be buried. A wooden statue is made and placed in a sacred place alongside other statues. The ceremony is complete and the dead person takes its place among the ancestors.

(2) A Hindu Funeral

- The funeral ceremony aims to set free the atman (soul) for another incarnation.

- There are readings from the Holy Sanskrit Books and prayers are said.

- Sacred objects and significant symbols such as rice and gold are placed beside the body.

- The eldest son, or closest male relative, has the duty to ignite the funeral pyre (obviously this is not permitted in British crematoria).

- The eldest son collects the ashes which are scattered in the nearest river.

Cremation is normal but if friends of the deceased are sure that he has obtained Moksha (escape from reincarnation) he need not be cremated. Instead the deceased is buried in a seated position of meditation.

(3) A Jewish Funeral

'Within the Jewish religion burial rather than cremation is usual. Burial takes place as speedily as possible – as official mourning cannot take place until after the burial. Direct family members (i.e. children, brothers and sisters) of the deceased are the only ones who are involved officially. This means that directly after the funeral, where prayers and an eulogy are offered by the Minister, the men of the family say "Kaddish" – mourning prayer. Those in mourning sit on low chairs for seven days. Prayers are said within the home every evening and early morning prayers are said daily in the Synagogue. The family are visited daily and at any time of the day and for evening prayers visitors make a special effort to be with the family.

After seven days mourning are over, under religious law one is instructed to get on with living. For a whole year the men of the family pray (special mourning prayers) every morning and evening. At the end of a year a memorial stone is consecrated at the grave – where a "final service" is held. It is at this time that we are told by our Rabbi that the days of mourning are over.'

(4) A Christian Funeral

Christians choose either burial or cremation. During the funeral service the minister:

- commends the departed to God's care

- proclaims the belief in life after death seen in the resurrection of Jesus Christ

- reminds those attending the funeral of the certainty of their own coming death and judgement before God.

In the past Christians have sought burial rather than cremation because of the belief in the literal resurrection of the dead at the second coming of Jesus.

(5) An Islam Funeral

○ Muslims believe in resurrection and a Day of Judgement. Each personality is judged according to their deeds. The faithful entering paradise which is portrayed as a celestial garden of delights with cool streams and rivers of milk and honey. In contrast the unfaithful are thrown into hell – a fiery place where they are given scalding water to drink and bitter fruit to eat.

○ Muslims are not cremated because of their belief in a physical resurrection of the body.

○ If possible the burial takes place the day after the death has occurred or else at the first opportunity.

○ During the funeral service a prayer is said asking for God's forgiveness for the deceased.

○ The body is buried with the head facing Mecca, the holy city of Islam.

○ No extreme forms of mourning are permitted. Instead the reading of the Qur'an is encouraged. The period of mourning usually lasts from one week to three months.

Care of Hindu – Muslim – Jewish – Buddhist Children

Toddlers are allowed to stay and join in the ceremonies and rituals. This can include chanting prayers for the deceased before, during, and after the funeral, in the period of official mourning. An adult is made responsible for looking after the welfare of very young children.

All families observe the mourning period and children of all ages are trained to refrain from going to any social occasions/parties or merrymaking during this time. The anniversary of the death is usually observed.

Families have a day in the year when prayers are held for the dead, particularly so for close relatives. Regular visits to the cemetery are made – circumstances and distances permitting.

'How will mummy breathe and who will feed her?'

As part of his study of attachment and loss, **John Bowlby** reflects on children who mourn dead parents.

After a parent's death a child or adolescent commonly yearns as persistently as an adult. Children barely four years old are found to yearn for lost parents, to hope and at times to believe that they may yet return, and to feel sad and angry when it becomes clear that they will never do so.

Many children, it is known, insist on retaining an item of clothing or some other possession of a dead parent, and they especially value photographs. So far from forgetting, children—given encouragement and help—have no difficulty in recalling the dead parent. As they get older, they are eager to hear more about him or her in order to confirm and amplify the picture they have retained.

As an initial response to the news of their loss some children weep copiously, others hardly at all. Peter Marris recalls the accounts given by widowed mothers of their children's initial reactions, and he was impressed by their extreme variety. There were children who cried hysterically for weeks; others, especially some of the younger ones, seemed hardly to react. Others again became withdrawn and unsociable.

The reaction of one child, Wendy, was reported in a study by Marion Barnes. Wendy was four when her mother died in an acute exacerbation of a chronic illness. On the day her mother died, her father decided to tell the children what had happened, that the mother would be buried in the ground and that this was the end.

This he did during a ride in the car. Mother had stopped breathing, he told them, she could not feel anything, she was gone for ever and would never come back. She would be buried in the ground, protected in a box and nothing would hurt her—not the rain nor the snow (which was falling) nor the cold. Wendy asked, "How will she breathe and who will feed her?"

Father explained that when a person is dead they don't breathe any more and don't need food. There had already been general agreement that the children were too young to attend the funeral; but father showed them the cemetery, with a nearby water tower, which could be seen from their window.

That evening the children seemed relatively unaffected and for a time were busy playing "London Bridge is falling down." Relatives, who disagreed with father's candour and preferred to tell the children stories of heaven and angels, endeavoured to stifle their own sorrow and to enter gaily into the children's games.

During the days that followed, Wendy invented two games to play with her father, in both of which she would twirl around and then lie down on the floor. In one she would then quickly stand up with the remark, "You thought I was dead, didn't you?" In the other, in which she was supposed to rise when father gave the proper signal (which was her mother's first name), she remained prone. There were also occasions—for example, at meals—when Wendy cheerfully enacted the part of her mother with remarks such as "Daddy, this is such a pretty tie. Where did you get it," or "Anything interesting happen at the office today?"

Yet sorrow was not far away. A week after the mother's death the grandmother of another child became very emotional when talking about it in the car to Wendy's grandmother. Wendy paled and fell over on the seat. Her grandmother comforted her, held her, and they both cried. About the same time, on a visit to relatives, cousins assured Wendy her mother was an angel in heaven and then showed her her mother's picture. Wendy cried hysterically and said her mother was in the ground.

During the third week after her mother's death Wendy gave evidence that she was still hoping for mother's return. Sitting on the floor with her younger sister, Winnie, she chanted, "My mommy is coming back, my mommy is coming back. I know she's coming back." To this Winnie retorted in an adult-like monotone, "Mommy's dead and she's not coming back. She's in the ground by the "tower water." "Tsh, don't say that," retorted Wendy.

Wendy's fear of suffering the same fate as her mother manifested itself when, during the fourth week after mother's death, she insisted that she did not want to grow up and be a big lady and that if she had to grow up, she wished to be a boy and a daddy. She also wanted to know how old one is when one dies and how one gets ill.

On the therapist's encouragement, the father talked with Wendy about her fear that when she grew up she would die as

her mother had. He reassured her that her mother's illness was very rare. A few days later, Wendy inquired of her grandmother, "Grandma, are you strong?" When grandmother assured her she was, Wendy replied, "I'm only a baby." This provided grandmother with further opportunity to discuss Wendy's fear of the danger of growing up.

Bereaved children's fear that they may also die is found often to be a result of the fact that they are unclear about the causes of death. They suppose that whatever caused the parent's death might well cause their own too. Or they think that, because the parent died as a young man or woman, the same fate is likely to be theirs, also.

There are, it is true, many cases on record where a child is clearly identifying with a dead parent. Wendy at times treated her father in the same way as her mother had treated him, with remarks like her "Anything interesting happen at the office today?" Other children play at being a teacher, or take great pains over painting, evidently influenced by the fact that the dead father was a teacher or the dead mother a painter. But these examples do little more than show that a child whose parent is dead is no less disposed to emulate him or her than before the death.

As in the case of adults, some bereaved children have on occasion vivid images of their dead parent—linked, clearly, with

hopes and expectations of their return. Gerald Kliman, for example, reports the case of a six year old girl who, with her sister two years older, had witnessed her mother's sudden death from an intracranial haemorrhage. Before getting up in the morning this child frequently had the experience of her mother sitting on her bed talking quietly to her, much as she had when she was alive. Other episodes described in the literature—usually given as examples of children denying the reality of death—may also be explicable in terms of a child having had such an experience. Erna Furman, for example, describes how Bess, aged three and a half, who was thought to have been "well aware of the finality of her mother's death," announced one evening to her father, "Mummy called and said she'd have dinner with us," evidently believing it to be true.

Thus the evidence so far available suggests strongly that when conditions are favourable, the mourning of children—no less than of adults—is commonly characterised by persisting memories and images of the dead person and by repeated recurrences of yearning and sadness, especially at family reunions and anniversaries, or when a current relationship seems to be going wrong.

This conclusion is of great practical

Children are held beside their mother's body at a funeral in Czechoslovakia

importance, especially when a bereaved child is expected to make a new relationship. So far from its being a prerequisite for the success of the new relationship that the memory of the earlier one should fade, the evidence is that the more distinct the two relationships can be kept the better the new one is likely to prosper.

Anxiety and anger

Other features of childhood mourning which have great practical implications are the anxiety and anger which a bereavement habitually brings.

As regards anxiety, it is hardly surprising that children who have suffered one major loss should fear lest they suffer another. This will make them especially sensitive to any separation from whoever may be mothering them and also to any event or remark that seems to them to point to another loss. As a result they are likely often to be anxious and clinging in situations that appear to an adult to be innocuous, and more prone to seek comfort by resorting to some old familiar toy or blanket than might be expected at their age.

Similar considerations apply to anger, for there can be no doubt that some young children who lose a parent are made extremely angry by it. An example from English literature is of Richard Steele, of *Spectator* fame, who lost his father when he was four and who recalled how he had beaten on the coffin in a blind rage. In similar vein a student teacher describes how she reacted at the age of five when told that her father had been killed in the war. "I shouted at God all night. I just couldn't believe that he had let them kill my father. I loathed him for it."

How prone children are spontaneously to blame themselves for a loss is difficult to know. What, however, is certain is that a child makes a ready scapegoat and it is very easy for a distraught widow or widower to lay the blame on the child. In some cases, perhaps, a parent does this only once, in a sudden brief outburst; in other cases it may be done in a far more systematic and persistent way. In either case it is likely that the child so blamed will take the matter to heart, and therefore be prone to self-reproach and depression. Such influences seem likely to be responsible for a large majority of cases in which a bereaved child develops a morbid sense of guilt.

Nevertheless, there are certain circumstances surrounding a parent's death which can lead rather easily to a child reaching the conclusion that he is himself to blame, at least in part. Examples are when a child who has been suffering from an infectious illness has infected his parent; or when a child has been in a predicament and his parent, attempting rescue, has lost his life. In such cases only open discussion between the child and his surviving parent (or an appropriate substitute) will enable him or her to see the event and his share in it in a proper perspective.

If we are right that young children in their fourth and fifth years mourn in ways very similar to adults, we would confidently

Josef Koudelka/John Hillelson Agency

expect that older children and adolescents would do so too. Yet there is reason to believe that there are also true differences between the mourning of children and the mourning of adults.

Many differences arise from the fact that a child is even less his own master than a grownup is. For example, whereas an adult is likely either to be present at the time of a death or else to be given prompt and detailed information about it, in most cases a child is entirely dependent for his information on the decision of his surviving relatives: and he is in no position to institute inquiries as an adult would, should he be kept in the dark.

In a similar way, a child is at even greater disadvantage than an adult is if his relatives or other companions prove unsympathetic to his yearning, his sorrow and his anxiety. For, whereas an adult can, if he wishes, seek further for understanding and comfort if his first exchanges prove unhelpful, a child is rarely in a position to do so.

Other problems arise from a child having even less knowledge and understanding of issues of life and death than has an adult. So children are more apt to make false inferences from the information they receive, and to misunderstand the significance of events they observe and remarks they overhear. Figures of speech, in par-

young child has in recalling past events.

Few people will grieve continuously. Even an adult whose mourning is progressing healthily forgets his grief briefly when some more immediate interest catches hold of him. For a child, such occasions are likely to be more frequent than for an adult, and the periods during which he is consciously occupied with his loss will be correspondingly more transient. As a result his moods are more changeable and more easily misunderstood. Furthermore, because of these same characteristics, a young child is readily distracted, at least for the moment. This makes it easy for those caring for him to deceive themselves that he is not missing his parents.

It is inevitable that when one parent dies, the survivor's treatment of the children should change. Not only is the survivor likely to be in a distressed and emotional state, but he or she now has sole responsibility for the children instead of sharing it. The surviving parent now has to fill two roles, which in most families have been clearly differentiated.

The death of a child's parent is always untimely and often sudden. Not only is the parent likely to be young or in early middle age, but the cause is much more likely to be an accident or suicide than in later life. Sudden illness also is not uncommon. Thus for all the survivors, whether of the child's,

widows seen by Iva Glick and colleagues.

An opposite kind of reaction, which is also common, is for a widowed mother to seek comfort for herself from the children. In the study by Kliman no fewer than seven of the 18 children he studied "began an unprecedented custom of frequently sharing a bed with the surviving parent. This usually began quickly after the death and tended to persist." It is also easy for a lonely widow to burden an older child or adolescent with confidences and responsibilities which it is not easy for him to bear. In other cases she may require a child, usually a younger one, to become a replica either of his dead father or else, if an older child has died, of the dead child. Constant anxiety about the children's health and visits to the doctor, as much to obtain his support as for the children's treatment, occur commonly.

Not only is a widowed mother liable to be anxious about the children's health but she is likely also to worry about her own, with special reference to what would happen to the children were she to get ill or die too. Sometimes, as Glick reports, a mother will express such anxieties aloud and within earshot of the children. In the light of these findings it is not difficult to see why some bereaved children are apprehensive, refuse to attend school and become diagnosed as "school phobic."

Our knowledge of changes in the behaviour of widowed fathers towards their bereaved children is extremely scanty. No doubt those of them who care for the children mainly themselves are prone to changes in behaviour similar to those of widows. Especially when the children are female and/or adolescent, widowed fathers are apt to make excessive demands on them for company and comfort.

Should the children be young, however, their care is likely to be principally in other hands, in which case a widowed father may see much less of them than formerly. He may well be unaware of how they feel, or what their problems are.

A substantial proportion of the special difficulties which children experience after the loss of a parent are a direct result of the effect that the loss has had on the surviving parent's behaviour towards them. Nevertheless there are, fortunately, many other surviving parents who, despite their burdens, are able to maintain relationships with their children intact. They help them mourn the dead parent in such a way that they come through undamaged.

That others fail, however, can hardly surprise us. Even in small ways, it can be hard. One study reports on a little girl, of four, who visited her father's grave with her mother some six months after his death:

"She was in a conflict about going. They both wanted to go and also cried bitterly about doing so. After placing flowers on the grave, she began asking a succession of questions that mother found painful to answer: 'Are there snakes in the ground? Has the box come apart?' Mother struggled to help her to understand and express her feelings, but sometimes found the burden too great."

Mourning their mother: a Victorian view

ticular, are apt to mislead children. As a result, it is necessary for the adults caring for a bereaved child to give him even more opportunity to discuss what has happened, and its far-reaching implications, than it is with an adult.

In the great majority of cases in which children are described as having failed totally to respond to news of a parent's death, it seems more than likely that both the information given, and the opportunity to discuss its significance, were so inadequate that the child had failed to grasp the nature of what had happened.

Yet not all of the differences between childhood and adult mourning are due to circumstances. Some stem from a child's tendency to live more in the present than does an adult, and the relative difficulty a

the parent's or the grandparent's generation, the death is likely to come as a shock, and to shatter every plan and every hope of the future. As a result, just when a child needs most the patience and understanding of the adults around him, those adults are likely to be least fit to give it him.

A widow caring for her children is likely to be both sad and anxious. Preoccupied with her sorrows and the practical problems confronting her, it is far from easy for her to give the children as much time as she gave them formerly and all too easy for her to become impatient and angry when they claim attention and become whiny when they do not get it. A marked tendency to feel angry with their children was reported by about one in five of the

I CAN'T WRITE TO DADDY

How can you help a child whose mother or father has died?
Rosemary Wells – teacher, mother, widow – offers some suggestions.

Two seven-year-olds I teach at the local primary school were chatting away beside me in class one day.

"I'm writing a letter to my daddy. He lives in France."

"You're lucky. I can't write to *my* daddy."

"Why? Where does he live?"

"In heaven."

My heart went out to the little girls – Kate, whose parents had recently divorced, and Lucy, whose father had died of leukaemia. Both felt a sense of loss, both longed for their parents to be together again, but Lucy belongs to a group of youngsters whose longing can never, ever be satisfied – not at weekends, not in the holidays, not in her wildest hopes.

There is a tendency in the social services and in society in general to lump bereaved children and the children of divorced couples together as members of "one-parent families" but, without minimising the troubles faced by children whose parents have split up, it should be recognised that bereaved children have special problems that must be tackled if these children are not to suffer unduly, perhaps even into adulthood.

Several large-scale population studies link adult psychiatric disorder with the death of a parent in childhood. Dr Dora Black, a consultant child psychiatrist at Edgware General Hospital in Middlesex, confirms that "there is a higher incidence of depressive illness in adults who lose a parent before the age of 10 than in those whose parents live longer. Research suggests that the risk of depressive illness can be significantly lowered if the child is encouraged to express grief at the time of loss."

Emotional disturbances

Far from giving vent to her feelings, however, a bereaved child often bottles them up. She may seem unconcerned, even callous, about her loss. At the same time, she may start to misbehave at school and fall behind in class – sometimes for several terms. It's important to understand fully why this is

happening and that the child is probably suffering not just from grief but also from shock and a refusal to accept the parent's death. In extreme cases the child may need to be referred to a child guidance clinic for help, but most children respond to an understanding friend, relative or teacher.

After his mother died, 6-year-old William had appeared dry-eyed for weeks at the school where I teach. But he was quiet and withdrawn – not at all his usual self. His own teachers avoided talking about his mother for fear of upsetting him and embarrassing themselves. One playtime he took my hand and I sensed that he longed to talk about his mother but just didn't know where to start. I asked him where he went on holiday last summer and he began to tell me. "Did Mummy go swimming?" I asked, and he looked up at me in sudden excitement. "Yes! She had a smashing costume . . . it was red and had only one strap around the neck . . . and we tried surfing . . . and she said . . ." He was off – all the feelings he had been keeping to himself came tumbling out. Every day for weeks William talked to me about his beautiful young mother, and eventually he was able to settle down once more into his school routine.

It is quite normal for a bereaved child to feel anger towards the surviving parent, though of course this can be very distressing for the family. "Why are you still here?" "What did you do to Mummy/Daddy?" "Why did you let him/her die?" – these are all questions a child might blurt out under stress. The child's anger may even be directed at the dead parent for abandoning her and she may suffer from feelings of guilt – was it her fault that her parent died? This was the case with Sarah, who blamed herself for her father's death. "Dad said he'd work hard to make enough money to buy me a bike for Christmas. Then I heard Aunty say Dad died of overwork!" Guilt and anger are common reactions in anyone who has suffered a

bereavement, but a child needs an adult's help to express and overcome these feelings.

Obsession with death

Almost inevitably, at some stage, most bereaved children become obsessed with accidents, illness and death. They may be victims of night-time terrors – the fear that the surviving parent or a sibling might die or the even greater horror of their own death. The sight of a coffin, an ambulance or even a bonfire, could give rise to panic.

In these circumstances the child must be reassured that there is no reason why any other close relative should die suddenly.

No matter how she reacts, there comes a point when she will want some down-to-earth explanation of death. Before the age of 4, a child cannot understand that death is final. She only knows that when her parents go out, they come back again. "Daddy has gone to heaven" has no more significance for her than "Daddy has gone to London", and she will wait for him to return as usual. When he does not, the child might think he has run away or is lost. This needs gentle, honest discussion. Children have very literal minds and will take euphemistic explanations at face value. It's best not to describe death as "a long sleep", for instance, as they might then fear bedtime. Clinical evidence shows

that some children do suffer sleep disturbances when death is discussed in these terms. Even casual remarks can cause trouble. Wendy, aged 11, suddenly started losing her temper with Susie, her little sister. Susie was a lively, mischievous child and their mother used to tell her off, sometimes using the expression "you'll be the death of me". Wendy ended up believing that her sister really would cause their mother's death, and it took very careful probing and listening on the part of an understanding doctor to reassure her.

The role of religion

Religious beliefs may help a child look on death with less fear, but God and "life after death" should only be brought in if religion is already a part of family life. If it is not, the child is likely to be confused by such strange, unfamiliar stories. Better then to explain that death is the end of life and that the parent had an illness which the doctors could not cure.

For a small child from a family where religion is important, an image of heaven in the sky is comforting. One young child was told that her Mummy had gone to heaven "to help God look after Grandpa" which she accepted happily, though of course another child could blame a God who would take

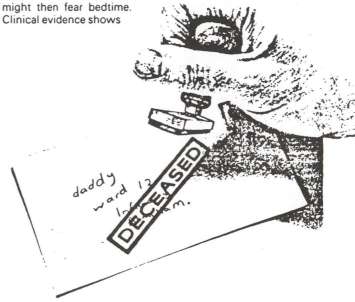

her mother away for such a purpose. It's important to get to the bottom of the child's own view of the event and to put right misconceptions.

An adolescent child may already have suffered the loss of a relative or friend, but nevertheless she will need help in coming to terms with the death of a parent. A teenager is old enough to worry about practical matters: whether there will be enough money for the family to live on, whether they will have to move house and whether she will be expected to look after the surviving

parent for the rest of her own life. She will also want desperately to comfort that parent, but may well be at a loss as how to go about it. It's almost impossible for the mother/father to instil confidence into a bewildered child while trying to face his or her own grief and cope with other problems. In Dr Black's words, "Bereaved children find themselves alone with a tearful, withdrawn parent whom they cannot contact or comfort and who no longer appears to meet their needs. The conspiracy of silence can be bewildering."

A friend in need

It may need the help of someone outside the immediate family to sit down with the child and reassure her about practicalities and explain that the remaining parent *will* gradually recover and return to normal. Close friends can play a useful role in encouraging all members of the family to express their sadness and to help them communicate with each other. They can try to ensure that family life continues as normally as possible by bringing a little cheer and fresh air

into the household. The important thing to remember, for parent, relative or friend, is that children need to talk about death, to ask questions and express all their feelings and emotions. A frank discussion will enable the family to share their grief, to dispel anxiety and anger and to keep alive the happy memories. It may be that a bereavement, despite the immediate misery it causes, will bring a family closer together. □

Further information

Current research into the effects of bereavement on children is sponsored by CRUSE

insert news p.205 book

Heavenly bodies

Thousands of people who have returned from the 'dead' describe passing into a timeless zone of peace and natural beauty. Is it really possible their soul entered another world, a new spiritual dimension? Chris Stonor investigates a fascinating phenomenon

'Dying has been the happiest experience of my life,' explained a very much alive Pat Burt. 'It has to be the best thing that's ever happened to me.' Pat, an ex-stewardess married to an airline captain, is adept at dying. She has 'died' four times, each time during a medical operation, but has then been resuscitated by doctors.

'The second time I died I fought hard not to come back. I experienced leaving my physical body and then travelling through a tunnel. I felt completely relaxed and unafraid. At the end of the tunnel was a bright light. As I merged with this light I had overwhelming feelings of peace and love—feelings so beautiful they were indescribable. I just wanted to stay there forever. Then I realised something was turning me around against my will and I sensed myself re-enter my physical body.

'When I came round in the hospital bed I cried and cried. I told the doctors, "I don't want to be back here again." I was deeply upset and very depressed for several days.'

It is easy to dismiss Pat as a case for the white coat brigade, but she is just one of tens of thousands of people throughout the world who have had what is now called a 'near death experience' (NDE). Forty per cent of people who clinically 'die' and later come back to life describe a continuation of consciousness after death and of entering a non-physical world.

These people include doctors, psychiatrists and well known personalities (such as Stephanie Beacham and Michael Bentine) whose experiences of what they feel to be an after-life often dramatically change their views on death—and life. As Pat said, 'I'm not frightened of dying any more. Death is simply a transition from one dimension to another, in my view.'

Death is still very much a taboo subject in our society. The prospect of our death is by far the biggest challenge we have to face up to in our lives, but as a society, we are emotionally unprepared for this eventuality. Why? When turning to orthodox science for consolation we are greeted with the belief that our consciousness and mind are one. When you die that's your lot. Death is seen as the ultimate symbol of failure and defeat, to be evaded and denied. Life must be prolonged where possible. As for Western religions and their belief in heaven and hell, we are caught up in a crossfire of views—where ignorance breeds fear and fear feeds ignorance.

The facts of death were the last thing on the mind of Mark Gagne, now twenty-three, when he went into hospital for a routine operation to remove his tonsils at the age of thirteen.

After being given a general anaesthetic, instead of waking up in the hospital bed after a successful operation, his first conscious awareness was of floating near the ceiling, above the operating table, watching the doctors at work.

'I wondered who the person was on the table,' Mark said, 'and then realised it was me. I could see and hear everything going on in the room, even the clock that said 8.05 am. Suddenly, I saw the anaesthetist tapping the dial and heard him say, "I'm losing him, I'm losing him." '

Mark next saw a nurse turn on the heart machine, a doctor massage his chest and then his body go rigid, and jump after

'Around forty per cent of people who clinically "die" and later come back to life describe a continuation of consciousness after death and of entering a non-physical world'

Heavenly bodies

being given an electric shock. Yet all the while, as Mark put it, 'I felt unafraid, just completely relaxed and at peace.' He next glanced at the clock at 8.36 am, when he saw the doctor pull the sheet over his physical head and phone through to say, 'Send Gagne's file to the office—I'm afraid I've lost him. You had better notify his family.'

'The next thing I remember,' Mark said, 'was going through a tunnel at great speed and seeing a light at the end. As I moved into this light I felt an incredible feeling of love and then became aware of my aunt, who had died some months before, asking me if I wanted to come with her. I then judged my life—no one else judged me—with complete honesty. I looked at the good things I had done and the bad. I decided that I hadn't learned enough from my life. I decided to come back.'

It was a nurse who heard Mark gasp. She pulled the sheet back and saw his eyelids flickering. Mark later told the doctors of his experience—the descriptions, times and events were all corroborated. One nurse exclaimed, 'How scary.'

From Jesus Christ's resurrection to the East's belief in reincarnation and Karma, religion has always promised eternal life—another conscious 'body' that survives physical death. In one

'I tried to grab the doctors and stop them. I felt happy where I was—but nothing happened. I grabbed one doctor but my hand just went through him'
Vietnam veteran

American study (by Michael Sabom) ninety-three per cent of near death experiencers perceived this 'soul' or separated self to be an invisible, non-physical entity.

Though orthodox science generally scoffs at the very idea of an NDE, it is, paradoxically, the increasing use of sophisticated resuscitation techniques that has led to a higher incidence of reports than ever before.

Yet, it is only now that the experiencers are coming out of the closet. As Margot Grey, a psychologist and author of the bestselling book *Return From Death*, explained, 'People before were afraid of being ridiculed or even being branded mentally unstable. Now there is a feeling that it is getting safer to talk. This is mainly due to the pioneering efforts of doctors like Elisabeth Kübler-Ross and Raymond Moody (author of *Life After Life*), who have questioned the orthodox viewpoint on death; done extensive research into the phenomenon; come up with new findings and had the courage to put their reputations on the line.'

These international findings are unanimous. It doesn't matter what creed, culture or background one originates from. For the majority, the next dimension is a heaven of a place to be in. The psychologist Carl Jung wrote (in *Memories, Dreams and Reflections*, first published in Great Britain in 1963) of the next world, after his own NDE in 1944. 'Once inside, you taste of such completeness,

peace and fulfilment that you don't want to return.'

But before you begin to imagine that the next world is all *that* attractive, be warned. Suicides can have a bad time. As one man explained, who experienced moving into a grey wilderness during a failed attempt: 'I realised I had broken the rules. Life is precious and not to be taken. I would only have had to face the same problems all over again.'

Also, it has to be said that some people experience a negative type of NDE. Fear, panic and a sense of evil are sometimes felt, with a few experiencing a hell-like environment.

Margot Grey told me, 'It is in no way a punishment. I feel these people choose to have this experience as it alerts them to some aspect of their life that needs changing.'

Not surprisingly, many people change after their NDE. For Mark Gagne his transformation was dramatic. From being a school bully, general trouble-maker and lazy pupil, overnight he became a 'do-gooder and swot'. 'My headmaster was so worried about me that I was sent to see a psychiatrist,' laughed Mark. 'Yet for the first time my life made sense. Things just fitted into place.'

He became very perceptive and was known as 'the little wise man'. He later attended a church that follows no set religion. 'Whether you are a Christian, Muslim or Buddhist, you are all part of the same God. Religion just creates barriers between people.'

Spiritual values become increasingly important in some experiencers' lives. They enjoy

and appreciate life more; become more understanding and sympathetic; have more self-respect. Some discover psychic or healing abilities.

Most orthodox doctors pass this evidence off as exceptional or unreliable, while others, like Dr Ian Judson of the Royal Marsden Hospital in London, are less defensive. 'Some cases are very hard to explain,' he told me. 'I feel we should keep an open mind.' But, generally, doctors tell us we only have a body. They say the NDE is an hallucination or delusion, lack of oxygen to the brain, temporal lobe seizure, anaesthesia or just plain fabrication.

The simple truth is that orthodox medicine has done very little research into the NDE. Why? David Lorimer, author of the book *Survival* and Vice-chairman of the British affiliation of the International Association of Near Death Studies (IANDS), remarked, 'The medical profession is afraid to. They know the findings will seriously challenge their beliefs. Changes in brain chemistry are certainly not enough to explain away the complexities of an NDE.' Adding, with a deft jab, 'Also their promotional prospects can be seriously hampered if they are known to be dabbling in psychic research.'

One sceptic, cardiologist Michael Sabom, changed his opinion after conducting his own scientific study. In his book *Recollections of Death*, he concludes that the medical explanations so far proposed for NDEs are insufficient to account for them as a whole.

The spiritual corner packs a harder punch when it comes to

Heavenly bodies

evidence. There are quite a few authenticated cases of blind people who regain their sight on leaving the physical body. They see people in the earthly sphere entering and moving around the room, note the colour of their hair. Once back in their body and blind again, their extensive and detailed descriptions are all corroborated. There are also cases of people meeting a friend or relative whom they didn't know had died.

There are five distinct NDE stages that most soul travellers report: feeling peaceful and calm; leaving the physical body; going through a tunnel; merging into light—reviewing and judging their life; meeting dead relatives and friends—being told they must go back. In this non-physical dimension there is no sense of time. Communication is telepathic. The senses are magnified a hundred-fold. Movement is by a sort of thought projection—think of a place and you're there in seconds. Tremendous insights and knowledge are gained in moments. A feeling of love for fellow man pervades. Awareness of a higher spiritual self is strongly felt.

Only about a third of so-called soul travellers experience this last phase on temporarily departing the body: 'I found myself in a beautiful country lane. I was strolling down the lane slowly and I felt I had all the time in the world. I could hear the skylarks singing and I thought, "Oh, how lovely".'

'I saw a beautiful landscape—the flowers, trees, the colours were indescribable, not at all like the colours you see here. The peace and joy were overpowering. Somewhere I heard the most wonderful music and there was an organ playing. I felt embraced by such love, it's beyond description.'

'In this place I saw people that I knew had died. There were no words spoken, but it was as if I knew what they were thinking and at the same time I knew *they* knew what I was thinking. I saw my parents approaching me; they appeared as I remembered them. They seemed not at all surprised to see me . . . I communicated with them by some form of telepathy.'

A thirty-three-year-old Vietnam veteran reports that, after a mine explosion in which both his legs and one arm were lost, he followed his body from the battlefield to a helicopter which then took it to a nearby field hospital. He remained with his body all the time. He then watched his own operation. 'I tried to grab the doctors and stop them. I felt happy where I was—but nothing happened. I grabbed one doctor but my hands just went straight through him.'

One aspect of the final phase is the 'being of light' which some claim they encounter. Some see this light as Christ, others as Buddha. 'Their interpretation of it is coloured by their own cultural background,' says Margot Grey. 'You see what you believe in.'

A fifty-five-year-old Protestant Florida woman explained: 'Just as clear and plain the Lord came and stood and held his hands out for me . . . He stood there and looked down and it was all bright then . . . He was tall with his hands stretched out and he had all white on, like he had a white robe on . . . [His face] was more beautiful than anything you've ever seen . . . His skin was almost glowing and it was absolutely flawless . . . He just looked down at me and smiled.'

In an American census, eighty per cent of experiencers regretted 'not having loved more' at the time of their clinical death and ten per cent realised they had squandered their talents and 'become aware of their enormous potential'.

One woman said, 'My whole life was just going in front of me as I "died" like a very fast computer and I kept thinking about all the different things I had done or perhaps I hadn't done.'

Numerous celebrities have claimed to have had an NDE. Actress Stephanie Beacham of *The Colbys* experienced 'dying' after a routine operation had gone wrong. 'I felt that I was being led away by cloaked figures. But suddenly I saw a close-up of one of the eyes of my daughter Chloe. That told me I wasn't to go. Then everything was like a film being wound backwards, and I became conscious enough to press the emergency button and nurses came running.'

Has the experience changed her? 'It has affected me in all sorts of ways. And I am forced to conclude that there is life after death, and that I will be going somewhere else.'

Comedian Michael Bentine has 'died' three times. On one occasion he realised that he'd entered another dimension: 'Looking down, I saw that I was attached to a silver chord that stretched downwards for miles. It was quite an amazing experience—beyond all fear or terror. Next I remember seeing a light. Then I experienced sitting in what I took to be a reception room and I remember distinctly waiting for someone, a guide perhaps. Next thing I knew was being drawn back into my body and waking up to see what I took to be an angel. It turned out to be a nurse.'

Whatever your views are, near death experiencers are in no doubt. As Pat Burt said, 'I've actually been there and it's a beautiful place.' And, as an almost smug yet sincere afterthought, 'Please never be frightened of dying. It's going to be the nicest thing that's ever happened to you.' □

> 'I was going through a tunnel at great speed and seeing a light at the end. As I moved into this light I felt an incredible feeling of love, and then became aware of my aunt who had died some months before' Mark Gagne

For further information:
IANDS (UK), PO Box 193, London SW1.
Cases taken from:
Life After Life *by Dr Raymond Moody (Bantam)*
Recollections of Death *by Dr Michael Sabom (Corgi)*
Return from Death *by Margot Grey (Arkana)*
Reflections on Life after Life *by Dr Raymond Moody (Bantam).*

THIS ARTICLE IS REPRINTED FROM Azarnoff, Pat, Ed.
Medically-Oriented Play for Children in Health Care: The Issues
Santa Monica, California (PO Box 1880): Pediatric Projects Inc., 1986.

Value of Hospitalized Children's Artwork

Susan Harvey, Cert.Ed., Dip.N.F.F.

The German poet and historian, Friedrich von Schiller (1759-1805) said, "Children paint what they experience and experience what they paint." He was observant of children's behaviour and showed insight into their pressing need to play. He expressed the idea that the origin of all art was to be found in play. Many people would still agree with him that the end products of play are to be found in all arts, sciences and social services.

Play is an expression of feelings and skills.

In early childhood, painting, daubing, scrubbing, drawing, cutting up scraps of various materials, sticking bits and pieces together are all aspects of play and are expressions of feelings and skills. These activities are part of everyday life and reflect the normal stages of children's development.

The growth of artistic expression

Most infants and young children are exuberant with their first artistic expressions. This universal fact can be seen in remote and isolated communities around the world as well as in highly populated and industrialized countries.

The limitations imposed on children probably come first from their attendant adults. Babies make their first marks with any material within their grasp. It can be dribble, baby food, jam, water, urine or faeces. They begin to draw with fingers, sticks, stones and other objects on a wide variety of surfaces, such as sand, dust, mud, rocks, walls, furniture and even paper. They seek out a smooth surface and set to work on it.

Recently I watched a group of seven Portugese children absorbed in making elaborate drawings with long bamboo sticks on a smooth sandy beach. The drawings covered several square metres of sand until the tide washed them away. Perhaps children's imaginations are limited by expecting them to use manufactured materials such as chalks, pencils, brushes, pens and sheets of rectangular paper, when we provide for their creative adventures.

A universal sequence of development in children's art [1] begins with scribbling at a few-months-old to five-years-old, depending on the encouragement received at home or the circumstances of living. When children make a circle or oval shape and say mum, mama, maman, madre, or mutter, mother has been "caught" and portrayed in a confined space and symbolism has begun.

Usually mum is first given two eyes, among the first features that babies recognize. Since arms and hands play an important part in the care of infants, toddlers and pre-school children, these parts are next depicted. Legs and bodies are added at random to the figure as the drawings become more sophisticated.

An example of the eagerness of people to interpret children's work happened in the nursery school where I once worked. A student saw three-and-a-half-year-old Charley sloshing away with black paint. She immediately said, "He must be depressed, using black all the time." Nothing was further from the truth. I had known Charley and his family for several years. He was a lively and robust child who loved trying out new things and experimenting. This was the first time he had a chance to use black paint and was thoroughly enjoying a new experience.

Pictures give clues about what children think that can be used for discussion. They may lead us to help with problems which children cannot express in words. For example, Joe, nearly three-years-old, and in nursery school, had alopecia. He had lost all the hair on his head, including eyebrows and eyelashes, as a result of a fall down a steep flight of stairs when he was eighteen-months-old. He had received medical treatment to no avail. One day he drew the typical oval shape and said, "My mum." He gave her two eyes, then fastidiously drew line by line each hair of her head, eyebrows and eyelashes. It was unusual for so young a child to emphasize in such detail the hairy features of the face. Having done the drawing, Joe was able to talk about his own hairless state without any prompting.

Young children paint their problems, where adults might use words. Both would feel better for having unloaded their pent-up feelings. Since this happens in everyday life, small wonder that drawings have special significance and value for children under stress of illness, pain and separation in hospital.

In another example, Patrick, age seven, was lying in bed, his leg in plaster, injured from a car accident. Two days after admission he was refusing to eat, talk or accept companionship and was becoming increasingly withdrawn. He did agree to draw, making an enormous car and several smaller ones. "That's interesting," I said. "I wonder why one is so much larger than the others." Children often express important features in life by enlarging them in pictures. "Because it knocked me down," he said. "That's the one that knocked me over."

It did not take long for the whole story to pour out. Patrick had gone out to fetch the newspaper, with a friend who had urged him to run across the road without looking carefully to see whether cars were coming. Patrick felt very guilty and blamed himself severely for all that had happened. Once we discussed the accident he became more lively, cooperative and enjoyed his food. The painting and discussion had a confessional or cathartic effect.

Peter, five-years-old [2] was admitted to hospital with vomiting and abdominal pain. The physical illness was rapidly cured but there remained an ailing and miserable child. He drew a typical picture, showing a mother holding the minute figure of an infant at arm's length. He cried as he drew. Between his sobs he said, "When my mum came out of the hospital, she came home with a screaming baby and I don't want one of those." When I explained to him that little boys could not have babies, he was immensely relieved and returned to normal life style.

Peter's drawing of mother and infant.

Julie, six-years-old, had been in a small local hospital frequently. When she was admitted to a large hospital she showed many symptoms of panic. She clung to the hospital play specialist, who was a large woman. They sat together and Julie said, as she worked away with a brush and paint, "I'll do a picture of you. A small person like me needs a large person like you in a place like this. I might get lost." Her fear was not overtly of illness but of a menacing and incompatible building.

Julie's drawing of the hospital play specialist.

In an inner-city hospital where many patients brought their social problems with them as well as their illnesses, Fred, age seven, was a destructive and aggressive boy. He broke two windows in the ward, kicked a nurse and threw food on the floor. Two student nurses were off duty "sick" because they could not cope with him.

I sat beside Fred in the playroom, saying nothing, but observing. He drew a miserable picture of a black beast on a dirty green patch of ground and said, "You're a bitch. It's shit in here." After a pause, he said anxiously, "I'm a good boy, I'm a good boy."

I reply, "I know you're a good boy and it's horrible to be in hospital. We're trying to make you better." He held out his hand and asked me to go with him when he had an X-ray.

This was the first step towards a positive and friendly relationship with an anxious and aggressive child, coping the only way he could with enormous personal and social problems. The painting had paved the way to a better understanding and to improved behaviour.

Fred's drawing of an animal.

Children's art in clinics

Two patients attending a leukaemia clinic drew pictures about their illnesses. A six-year-old girl in remission had been admitted frequently to hospital and was well-known by the staff. She said, "I'm going to draw my guinea pig," her favourite pet. She drew the animal, covered it with spots and said, "I felt really ill when I had chicken pox and was covered with spots like this. Now I feel better." She may have been transposing her own feelings upon her pet animal.

Janet, eight-years-old, drew a picture of her friend, Robby, whom she had met in hospital. As she painted, she said, "He's in the cemetery, but I'm still here."

These drawings were discussed at case conferences with the consultant and clinical psychologist to share the insights obtained into the children's ideas and feelings about their conditions. There are opportunities to help children when we have watched, listened and taken our cues from what they have said or done while they painted or played. The fact of playing out or externalizing fears, is, in itself, a therapeutic act. It may easily lead to exposing problems which can be discussed, explained and frequently resolved. Drawing and painting bring hidden problems to the surface where words fail.

Children's art used for diagnosis

Children's pictures can be used for diagnostic and teaching purposes. For example, three pictures painted by a three-year-old Nigerian child over a period of six months were used in a medical school to demonstrate to medical students and nurses that essential evidence and information, not always to be found by physical examination and tests, can be found in patients' play activities.

Zola, two-and-a-half-years, came from a single-parent home, lacked adequate parental care and was infrequently visited in hospital. She had sickle cell anaemia, right-sided hemiparesis and left-sided hemianopia. Her poor language development and home conditions added to the stress of hospitalization. She received regular physiotherapy but was resistant to developmental tests and the clinical psychologist.

Zola at the
easel.

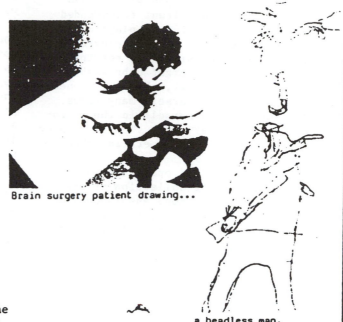

Brain surgery patient drawing...

a headless man.

Zola enjoyed painting on a low easel in the
playroom. Sometimes she could not control
the brush but usually she managed successfully to produce stripes and blotches of
brilliant colour. Initially her painting
only covered one-third of the paper, demon-
strating the limitations of her vision.
Over several months the area covered showed
improving vision; eventually she could
cover the entire page. Painting showed the
progress she was making, while other forms
of testing had not.

A boy, eight years of age, was admitted for
brain surgery. (2) The first picture shows
him sitting on the floor drawing with felt
pen a portrait of a headless man. The
second is a "close-up view" of the drawing.
There is the outline figure of the man, a
large scimitar or knife hanging over the
headless figure. The head is on the floor.
Although the drawing was done primarily
with a black pen, there are two blotches of
red, one around the neck area where the
head has been severed and one on the neck
of the head rolling on the floor.

Although the child did not indicate panic,
the drawing was horrific. The play
specialist and senior nurse who cared for
Tom during a previous surgery as well as
this one, conferred over the drawing.
Although the nurse had thought she had carefully prepared Tom for the ordeal of surgery, she decided, upon seeing the drawing,
that further discussion would be needed.

Children's art from various cultures

Often, people who work in hospital do not
understand other customs, languages, or
communication styles. It is then that
drawings can be used to build friendship
and trust.

Masha was admitted to Moorfields Eye Hospital from an Arab country. Her brother was
her interpreter at times, as Masha had no
sight, spoke no English and had never left
her country before. After her surgery she
lay very still and quiet in a "postured"
position for two days.

The play specialist, Mary Digby, wanted to
make contact with Masha, who remained lying
on her abdomen with one eye beyond recovery
and the other eye padded and recovering.
On the fourth day after surgery, she was
given a telephone to play with. She gradually began to feel it, poking the dial,
whispering to herself. Suddenly she made a
phone noise, "burr, burr, burr," several
times. Then she picked up the receiver and
burst into conversation. Kneeling on her
bed, smiling and laughing she touched various parts of her face and hands. After a
few minutes, she contentedly lay back in
the "postured" position and rested.

Later, she picked up the telephone again and, full of smiles, began another animated conversation. When the pad was removed from her eye, the consultant recommended that Masha spend time in the playroom each morning and afternoon. In the playroom, it was obvious that her sight was returning. She peered at a lightweight unbreakable mirror, gazed at herself, shut and opened her eyes and greeted herself many times. Each day she checked herself in the mirror before tackling other toys. Ten days later she had to return to the operating theatre.

It was after her second operation that Masha made an amazing collection of drawings, with sophistication, assurance and technical skill. Her drawings became her way of telling the play specialist about her family and home and how she had been looked after in the hospital.

Summary

There are many more ways of using children's painting in hospitals and clinics, for understanding and diagnosis.
Children will present facts in their pictures that surprise the adults who care for them. It is a rash person who makes assumptions about their patients' work. Instead, observe and listen. Painting is an involuntary means of communication. We must be alert to assess, deduce and evaluate what is going on. ●

REFERENCES

1. Jameson,K. Pre-school and infant art. Studio Vista, 1968.
2. Lind,J., Harvey,S. & Newman,L., eds. Children and parents in hospital. S. Karger, 1980.

Moving Mural

PROBLEM:-
How to provide a mural that continuously involved patients and staff, was not static, and was cheap, preferably free.

This was our goal when we decided to have a new mural for our adolescent unit. It was felt that the existing one, although enjoyed by many, needed refurbishment. The original idea was to have graffiti art.
The basic artwork was to be done by young people in the community who had proved themselves talented at this type of work.
This would help to break down some of the barriers between the community and the hospital. The patients could then add to it as they were admitted. Unfortunately "street cred" does not come cheap these days; spray paint is very expensive and so was the labour - so we had to think again.

The activity worker at that time (H.P.S.) contacted a group called S.H.A.P.E. This is a group of artists who work with handicapped and able bodied people in various institutions and have obtained funding from the Westminster Arts Council. It was agreed that they would do a six week project, which they would basically fund (we supplied some of the materials). After several meetings the format was decided, taking into account issues like shortness of patient's stay, etc. The patients would each work directly on to a piece of board - this included painting, collage work, paper mache, drawings and screen printing.

Plastic curtain runners were affixed to the wall by the hospital carpenters, and the finished boards were then slotted along the runners. The result is a constantly changing mural because the boards can be moved around and young people coming in can add to it. It has caused a lot of interest and doctors have requested to join in the sessions, thoroughly enjoying it.

After several visits from H.P.S.s and others, many of whom expressed an interest in the way this work was displayed, I felt that it might be of wider interest. It is ideal for corridors where, in my experience, children's work very quickly gets ragged, torn or falls of the wall altogether with the constant passage of people, theatre trolleys, etc. The leaders of the project were both talented artists, one able bodied and one handicapped, and taught the young people new skills without imposing their ideas on them. They also helped patients with the cover of our ward Newsletter which goes to Out patients as well as In patients. It was a very successful enterprise!

KAY WOODS, Play Co-ordinator
Westminster Children's Hospital

The universal sequence of development in children's art.

Children have definate ideas about their early communications. They know mother has two eyes and will draw them from whichever angle the figure is seen. Vehicles are similarly given four wheels even when seen from one side. The sky is above our heads and the earth is beneath our feet.

Children's art in hospital

Drawing and painting is of prime importance to nearly all patients, not only for fun but also as an outlet for feelings and a way of telling facts which they cannot express in words. Working with young children is a continuous process of two-way communication, trying to understand them through what they are and what they do.

A professionally trained teacher or play specialist works on a precipice, balanced between skilled intervention and non-intervention, ready to take every chance to extend children's experiences. There are three separate, but related, ways which, if delicately used, can help adults to know something about what is happening in children's minds:
1. The content of the paintings
2. What children say to themselves while painting and drawing
3. What children say to the adult about the paintings and drawings

Interpreting children's drawings

No one who has neither training nor sufficient information should try to interpret children's drawings at unconscious levels. The job of play specialists is, instead, to listen, express interest, appreciate results and write down immediately afterward what children said about their drawings. One useful way to learn more about children's inner world is by saying, "That's interesting. Tell me more about your picture." This is preferred to the blunt question, "What's that?"

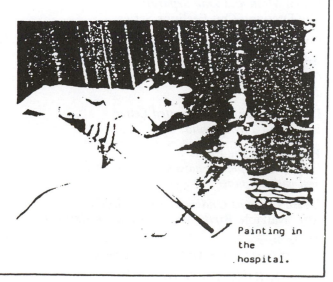

Painting in the hospital.

Additional Resources
(See also Book List)

Whilst recognizing that the best resources in any programme will be the children, staff, and surrounding community, a wide variety of other resources is now available. These include teaching packs, videos, books, radio and TV broadcasts, and visitors.

Note: BY means available from Being Yourself (see address at end of list).

Check List for Using Resources

(1) Do they fit your aims and objectives?

(2) Are they suitable, given the abilities of the children?

(3) Will they need adapting to suit your purpose?

(4) Where are they kept, and how are they obtained?

Supporting Bereaved Children and Families *Practical ways of helping children to express loss, and setting up groups of bereaved children.*	D. Black (ed)	Cruse (1993)
When Someone Very Special Dies The Drawing Out Feelings Series	M. Heegaard	Being Yourself/Cruse
When Someone Has a Very Serious Illness The Drawing Out Feelings Series	M. Heegaard	Being Yourself/Cruse
When Something Terrible Happens The Drawing Out Feelings Series	M. Heegaard	Being Yourself/Cruse
When Mom and Dad Separate The Drawing Out Feelings Series	M. Heegaard	Being Yourself/Cruse
Oxford Book of Death	D.J. Enright (ed)	Oxford University Press
Am I Allowed to Cry *Guidelines for bereaved people who have learning disabilities*	M. Oswin	London: Souvenir Press
Dougy Letter: An Illustrated Letter *Written to a dying child*	E. Kubler Ross	MacMillan Education
Wise Before the Event *Helps schools plan in advance how they will deal with a disaster*	W. Yule and A. Gold	Caloustie Gulbenkian Foundation
Death Customs Understanding Religions Also available ***Birth, Marriage*** and ***Initiation Customs***		Wayland
Milestones *Rites of Passage in a Multi-Faith Community*	C. Collinson and C. Miller	London: Arnold
Will My Rabbit Go To Heaven? *And other questions children ask*	Hughes, J.	London: Lion.

Play Therapy: Where the Sky Meets the Underworld This book shows how children can use play as a therapeutic process	A. Cattanach	London: Jessica Kingsley (1994)
Homemade Books to Help Children Cope. These books can be used by parents and professionals to help children face an almost unlimited variety of life situations	R.G. Ziegler	(BY)
Cartoon Magic Using cartoon characters to help children solve their problems.	R.J. Crowley and J.C. Mills	(BY)
More Annie Stories Therapeutic storytelling techniques	D. Brett	(BY)
Self Esteem 1 and 2 A Classroom Affair	M. Borba and C. Borba	(BY)
Building Self Esteem in Children	P. Burne and L.M. Savary	(BY)
Chain Reaction: Children and Divorce Case studies are used to illustrate a range of methods to help children come to terms with separation/divorce and remarriage of their parents	O. Ayalon and A. Flasher	London: Jessica Kingsley (1993)
This is Me and My Single Parent A Discovery Workbook for Children and Single Parents	M.D. Evans	(BY)
This is Me and My Two Families An Awareness Scrapbook/Journal for Children living in stepfamilies	M.D. Evans	(BY)
Foundations for HIV/AIDS Education in Primary Schools	P. Helson	irmingham Health Education B Unit, Martineau Ed. Cre, 74 Balden Rd, Harborne Brimingham

Books with a Holistic Approach to Education

Psychosynthesis and Education: A Guide to the Joy of Learning	D. Whitmore	Turnstone
He Hit Me Back First Creative Visualization for Parents and Teachers	E.D. Fugitt	Jalmar Press, USA
Windows to our Children A Gestalt therapy approach	V. Oaklander	Real People Press, USA

Videos (see also end of Children's book list)

The Fall of Freddie the Leaf This video follows Freddie from Spring to Autumn as he questions the meaning of life and death	E/M/VIDEO, 235 Imperial Drive, Rayners Lane, Harrow, Middlesex, HA2 7HE. Tel: 0181 868 1908
That Morning I Went To School This video features a bereavement group for children who have lost by death a parent or sibling	Northampton Health Authority, Highfield, Cliftonville Road, Northampton, NN1 5DN

Games

All About Me   Barnados
A non competitive board game for therapists to use with children to help them explore their feelings around bereavement

Un Game
Over a million copies of the Un Game have been sold to those interested in facilitating communication.

Memory Store

The memory store provides a practical way of bringing together important information for children who are losing contact with their parents. Originally developed for families affected by HIV it can be used in many other situations such as adoption, marriage break up or other illnesses.

Book available from: 'Being Yourself', 73 Liverpool Road, Deal, Kent, CT14 7NN. 0304 381333.

Being Yourself
is an independent resource centre, offering a wide range of teaching and therapeutic aids for professionals and parents. A free catalogue is available.

Books for Bereaved Children

Barbara Greenall Halley Stewart Library, St Christopher's Hospice, Lawrie Park Road, London SE26 6DZ

The ways in which books may be used to help bereaved children to understand death are discussed. Books written for children which deal with the themes of death and grief are described briefly.

Every year in this country thousands of children are bereaved through the death of a parent, grandparent, friend or sibling. They are surrounded by caring adults who try to help the child cope with the situation, but are themselves often struggling with their own grief and are at a loss as to how to assist the child. At such times the adult might try to find a book which will help the bereaved child make sense out of what is happening. The purpose of this paper is to look at some of the available books and to see how they can be used in the bereaved child's situation.

Why Do We Turn to Books?

As adults we like to think that we have a philosophy of life which enables us to interpret various experiences. We feel secure in knowing facts and being able to answer questions, but when death intervenes we find ourselves in a situation beyond our control and we realize that there are no definite cut and dried answers. Bert Wood, speaking at a Reading Therapy Sub-Group meeting, movingly described his attempt to 'give sorrow words' after his son's death in a climbing accident.[1] Death is a mystery to us all and reminds us of our own mortality and the fragility of the life we enjoy. Fear of the unknown affects adults as much as children, and we realize that the latter are questioning us on a subject that we would rather avoid, and concerning which we do not have ready answers. In other areas of life we may turn to books to assist our understanding and increase our sense of being in control and we may do the same in this situation. Books about death provide us with pegs on which to base our explanations to children, but they also enable both the children and ourselves to explore a potentially frightening topic in a less threatening way.

Children's Experience of Death

The bereaved child is unlikely to have had any previous experience of people dying, except what has been seen on television, which gives rise to the belief that death is likely to be sudden, violent and painful. He has probably seen a dead bird and might have mourned a beloved pet. Even the latter event will probably not have affected him as deeply as the death of a significant person in his life, whether it be grandparent, parent, friend or sibling. In the case of the dead pet, he was probably given another one as soon as possible to replace it, by parents wanting to save him from grief and unhappiness.

However, when it comes to a person dying, no such replacement is possible and children find themselves in a situation for which they are likely to be totally unprepared.

The Bereaved Child's Situation

Whether death is sudden or expected, the bereaved child finds himself without warning in a world which seems completely different from his normal experience. Familiar people behave strangely and routines are disrupted so that life no longer follows a predictable pattern. The child often does not understand what is happening and feels very insecure as a result. He is also likely to feel very isolated and apart from other children if he does not know anybody else who has had a similar experience. The child will probably find that he is experiencing strong emotions which are sometimes overwhelming and frightening. He might behave out of character in response to the situation and is very likely to have fears about the future, particularly concerning his own death and the death of others close to him.

Such a bereaved child needs to understand what is happening and to have the opportunity to express his own feelings, fears and questions and to work through his grief at his own pace. He needs to know that it is quite natural for him to cry and be sad or to express anger against God or against the dead person for leaving him. Perhaps most of all he needs explanation about what has happened in terms that are appropriate to his stage of development and which do not include ideas that are completely new to him.

Explaining Death to Children

It is important to be honest with children, to admit that we do not have all the answers and not to use euphemisms which may confuse or frighten nor tell them things that they will later have to discover are not true. A book called *Nana Upstairs and Nana Downstairs* is, for example, one to be avoided because of misleading explanations given to the boy when his great-grand-mother dies.

It is also important that children should be told a person has died rather than assuming that they are temporarily absent and will be back some day. This point comes out in the book *My Grandson Lew* [4] when Lew's mother does not tell him that Grandpa has died, thinking he is too young to have remembered him. Lew makes it plain that he has very clear memories and has been waiting for Grandpa to visit them again, being unaware that he has died.

Probably the most difficult question asked by the bereaved child is likely to be 'What happens when you die?' or 'Where is ... Grandpa, Mummy, little brother?' The answers given to this question can vary enormously but if we are honest with ourselves and with the child, we have to say 'I don't really know but ... ' If the child has had a Christian upbringing and is familiar with the concept of heaven, then to say that the dead person is with Jesus in heaven would be an appropriate explanation.

However, if a child has never heard of God or heaven, introducing these concepts will probably only lead to confusion. In such circumstances it might be better to emphasize that the person is no longer ill or in pain as they were before they died. Interestingly enough none of the books mentioned later deal much with this most difficult aspect of death. However, a helpful book is *Talking About Death: A Dialogue Between Parent and Child*,[2] which contains a great deal of useful discussion material and includes guidelines for parents on how it may be used most effectively.

Themes in Children's Books About Death

Several themes recur in children's books about death and eight of these have been selected. The frequency with which different themes occur has been recorded for books which cover the death of a pet, grandparent, uncle, father or friend. Table 1 shows the frequency of each theme in the books analysed and the square-bracketed numbers in the text indicate to which book reference is being made. It is interesting that nearly half these books deal with the death of a grandparent, emphasizing that experience of such a death is considered to be more or less a normal part of childhood.

Turning to the themes in Table 1 these can each be illustrated with examples from different books. First of all anger is an emotion which is commonly experienced by bereaved people, but is often considered to be less acceptable than sadness. It was encouraging to find anger being expressed in several books even though it was only explored to any depth in *Bridge to Terabithia* [9] when Jess is furious at his friend Leslie for getting drowned. Helen is angry with her parents when her grandma dies in *Why did Grandma die?* [5] and Uncle Bob's niece is angry with him for dying because he was not old and his death made them all so unhappy [8]. It is natural for the bereaved child to be angry that the dead person has gone away and left them or to blame the doctors for not making the person well again. This theme is dealt with again in *Dusty Was My Friend* [10]. Helen's father points out that she will always have a link with her Grandma because of the skill at making model horses which Grandma had given to her [5]. When Badger dies the other animals remind themselves how he taught them to cook, skate and other useful accomplishments [7].

Table 1 Themes which occur in books for bereaved children

Title of book	Recurring themes							
	A	B	C	D	F	M	N	S
[1] Emma's Cat Dies						x		x
[2] The Tenth Good Thing about Barney		x			x	x		x
[3] Grandpa and Me					x	x		x
[4] My Grandson Lew						x		x
[5] Why Did Grandma Die?	x	x	x		x	x	x	x
[6] My Grandpa Died Today						x		x
[7] Badger's Parting Gifts						x		x
[8] When Uncle Bob Died	x		x	x	x	x		x
[9] Bridge to Terabithia	x	x	x	x		x		x
[10] Dusty was My Friend	x	x	x	x		x	x	x
[11] Mama's Going to Buy You a Mocking Bird	x	x	x		x	x		x

A: Expressing anger, B: behaviour out of character, C: coming to terms with the reality of what happened, D: fear of others dying, F: significance of funeral, M: memories, N: need to say goodbye, S: expressing sadness.

Sharing Grief

Mention has been made of shared memories, but it is also important to express fear and other emotions when grieving for a loved one. It is to be hoped that these books may enable adult and child to explore and discuss different aspects of grief and perhaps help the child to communicate his fears and feelings more openly. One of the reasons we may read novels is to identify with a character and to share his or her experiences vicariously. In such a way the child's sense of isolation or of being different might be reduced, as he realizes that other children have been through similar experiences, even if these are only in books.

It is very important that the bereaved child should read these books with an adult rather than being left alone to read. The following incident demonstrates the importance of sharing experiences.

Four-year-old Jenny asked her father to read *The Three Little Pigs* to her every night at bedtime. After a week, Dad tired of the same story and hit on what seemed a brilliant idea. He taped the whole book and when Jenny wanted her bedtime story he sat her in the chair, switched on the tape recorder and left her to listen while he got on with some woodwork. He did the same the next night but on the third evening Jenny rebelled at this treatment and told her Dad that the 'thing' (tape-recorder) was not nice and cuddly! A very important part of the bedtime story ritual was sitting on Dad's knee while he read to her, because she then felt secure as they both enjoyed the story together. Such security is even more vital when handling sensitive issues like death as in the case of the bereaved child. No book can ever substitute for a loving, concerned adult trying to help the child come to terms with his situation, but it might assist the child to feel able to discuss some of the problems that are troubling him.

This paper has briefly examined some of the books which might help a bereaved child, but there are still very few suitable titles from which to choose. Hardly any are written by British authors, meaning that a cultural barrier has to be crossed in terms of language used and geographical setting of the story. Another major problem is that books on this topic understandably have a limited appeal and so tend to go out of print very quickly. This makes it difficult to recommend them to families with bereaved children, because one is only too aware that they will be difficult to obtain. However, there does seem to be a growing awareness among publishers of children's books that such topics as death, divorce and other kinds of loss can be sensitively handled in fictional form, in ways which can help children adjust to what seems to them to be a strange situation.

Further Reading

Anthony, S. (1973) *The Discovery of Death in Childhood and After*. Penguin: Harmondsworth.

Krementz, J. (1983) *How it Feels When a Parent Dies*. London: Gollancz.

Rosen, H. (1986) *Unspoken Grief: Coping with Childhood Sibling Loss*. Lexington, MA: D.C. Heath and Co.

Wynne Jones, P. (1985) *Children, Death and Bereavement*. London: Scripture Union.

Appendix (May 1987)
Books for Bereaved Children: Summary of Content and Indication of Age Group

[1] *Emma's Cat Dies*   N. Snell   Hamish Hamilton (1984)
Emma enjoys playing with her kitten and is upset when he gets run over. Suitable for ages 4–7. Out of print

[2] *The Tenth Good Thing About Barney*   J. Viorst   Collins (1971)
Tom tries to think of 10 good things to say about Barney his cat, at Barney's funeral. Suitable for ages 4–7.

[3] *Grandpa and Me*   M. Alex and B. Alex   Lion (1983)
A specifically Christian approach to the death of a grandparent. Set in Scandinavia, this book contains many beautiful photographs. Suitable for ages 4–7.

[4] *My Grandson Lew*   C. Zolotow   World's Work (1976)
Lew's mother is surprised how well he remembers his grandfather, even though Lew was very young when he died. Suitable for ages 3–6.

[5] *Why Did Grandma Die?*   T. Madler   Raintree: Blackwell (1982)
Trudy's grandmother dies unexpectedly and she tries to come to terms with what has happened. Suitable for ages 5–9. Out of print.

[6] *My Grandpa Died Today*   J. Fassler   New York: Human Sciences Press (1983)
David remembers his grandfather's death and describes his own reactions afterwards. Suitable for ages 5–9.

[7] *Badger's Parting Gifts*   S. Varley   Collins (1985)
All the animals are very sad when Badger dies but they comfort themselves by remembering how he had helped them in various ways. Suitable for ages 4–8.

[8] *When Uncle Bob Died*   Althea   Overton, Cambridge: Dinosaur Publications. (1982)
Uncle Bob's niece explains what happened after he died and how she tries to adjust to his death. Suitable for ages 4–8.

[9] *Bridge to Terabithia*   K. Paterson   Gollancz (1982)
Jess and Leslie enjoy a wonderful summer in their fantasy kingdom, but when Leslie is drowned, Jess has to come to terms with her death. Suitable for ages 9–13.

[10] *Dusty was my Friend: Coming to Terms with Loss*   A.F. Clardy   New York: Human Sciences Press (1984)
Benjamin finds it very hard adjusting to life after his friend's death. Suitable for ages 5–9.

[11] *Mama's Going to Buy You a Mockingbird*   J. Little   Harmondsworth: Penguin (1985)
The summer their father dies of cancer is a hard one for Jeremy and Sarah, but with the help of a new friend, they gradually begin to adjust to life without him. Suitable for ages 9–13.

Children's Booklist
(See also Additional Resources)

Many of these books should also be available through your local library service. If bookshops can't supply because titles are out of print, try local library.

The books have been put under different headings for each reference, but may also fit under other headings too.

(**)   =   specially recommended

(M)   =   multi-cultural

(J)   =   suitable for Juniors only

(BY)   =   Available from Being Yourself (see end of Additional Resources)

(C)   =   Available from Cruse.

Feelings

Blubber *Problems of bullying in an American classroom*	J. Blume	Heinemann	(J)
Gorilla *A girl's often difficult relationship with her father, a single paren.*	A. Browne	J. MacRae	(**)
Piggy Book *An over-worked Mum gets her own back on the family that takes her for granted*	A. Browne	J. MacRae	(**) (J)
Double-Dip Feelings *A book to help children understand emotions*	B. Cain		(BY)
Say Cheese *Ben feels left out as he is the only one in his class left with his baby teeth*	C. Dinan	Faber and Faber	
Poems about Feelings *Selected by Danielle Sersier*	A. Earl	Wayland	(**)
It's Your Turn Roger *Roger the pig learns that he must pull his weight in the family*	S. Gretz	Bodley Head	
Roger Takes Charge	S. Gretz	Bodley Head	
What Feels Best *A young kangaroo learns about sharing*	A. Harper	Piccadilly	(**)
Alfie Gives a Hand *Alfie helps a shy girl at a party*	S. Hughes	Bodley Head	
Beware Beware *Short listed for Greenaway Medal 1993*	S. Hill	Walker Books	(**)

Comfort Herself *Comfort, daughter of a white mother and black father, must choose between an English or Kenyan way of life*	G. Kaye	Deutsch	(JM)
Angry Arthur Not Now, Bernard *Bernard can't get his parents' attention, even when threatened by a monster. Also available in dual-language editions (Bengali, Gujarati, Urdu)*	H. Oram D. Mckee	Andersen Press Andersen Press	(★★) (M)
Would You Be Scared	J. Oakley	Deutch	
Would You Be Angry	J. Oakley	Deutch	
Your Emotions: I Feel Angry	J. Oakley	Wayland	
Your Emotions: I Feel Frightened	J. Oakley	Wayland	
Your Emotions: I Feel Jealous	J. Oakley	Wayland	
Your Emotions: I Feel Sad	J. Oakley	Wayland	

Fears and Phobias

Otherwise Known as Sheila The Great *Sheila is scared of many things (for example, dogs, thunderstorms) but a holiday in the country and a new friend help her to overcome them*	J. Blume	Bodley Head	
The Eighteenth Emergency *Mouse is threatened by the school bully and must eventually face up to him*	B. Byars	Bodley Head	(★★) (J)
Scardey Cat	A. Fine	Heinemann	(J)
The Red Woollen Blanket *Julia is very attached to her blanket, which is finally outgrown when she starts school*	B. Graham	Walker Books	
I'll Take You To Mrs. Cole *A little boy overcomes his fear of a neighbour and her family, and makes many new friends. (Illustrated by Michael Foreman)*	N. Gray	Andersen Press	(M) (J)
Mother's Magic *A mother's magic helps a child overcome various fears*	S. Hill	Hamilton	
One Night At A Time *Tom's mother helps him chase away nightmares caused by his vivid imagination*	S. Hill	Hamilton	(★★)
Alexander and the Dragon *The only thing that scares Alexander is the dark, when the imagination that he enjoys all day begins to play tricks on him. He thinks there's a dragon under his bed*	K. Holabird and H. Craig	Aurum Books	
Where the Wild Things Are *Classic tale of nightmares and monsters*	M. Sendak	Bodley Head	(★★)
Cat's Got Your Tongue *A story for children afraid to speak*	C. Schaffer		(★★)
Danny is Afraid of the Dark	N. Snell	Hamilton	(BY)
Bedtime for Bear	S. Stoddard	Hodder and Stoughton	
The Owl Who was Afraid of the Dark	J. Tomlinson	Methuen	(★★) (J)
Brenda the Bold	J. Ure	Heinemann	(J)
Can't you Sleep, Little Bear	M. Waddell	Walker Books	

Let's Go Home, Little Bear   M. Waddell   Walker Books

Video

Where the Wild Things Are   M. Sendak   Weston Woods

Friends

The Bear Nobody Wanted   J. Aliberg and   Puffin.
The tale of a teddy in search of an owner who will make   Aliberg, A.
him feel wanted – as all bears and children should be

Who Will Play with Me   M. Coxon   Blackie
The story of how a lonely young boy and a
cat become friends and play together

Jamaica Tag-Along   J. Havill   Little Mammoth
Jamaica feels left out when her big brother and friends
won't let her join in their ball game. When Berto
tries to join her game, she makes sure he doesn't feel left out

Growing and Changing

The Snowman	R. Briggs	Hamilton	(**)
The Snowman Story Book	R. Briggs	Hamilton	
Arthur's Tooth	M. Brown	Piccadilly Press	
The Very Hungry Caterpillar	E. Carle	Hamilton	(**)

Metamorphosis explained, in a favorite picture book

Now One Foot, Now the Other   T. de Paola   Methuen
After a stroke, grandfather is helped to walk
again by the boy he taught as a baby

Ben's Brand New Glasses	C. Dinan	Faber and Faber	(**)
Titch	P. Hutchins	Puffin	
Bruce's Story	M. Thom and	The Children's Society	(**)
	L. Macliver		

The story of a dog and some changes in his life

My Great Grandpa	M. Waddell	Walker	
The Selfish Giant	O. Wilde	Kaye and Ward	

Many other editions of this famous story are available

Seasons	B. Wildsmith	Oxford	
Poppy's First Year	S. Williams	Marilyn Malin	

All the different stages of Poppy's first year and Sam,
her big brother's reactions

Non-Fiction

Earth Calendar   U. Jacobs   Black   (**)
A beautifully illustrated book

Growing Up   D. James and   Two-can   (**)
     S. Lynn

Getting Lost

Jessy Runs Away *A young girl with Down's Syndrome gets lost in a shop.*	R. Anderson	Black	
Polly's Puffin *Polly's toy puffin is lost at the shops*	S. Garland	Bodley Head	(**)
Dogger *A favorite toy is given to a jumble sale by mistake,* *much to the dismay of his owner*	S. Hughes	Bodley Head	(**)
Lost and Found	C. Jessel	Methuen	
Lost and Found *Teddy gets left on the train and finds himself in* *the lost property office*	J. Mogensen	Hamilton	
Jamaica Lost and Found	J. Havill	Little Mammoth	(M)

Moving House/Friends Moving Away

Moving House	N. Daw	Black	
Understanding Feelings about Moving	Gesec		(BY)
Moving Molly	S. Hughes	Bodley Head	
Moving House	C. Jessel	Methuen	
Moving	M. Rosen	Viking	

Staying the Night

Away for the Night	C. Jessel	Methuen	
Spot Stays the Night *Another in the popular series 'Spot, the dog'*	E. Hill	Heinemann	

Starting Playgroup/School and Changing School

My Special Playgroup	P. Dowling	Hamish Hamilton	
Emmie and the Purple Paint *Emmie visits playgroup and doesn't want to stay* *at first, but later realises what a fun place it is*	D. Edwards	Methuen	(**)
When Robert went to Playgroup *Stories to read aloud*	A. Rooke	Magnet	
Starting School *The first term at school told in pictures*	A. Ahlberg and J. Ahlberg	Kestrel	(**)
Starting School	P. Heaslip and F. Pragoff	Methuen	
My School *Also available in dual language editions -* *Bengali, Gujarati, Punjabi and Urdu*	J. Ingham	Blackie	(**M)
Into the Great Forest *A story for children away from parents for the first time*	I. Marcus Wineman and P. Marcus		
First Day at School *Also available in dual language editions* *- Gujarati and Urdu*	A. Scarsbrook and A. Scarsbrook	Black	(M)

I Hate Roland Roberts *Rosie has started a new school and Roland a revolting* *girl hater has been assigned to look after her*	M. Selway	Hutchinson	
Timothy Goes to School	R. Wells	Viking Kestrel	

New Sibling/Sibling Relationships

The Pain and the Great One *Sibling rivalry told in picture form, for junior readers*	J. Blume	Heinemann	(J)
Superfudge *Various problems, often amusing, caused by the* *arrival in an American family of a new sister*	J. Blume	Bodley Head	(**J)
The Baby	J. Burningham	Cape	
Ben's Baby	M. Foreman	Andersen Press	
Henry's Baby *Henry is embarrassed to introduce his friends* *to his baby brother*	M. Hoffman	Dorling Kindersley	(**)
Angel Mae *Story of a new baby born at Christmas time*	S. Hughes	Walker Books	
I Feel Jealous *In same series: I Feel Sad / Angry / Frightened*	B. Moses	Wayland	
Janine and the New Baby	I. Thomas	Deutsch	(**M)
Rosie's Babies *Winner of the Best Books for Babies Award and* *shortlisted for the Kate Greenaway Medal*	M. Waddell and P. Dale	Walker Books	(**)

Non-Fiction

New Baby	J. Baskerville	Black	(**)
Brothers and Sisters *A multi-racial class learn about the festival of* *Raksha Bandhan, a Hindu/Sikh festival* *celebrating family relationships*	S. Perry and N. Wildman	Black	(M)

Adoption

Jane is Adopted	Althea	Dinosaur	
The Finding *An adopted boy's search for his past*	N. Bawden	Gollancz	(J)
Zachary's New Home *Explores the experiences and emotions of the* *young foster or adopted child*	M.S.W. Blomquist and P. Blomquist		
Robert goes to Fetch a Sister	D. Edwards	Methuen	(M)
Michael and the Jumble-Sale Cat *Michael is adopted from a children's home*	M. Newman	Young Puffin	(J)
Why was I Adopted?	C. Livingstone	Angus and Robertson	(J)
What's Happening - Adoption	C. Livingstone	Wayland	(J)

Single Parent, Divorce and Step-Parents

My Daddy is a Stranger	Centering Company		
Sometimes a family just has to split up	Centering Company		
Are We Nearly There? A young boy travels home with Dad after a day out together, but must say goodbye at the front door	L. Baum	Bodley Head	(**)
Tell Me a Story, Paint Me the Sun When a girl feels ignored by her father			(BY J)
My Mother's Getting Married	J. Drescher	Methuen	(J)
What's Going to Happen to Me?	E. LeShan		(J BY)
The Visitors Who Came to Stay Picture book illustrated by Anthony Browne showing tensions within a modern family situation	A. Macaffee	Hamilton	(**J)
Mike's Lonely Summer Divorce in the family from a Christian viewpoint	C. Nystrom	Lion	
What's Happening - Splitting Up, Step Families	C. Nystrom	Wayland	

Non-Fiction

What am I Doing in a Step-Family?	C. Berman	Angus and Robertson	(J)
The Divorce Workbook		Waterfront Books	(BY)
My Kind of Family		Waterfront Books	
Changing Families		Waterfront Books	

Special Needs/Illness/Hospital

I Have Epilepsy (Many others in series also available)	Althea	Dinosaur	
I Have Asthma (Many others in series also useful)	C. Fairclough	Franklin Watts	
Blabber Mouth The humorous story of an Australian girl who is dumb	M. Gleitzman	MacMillan	(J)
See Ya' Simon Award winning book about the death of Simon who was physically disabled	D. Hill		
Home in Bed	P. Heaslip	Methuen (M)	
Spot's Hospital Visit	E. Hill	Heinemann	
Going to Hospital	C. Jessel	Methuen	
Sammy's Mommy Has Cancer A warm, straightforward and sensitively illustrated story telling Sammy that his mother has a life threatening illness	S. Kohlenberg		(BY)
Speccy Four-Eyes	C. Lloyd	Julie MacRae	
Gentle Willow Gentle Willow is a loving and tender story written for children who may not survive their illnesses	J.C. Mills		(BY)
Little Tree A story for children with serious medical problems	J.C. Mills		(BY)
Sarah and Puffle A story for children about diabetes	L. Mulder		(BY)

Cool Simon *Simon has a hearing difficulty*	J. Ure	Corgi Books	

Non-Fiction

Mummy Goes into Hospital	E. Elliott	Hamilton

My Tummy Has a Headache. Helping Children Understand Illness. Booklist compiled by Beverley Mathis and Desmond Spiers. Available from: National Library for the Handicapped Child.

Child Abuse/Strangers

Your Guess is as Good as Mine *The perils of accepting a lift from a stranger*	B. Ashley	Corgi	(J)
A Very Touching Book for Little People	J. Hindman		(BY)
Can't You Sleep Little Bear	Waddell and Frith		
What's Happening? Child Abuse	Waddell and Frith		Wayland

Non-Fiction

The Willow Street Kids: It's Your Right to be Safe *A class of junior age children discuss variousthreatening situations with their teacher, eg. bullying, obscene phone calls, flashing*	M. Elliott	Deutsch	(**J)
We Can Say No!	D. Pithers and S. Greene	Hutchinson	
No More Secrets For Me *Deals with some of the most common situations which threaten children, eg. possible abduction, homosexual advances and incest. Companion volume for adults also available*	O. Wachter	Viking Kestrel	(J)

Being Yourself has an excellent selection of books and materials on this subject. (See address at end of Additional Resources).

Death and Dying (see also Special Needs etc)

Grandpa and Me *The death of a grandparent seen from a Christian viewpoint*	M. Alex and B. Alex	Lion	
When Uncle Bob Died *Useful in dealing with the death of a younger relative*	Althea	Dinosaur	
Tuck Everlasting *The Tuck's have accidentally become immortal. Good for discussing life after death*	N. Babbitt	Collins	(J **)
Timothy Duck *A beautifully illustrated story of how Timothy Duck comes to terms with the sickness and death of his best person-friend*	L. Blackburn		(BY)
Grandpa *Poignant story, told in very few words, of a young girl's relationship with her grandfather*	J. Burningham	Cape	(** C)

Fall of Freddie the Leaf	L. Buscaglia		(BY)
Nana Upstairs and Nana Downstairs	T. de Paola	Methuen.	
John's Book *John is 10 when his father dies suddenly. He goes* *through a turbulent period before learning to trust again*	J. Fuller		(C)
Grandpa's Slideshow *This moving story shows the very special relationship* *which grows between the young and old*	D. Gould	Viking/Kestrel	(★★)
Dada Maa Dies *The death of a grandparent in a Hindu family*	J. Jones	Blackie	(M)
Lettuce - A Head of Her Time *A charming and engaging story that invites us* *to smile through our pain*	P. Loring and J. Johnson		(BY)
One the Wings of a Butterfly *A story about Life and Death*	M. Maple		(BY)
Bridge to Terabithia *Jess and Leslie invent the land of 'Terabithia'. When* *Leslie dies Jess uses the land as a source of strength*	K. Paterson	Gollancz/Puffin	(J)
A Taste of Blackberries *A very sympathetic account of the death of a* *friend (caused by an allergy to bee-stings)*	D.B. Smith	Penguin	(★★ J)
I Heard Your Mommy Died	M. Scrivani	(BY)	
The Velveteen Rabbit *A child's view of the survival of the spirit*	M. Williams	Heinemann	
Badger's Parting Gifts *The animals come to terms with the death of their* *friend Badger and remember all he has done for them*	S. Varley	Andersen	(★★ BY C)
The Tenth Good Thing About Barney *A young boy mourns the death of his cat*	J. Viorst	Collins	(★★)
Charlotte's Web	E.B. White	Hamilton	(J C)
I'll Always Love You *A moving story about the death of a much loved dog*	H. Wilhelm	Hodder	(★★ C)

Non-Fiction

Remembering Mum *True story about Sam 4 and Eddy 6, a year after* *their Mum died*	L. Morris and G. Perkins	A C Black	(C)
Gran Gran's Best Trick *A story for children who have lost someone they love*	D. Holden		(BY)
Waterbugs and Dragonflies: Explaining *Death of Children* *Highly recommended by workers in the field*	D. Stickney	Mowbray	(★★ C)

For more detailed information, contact the following:

Being Yourself has a free catalogue (see end of Additional Resources)

The Compassionate Friends have a 'Library List' available at £2.50 (includes postage and packing).

Cruse have 'Children and Bereavement - A Reading List.' Send £1 to cover postage and packing.

Educator's Book List

All in the End is Harvest *An anthology for those who grieve*	A. Whitaker	London: Darton Longman Todd/Cruse (1984)
The Bereaved Parent	H. Sharnoff Schiff	London: Souvenir Press (1977)
Body, Mind and Death *In the Light of Psychic Experience*	D. Lorimer	London: Routledge and Kegan Paul (1984)
Caring for Dying People of Different Faiths	Rabbi J. Neuberger	Austin Cornish (1990)
Childhood and Death	H. Wass and C.A. Cott	Hemisphere: New York (1985)
Conciliation and Divorce *A father's letter to his children*	B. Grant	Barry Rose
The Courage to Grieve	J. Tatelbaum	London: Heinemann (1981)
The Daniel Diary	A. Fabian	London: Grafton Books (1988)
Death and the Family	L. Pincus	London: Faber (1961)
Disasters Planning for a Caring Response	HMSO	London: HMSO (1991)
Divorce Parenting – How to make it work	S. Goldstein	London: Methuen (1987)
The Dying and Bereaved Teenager	J.D. Morgan	Charles Press (1990)
Facing Grief, Bereavement and the Young Adult	S. Wallbank	London: Lutterworth Press (1991)
The Forgotten Mourners	M. Pennells S.C. Smith	London: Jessica Kingsley (1994)
Grief Counselling and Grief Therapy	W. Worden	London: Tavistock (1983)
Grief in Children	A. Dyregrov	London: Jessica Kingsley (1990)
A Grief Observed	C.S. Lewis	London: Faber
Helping Children Cope with Divorce	R. Wells	Sheldon (1993)
Helping Children Cope with Grief	R. Wells	Sheldon (1995)
Helping Children Cope with Separation and Loss	C. Jewett	London: Batsford (1984)
Holistic Living – A Guide to Self-Care	Dr P. Pietroni	London: Dent (1987)
How Differing Religions view Death and the After Life	J. Johnson and M. McGee	The Charles Press 1991
How it Feels to be Adopted	J. Krementz	London: Gollancz (1984)
How it Feels When a Parent Dies	J. Krementz	London: Gollancz (1983)
The Illness and Death of a Child	Mother F. Dominica	The Church Literature Association (1988)
I Only Want What's Best for You *A parent's guide to raising well adjusted children*	J. Brown	Kingswood Press (1987)
In Search of the Dead *A scientific investigation of evidence of life after death*	J. Iverson	London: BBC Books (1992)
Life After Death	N. Randall	London: Corgi Books (1980)

The Light Beyond	R. Moody, R. and P. Perry	London: Macmillan (1991)
Living with Death and Dying	E. Kubler Ross	London: Souvenir (1982)
Living with Loss	L. McNeil Taylor	London: Fontana (1983)
Losing a Parent	F. Marshall	Insight (1993)
Loss and Grief in Medicine	P. Speck	London: Bailliere and Tindell (1978)
Love, Medicine and Miracles	B. Siegal	London: Century (1988)
The Needs of Children	M. Kellmer Pringle	London: Hutchinson (1987)
On Children and Death	E. Kubler Ross	London: Macmillan (1985)
Parents are Forever	Relate (Marriage Guidance)	London: Relate (1985)
Perspectives for Living	B. Mooney	London: Murray (1992)
The Private Worlds of Dying Children	M. Bluebond-Langer	Princeton University Press (1977)
Recovery From Bereavement	C. Murray Parkes	NY: Basic Books (1983)
A Special Scar *The experiences of people bereaved by suicide*	A. Wertheimer	London: Routledge (1991)
Standpoints - Death	M. Ball	Oxford: Oxford University Press (1976)
So Will I Comfort You	J. Kander	Gracewing (1991)
The Tibetan Book of Living and Dying	R. Sogyal	Rider (1992)
Through Grief, The Bereavement Journey	E. Collick	London: Darton Longman and Todd/Cruse (1986)
When Bad Things Happen to Good People	H.S. Kushner	London: Pan (1982)
When Parents Die	R. Abrams	London: Letts (1992)

Booklets

What to do When Someone Dies. Consumer Association Publication - Revised annually.

What to do After Death. Free DHSS Leaflet No. D49

The Right to Grieve. A leaflet to help mentally handicapped people who are bereaved. From the King's Fund Centre.

On Divorce. The Children's Society.

On Death and On Divorce. National Children's Bureau.
Handicap and Bereavement. Friends Book Centre, Euston Road, London.

Someone Special Has Died. St. Christopher's Hospice.

Journals

Bereavement Care. Cruse Publication - Periodical.
Newsletter. Compassionate Friends - Periodical.
Journal on Death/Divorce. National Children's Bureau.

Articles

Lists on Aspects of Loss and Death and Dying available from: Compassionate Friends, Cruse, National Children's Bureau, National Association for the Welfare of Children in Hospital, Relate (previously Marriage Guidance).

Care of Dying Children and Their Families. Guidelines from British Paediatric Assn. of King Edward's Fund for London and National Association of Health Authorities, NAHA, Garth House, 47 Edgbaston Road, Birmingham, B15 2RS.

Reactions to Death. Teaching and Training 1984 22 (1) p.10 - 17. Can the Mentally Handicapped grieve? Some experiences of those who did.

Useful Addresses

Abortion Law Reform Association (ALRA)
27-35 Mortimer Street
London W1N 7RJ
Tel: 0171 637 7264

Action for Sick Children (NAWCH)
Argyle House
29/31 Euston Road
London NW1 2SD
Tel: 0171 833 2041

Age Concern (Cymru)
4th Floor
1 Cathedral Road
Cardiff CF1 9SD
S. Glamorgan
Tel: (01222) 371566

Age Concern (England)
Astral House
1268 London Road
London SW16 4ER
Tel: 0181 679 8000

Age Concern (N. Ireland)
3 Lower Crescent
Belfast BT7 1NR
Tel: (0.1232) 245729

Age Concern (Scotland)
113 Rose Street
Edinburgh EH2 3DT
Tel: 0131 220 3345

**Association for Children with Life
Threatening Terminal Conditions
and their Families (ACT)**
65 St Michael's Hill
Bristol BS2 8DZ
Tel: 0117 922 1556
*ACT aims to inform families and professionals of available
services both in the statutory and voluntary sectors through its
national database and literature resource.*

**BACUP (Cancer), for patients
and families**
3 Bath Place
Rivington Street
London EC2A 3JR
Tel: 0171 696 9000 (Counselling)
Tel: 0171 613 2121 (Cancer Information)
Freephone: 0800 181199

Barnardo's
Tanners Lane
Barkingside
Ilford,
Essex IG6 1QG
Tel: 0181 550 8822

**British Agencies for Adoption
and Fostering (BAAF)**
Skyline House
200 Union Street
London SE1 0LX
Tel: 0171 593 2000

British Association for Counselling (BAC)
1 Regent Place
Rugby
Warwickshire CV21 2PJ
Tel: (01788) 578328/9

**British Association for Early Childhood
Education (Promoting quality
in the early years)**
111 City View House
463 Bethnal Green Road
London E2 9QY
Tel/Fax: 0171 739 7594

British Humanist Association
47 Theobald's Road
London WC1X 8SP
Tel: 0171 430 0908
Advice on non-religious funerals

British Institute of Learning Disabilities
Wolverhampton Road
Kidderminster
Worcestershire DY10 3PP
Tel: (01562) 850251

British Organ Donor Society (BODY)
Balsham
Cambridge
CB1 6DL
Tel: (01223) 893636

British Society for Music Therapy
25 Rosslyn Avenue
East Barnet
Hertfordshire EN4 8DH
Tel/Fax: 0181 368 8879

Cancer Link
17 Britannia Street
London WC1X 9JN
Tel: 0171 833 2451

Cancer Relief Macmillan Fund
Anchor House
15/19 Britten Street
London SW3 3TZ
Tel: 0171 351 7811

Carers National Association
Ruth Pitter House
20/25 Glasshouse Yard
London EC1A 4JS
Tel: 0171 490 8818
Carers helpline: 0171 490 8898
(Mon-Fri 1-4pm)

Centre for Multi-Cultural Education
Institute of Education
London University
20 Bedford Way
London WC12H 0AL
Tel: 0171 612 6721/2

Child to Child Trust
(A Worldwide Health Education Network)
The Coordinator
Institute of Education
20 Bedford Way,
London WC1H 0AL
Tel: 0171 612 6648

Childline
2nd Floor
Royal Mail Building
Studd Street
London N1 0QW
Tel: 0171 239 1000 (Office)
Tel: (0800) 1111 (Children's Line)

Citizens Advice Bureau
(see local telephone directory
for address and telephone number)

Community Health Council
(see local telephone directory
for address and telephone number)

The Compassionate Friends
(Head Office)
53 North Street
Bristol BS3 1EN
Helpline: 0117 953 9639
Admin: 0117 966 5202

Contact a Family
(Support Special Needs)
170 Tottenham Court Road
London W1P 0HA
Tel: 0171 383 3555

Cremation Society of Great Britain
2nd Floor
16/16a Albion Place
Maidstone
Kent ME14 5DZ
Tel: (01622) 688292

Crisis Management and Education
Roselyn House
93 Old Newtown Road
Newbury
Berkshire RG14 7DE
Tel: (01635) 30644

Cruse – Bereavement Care
Cruse House
126 Sheen Road
Richmond
Surrey TW9 1UR
Tel: 0181 940 4818/9042

Department of Social Security
(see local telephone directory)

Equal Opportunities Commission (EOC)
Quay Street
Manchester M3 3HN
Tel: 0161 833 9244

Exploring Parenthood
4 Ivory Place
20a Threadgold Street
London W11 4BP
Tel (advice): 0171 221 6681 (10-4pm)
Tel (enquiries): 0171 221 4471

The Foundation for Study
of Infant Deaths
14 Halkin Street
London SW1X 7DP
Tel: 0171 235 1721 (Helpline)
Tel: 0171 235 0965 (Enquiries)

Gingerbread
16-17 Clerkenwell Close
London EC1R 0AA
Tel: 0171 336 8183
Advice Line: 0171 336 8184

Good Bears of the World
Mrs Audrey Duck
256 St. Margaret's Road
Twickenham
Middlesex TW1 1PR
Tel: 0181 891 5746 (evenings only)
Provides teddies for traumatized children

Grandparents Contacts
Mrs Dallas Warren
Quarry Lodge
1b Haggstones Drive
Oughtibridge
Sheffield S30 3GL
Tel: 0114 286 2883
for those bereaved of their grandchildren.

Graham and Mary Stephens
Tree Tops, Church Street
Wellesbourne
Warwick CV35 9LS
Tel: (01789) 840622
For those whose child died leaving grandchildren.

Health Education Authority
Hamilton House
Mabledon Place
London WC1H 9TX
Tel: 0171 383 3833

Help the Aged
St. James Walk
London EC1R 0BE
Minicom (for deaf users only): (0800) 269626
Advice Line: (0800) 289404
Head Office: 0171 253 0253

Hospice Information
St. Christophers Hospice
51–59 Lawrie Park Road
Sydenham
London SE26 6DZ
Tel: 0181 778 9252

Institute of Family Therapy
43 New Cavendish Street
London W1M 7RG
Tel: 0171 935 1651

Jewish Bereavement Counselling Service
PO Box 6748
London N3 3BX
Tel: 0181 349 0839

Lesbian and Gay Bereavement Project
Vaughan M. Williams Centre
Colindale Hospital
London NW9 5HG
Tel: 0181 200 0511
Tel: 0181 455 8894 (Helpline)

Kings Fund
11-13 Cavendish Square
London W1M 0AN
Tel: 0171 307 2400

The Memorial Advisory Bureau
c/o Michael Dewar
Albemarle Connection
99 Charterhouse Street
Lonfon EC1M 6HR
Tel: 0171 251 5911

Memorials by Artists
Harriet Frazer
Snape Priory
Saxmundham
Suffolk IP17 1SA
Tel: (01728) 688934
For free leaflet or advice – this is a nationwide service.

**MIND (National Association
for Mental Health)**
Granta House
15–19 Broadway
London E15 4BQ
Tel: 0181 519 2122

Miscarriage Association
c/o Clayton Hospital
Northgate
Wakefield
West Yorks WF1 3JS
Tel: (01924) 200799

Multiple Death's Foundation
Queen Charlotte's and Chelsea Hospital
Goldhawk Road
London W6 OXG
Tel: 0181 740 3519/3520National AIDS Helpline
Tel: (0800) 567123 (Freephone)

**National Association
of Bereavement Services**
20 Norton Folgate
Bishopsgate
London E1 6DB
Helpline tel: (Refferals) 0171 247 1080
Tel/Fax (Admin): 0171 247 0617

National Association of Funeral Directors
618 Warwick Road
Solihull
West Midlands B91 1AA
Tel: 0121 711 1343

**National Association of Hospital
Play Staff**
40 High Street
Landbeach
Camb CB4 4DT

**National Association for the Prevention of
Cruelty to Children (NSPCC)**
National Centre
42 Curtain Road
London EC2A 3NH
Tel: 0171 825 2500
Tel: (0800) 800500
(24hrs Emergency Number)

**National Association of Toy
and Leisure Libraries**
68 Churchway
London NW1 1LT
Tel: 0171 387 9592
Fax: 0171 383 2714
(Details of local toy libraries are available from the
National Association of Toy and Leisure Libraries)

National Children's Bureau
8 Wakley Street
London EC1V 7QE
Tel: 0171 843 6000

National Council for One Parent Families
255 Kentish Town Road
London NW5 2LX
Tel: 0171 267 1361

National Forum on AIDS and Children
National Childrens Bureau
8 Wakley Street
London EC1V 7QE
Tel: 0171 843 6057

National HIV Prevention Information Service
Health Education Authority
Hamilton House
Mabledon Place
London WC1H 9TX
Tel: 0171 388 9855
National Helpline: (0800) 567123

National Library for the Handicapped Child
Wellington House
Wellington Road
Wokingham
Berks RG40 2AG
Tel (voice and text): (01734) 891101
Fax: (01734) 790989

The National StepFamily Association
Chapel House
18 Hatton Place
London EC1N 8RU
Tel (Office): 0171 372 0846
Helpline Tel: 0171 209 2464

Natural Death Centre
20 Heber Road
London NW2 6AA
Tel: 0181 208 2853
*Please enclose six first class stamps when requesting an
information pack.*

Neti Neti Theatre Co.
George Orwell School
Turle Road
London N4 3LS
Tel: 0171 272 7302

**Northern Ireland Pre-School
Playgroups Association**
Enterprize House
Boucher Crescent
Boucher Road
Belfast BT12 6HU
Tel: (01232) 662825

The Open University
Walton Hall
Milton Keynes
MK7 6AA
Tel: (01908) 274066

**Parents of Murdered Children
Support Group**
(see Compassionate Friends)

Pet Bereavement Counselling Service
Aine Wellard
25 Townsend Street
Dublin 2
Tel: 00 3531 677 5097

Pre-school Playgroups Association
61–63 Kings Cross Road
London WC1X 9LL
Tel: 0171 833 0991
(also see Northern Ireland Pre-School and Scottish
Pre-School Playgroups Assocation)

Rape Crisis Centre
PO Box 69
London WC1X 9NJ
Tel: 0171 916 5466 (Office)
Tel: 0171 837 1600 (24-hour emergency)

Relate Bookshop (formerly Marriage Guidance)
Herbert Gray College
Little Church Street
Rugby CV21 3AP
Tel: (01788) 573241

**Research Trust for Metabolic Diseases
in Children**
Golden Gate Lodge
Weston Road
Crew
Cheshire CW1 1XN
Tel: (01270) 629782

Samaritans (Head Office)
10 The Grove
Slough
Berks SL1 1QP
Tel: (01753) 532713
Tel from 2nd Nov 1995: (0345) 909090

**SANDS
(Stillbirth and Neonatal Death Society)**
28 Portland Place,
London W1N 4DE
Helpline Tel: 0171 436 5881
Tel (Admin): 0171 436 7940

Schools Outreach
10 High Street
Bromsgrove
Worcs B61 8HQ
Tel: (01527) 574404

Scottish Pre-school Playgroups Association
14 Elliot Place
Glasgow G3 8EP
Tel: 0141 221 4148/9

Shadow of Suicide
(see compassionate friends)

**Society for the Protection
of Unborn Children**
7 Tufton Street
London SW1P 3QN
Tel: 0171 222 5845

Terence Higgins Trust
52–54 Grays Inn Road
London WC1X 8JU
Tel: 0171 831 0330

**Twins and Multiple Births Association
(TAMBA)**
PO Box 30
Little Sutton
South Wirral
L66 1TH
Tel: (01732) 868000 (weekdays 7pm-11pm,
weekends 9am-11pm)
*For those with twins of multiple births and those having
suffered a bereavement within a multiple birth.*

Victim Support National Office
Cranmer House
39 Brixton Road
London SW9 6DZ
Tel: 0171 735 9166

Voluntary Euthanasia Society
13 Prince of Wales Terrace
London W8 5PG
Tel: 0171 937 7770

The Woodland Trust
(Plant a Tree Scheme to remember loved ones, also
Commemorative Groves)
Autumn Park
Dysart Road
Grantham
Lincolnshire NG31 6LL
Tel: (01476) 74297

Attributions

We are pleased to acknowledge the material listed below which can be found within the subject areas as shown.

Section 1: Background

Why Teach about Loss and Bereavement. © Health Education Authority. Reproduced with permission. *The saddest thing you can remember.*

Speck, P. *Understanding Loss.* Balliere Tindall. *Excerpt from Loss, Grief and Medicine.*

Professor Caplan. *Divorce and Separation.* © 1987 Archives of Disease in Childhood, BMA. *Helpful Hints for Parents.*

Mr and Mrs Turner. *Death of a Child – A School's Response.* *For Natalie.*

Section 2: Activities

Creative Activities

Violet Oaklander *Excerpt from 'Windows to our Children'.* Real Press.

'There is a Knot.' In *Have You Seen a Comet?* US Committee for UNICEF. John Days and Company.

Roger McGough 'First Day at School.' *You Tell Me.* McGough and Rosen.

Michael Rosen *Gone.*

Don't Put Mustard in the Custard. Deutsch.

John Agard 'Happy Birthday Dilroy' *I din do Nuttin.* Bodley Head/Magnet.

Demetroulla Vasslil *Don't Interrupt.*★

Accabre Huntley *At School Today.*★

P.S. Blackman Jnr *I thought a lot of you.*★

Karten Fitzgerald *First Day at the Nursery.*★

All from Childhood 5–10 and Pre School Child. © Open University.★

John Kitching/Trevor Dickinson *My Gerbil.*

Bishop Brent *The Ship.* Compassionate Friends.

Alison *Dear Grin Gran.*

Kate 'My Grandpa.' *For Such a Time as This.* *A Grief Journey by Felicity.*

John Foster/Derek Stuart 'Great Gran.' *Fifth Poetry Book.* Oxford University Press. *Reproduced by permission of the author.*

Graeme C. Young *The Journey.* Helen House.

D. Norris *Poor Little Joe.* Roan School for Boys.

D. Grant *Hope.*

Susan Wallbank (Cruse Counsellor) *If God had wanted a Gerbil.* *To Emily at Four.*

Sally Crosher *Teddy.* Why Me.

Sateke Faletan *Death.* King Alfred School Chronicle.

Joyce Grenfell *From Joyce*. Richard Scott Sirian Ltd.
Canon Scott Holland *Death is Nothing At All*.
Pam Ayres *In Defence of Hedgehogs*. 'All Pam's Poetry'. © *Pam Ayres*.
Michael Rosen 'Going Through the Old Photos.' *Quick let's get out of here*. Hutchinson.
David Houghton *You are a Lovely Cat*. Lady Bankes Junior.
Edward Lucie-Smith 'The Lesson.' *Oxford Book of 20th Century English Verse*. Oxford University Press.
Cathy Baker *There is a Baby on the Way*. Bishop Winnington and Ingram School.
Michael Rosen 'Today was not.' *Wouldn't you like to know*. Deutsch/Puffin.
Mike Gower 'Daddy and Rain.' *Swings and Roundabouts*. Collins.

What is Death

Frog Story. Adapted from 'Should Children Know.' Rudolph M. Schocken Books.
Your Own Personal Coat of Arms. Adapted from 'Think Well' Project.

Self-Esteem and Self-Image

Children Learn What They Live. Scottish Health Education Authority. Adapted from 'Parents Anonymous USA'.
D. Lawrence *Assessing Self Esteem*. 'Enhancing Self Esteem in the Classroom'. PCP Education

Section 3: Appendices

Sally Brompton *Unhappy Ever After*. The Times.
Kathleen Cox and Martin Desforge *Caught in the Middle*. The Times Educational Supplement.
What to Do When Someone Dies (Charts). Consumer Association.
David J. Williams *A Non-Religious Funeral Service*. British Humanist Association.
John Bowlby *How will Mummy breath and Who will feed her?* New Society.
Rosemary Wells (June 1984) *I Can't Write to Daddy*. Good Housekeeping.
Chris Stonor *Heavenly Bodies*. Woman's Journal.
Susan Harvey *Value of Hospitalized Children's Artwork*. Pat Arzanoff.
Barbara Greenall *Books for Bereaved Children*. Health Library Review.

Contributors

Zuby Bhagat is Team Leader of English as a Second Language, Hillingdon.

Helen Bona is Head Teacher of Oak Farm Infant School, Hillingdon.

Dave Burdett is Head Teacher of Oak Farm Junior School, Hillingdon.

Mary Conway is Head Teacher of Bourne School, Hillingdon.

Anita Courtman is a teacher at Pinkwell Junior School in Hillingdon. She also has a private counselling practice, and runs workshops for children and adults for the Psychosynthesis and Education Trust.

Jenny Chadwick is Advisor/Inspector for Hillingdon LEA. Her areas of responsibility include Personal, Social and Health Education and Child Development. She is also a mother of a nine-year-old child.

Mike Chomosky was Deputy Head of Townmead Comprehensive School in Hillingdon, and has a background in art.

Sue Chomosky is Head Teacher of Castleview Country Combined School, Slough, Berks.

Gill Combes is School Health Education Advisor, Birmingham. Her background includes 'special needs'.

Sally Crosher is a health visitor and a counsellor in Adlerian methods of family therapy. She has also a background in music.

Jenny Cutcliffe is a college lecturer in Health Studies, specialising in the Pre-Nursing Course. Her professional background as a RSCN, and health visitor, combined with her role as mother, led to an interest in, and work for, NAWCH (The National Association for Welfare of Children in Hospital).

Vera Hawkins is a class teacher at Lady Bankes Junior School, Hillingdon. She gives pastoral support as a Reader in the Parish of Uxbridge.

Margaret Hayworth is Newsletter Editor, and member of the national committee of The Compassionate Friends.

Pixie Holland is a music therapist. Her background includes organising music summer schools for young children, and working with autistic and handicapped children and parents.

Madeline Jones is a deputy head of a Junior School, Hillingdon.

Heather Lorusso and **Sarah Wilkie** are 'stock' co-ordinators in the Education and Young Department of Hillingdon Libraries.

Alison Moon and **Bill Rice** were with the organisation TACADE (Teacher's Advisory Council for Drug Education).

Laurel Newman is Deputy Head of Vanessa Nursery School. She has completed the in-depth training with Psycosynthesis in Education, and is responsible for some training with probationary teachers.

Beverley Walker is Head Teacher of The Priory School, First School, Moseley. She has attended courses on Counselling in Education, and Psychological Aspects in Education at the Tavistock Clinic.

Tessa Wilkinson formerly a bereavement visitor for Helen House Hospice for Children, Oxford. She has trained as a Montessori nursery teacher.